The Beach Boys

BYRON PREISS

BALLANTINE BOOKS • NEW YORK

This book is dedicated to my mother and father, with much love and continual delight.

ARTISTS' CREDITS
Surfin' /Illustration by Arnie Sawyer/Original design by Michael Pilla *409*/William Stout *Surfer Girl*/Michael Kanarek *Little Deuce Coupe*/Mac Evans-The Workshop *Fun*/Harvey Kurtzman *I Get Around*/Bill Nelson *In My Room*/Christof Blumrich *Don't Worry Baby*/Ralph Reese *Help Me Rhonda*/Alex Jay *Party*/Sean Earley *Good Vibrations*/John Pound *Heroes and Villains*/Dan Green *Cabinessense*/Wayne McLoughlin *Surf's Up*/Kenneth Smith *Vegetables* /Joey Epstein-Tom Hachtman/Photo by Ben Asen *Wind Chimes*/Mike Skaret-The Workshop *Country Air*/George Chastain *Darlin'* /John Collier *Busy Doin' Nothin'* /Edward Gorey *Carl and the Passions-So Tough*/David Willardson *I Went to Sleep*/Walter Simonson after Gorey *Winds of Change*/Wayne McLoughlin *This Whole World*/Denis Pohl *Cool Cool Water*/Bobby London *All This Is That*/Gabriel Csakany *Cuddle Up*/Jo Ellen Trilling/Photo by Ben Asen *Sail On Sailer*/Howard Chaykin *California Saga*/Lynda Jardine *Long Promised Road*/Steve Hofheimer *That Same Song*/Overton Loyd *15 Big Ones*/Overton Loyd *Dennis and Mike*/Bill Nelson

 *INTRODUCTION*

This book is about the spirit as well as the music of the Beach Boys. As the first authorized work on the band to appear, it is an effort to express both the Beach Boys' view of themselves and the image held by audiences who have made them the most successful American rock and roll group of the last seventeen years.

Producing a somewhat autobiographical work about a group of men with five very different personalities is a challenging experience, but it is hoped that the structure of this book will reflect, more comprehensively than has been done in the past, both the collective and individual character of the Beach Boys and their music. It is an attempt to record rock and roll history both visually and aurally. Designed as a kind of "visual soundtrack," the book is composed of *conversational extracts* (comments by the group); *a narrative* (historical text that reflects the group's understanding of themselves and their songs); *lyrics* (words to their compositions, many never before published); *photos* (tracing the history of the group); and *illustrations* (conceptual and decorative art keyed to specific songs and periods in the group's development).

It has been said that Brian Wilson invented the California myth and that the Beach Boys are America's foremost exponents of suburban soul music, inextricably linked with teenage fantasies. However, what seems more important to me is the very positive and instinctive response that the Beach Boys' music has always generated in young people. Searching for a way to convey this feeling here, I came upon an answer, unexpectedly, on a rainy night in midtown Manhattan. It was spring—cool, wet, and rather lonely. I stood with two or three others in front of the counter of a tiny pizza store. While I chewed my way through another slice, a twelve-year-old kid came in and ordered a pie. I watched him as the radio began to play "Help Me Rhonda." He moved slowly at first, embarrassed, to the rhythm of the song. Then his face began to light up, shyly, almost imperceptibly, with a slight smile. "Help me"—I saw it coming—"Rhonda!" He was singing; he was grinning. "Help me Rhonda!" Then he was really into it: "Help me get her out of my ..." He didn't know the words, but that sound, the beat, the spirit of youthfulness was as effective and beautiful as it had been in 1964. Fourteen years later and three thousand miles from California, it still made kids want to sing.

In *Mystery Train*, a seminal analysis of six rock related musicians, Greil Marcus wrote, "Unlike so many Hollywood groups, the Beach Boys have never been fakes. They celebrated the freedom of California ... looked for its limits, owned up to its failures....Their pleasures...have always radiated affection because these pleasures are firmly rooted in friendship." The Beach Boys' songs—and their lives—still retain a quality of youthfulness and innocence. In uncovering their story, I became involved again in the story of the sixties and early seventies, a time in which idealism and youth played central roles in the evolution of American society.

In the past twenty years rock and roll has acquired a history, yet there exists no central source for information about that history. There are the perennial collections of articles and back issues of magazines, but much of rock and roll's memory is still held only in personal reminiscences or rare clippings from suspended publications and fan journals. In compiling the raw material for this book and in coordinating its production with the Beach Boys' organization, I found that there are many people to whom I owe a deep and lasting appreciation. To mention just a few, my thanks, for their indulgence, to: Gary Johnson, Skip Brittanham, Steve Love, Diane Rovell, Marilyn Rovell, Janet Lent-Koop, Linda Jardine, Henry Fetter, John Branca, Susan Scharf and Eileen Rossner at Brother, Gary Nichamin at Caribou, Phil Caston, Ron Goldstein, Evan Meadow at A&M, Dave Berman, Chuck Britz, Jim Lockhart, Ed Engel, Marty Taber, Wayne Rodgers, Derek Bill, Mike Vossi, David Morris, Ward Mohrfeld, Paul Anbinder, Guy Webster, Dean Torrence, Earl Leaf, especially Peter Reum, Dorinda Morgan, Sandy Friedman, Alex Jay, Shirley Feldman, Basile Associates, Ben Asen, Jim McMullan, and Ralph Reese. My thanks also to those who have sympathetically covered the Beach Boys' story over the years—Gene Sculatti, Ken Barnes, Timothy White, Pete Fornatele, Tom Nolan, Richard Williams—and to Paul Williams, David Oppenheim, David Anderle's office at A&M, Ralph Newman (*Time-Barrier Express*, P.O. Box 206, Yonkers, New York 10710), and of course Edmund Preiss.

I must also single out Jeff Deutch, Beach Boys' aficionado, record producer, walking encyclopedia of rock and roll, and one of the nicest people in New York, for his help in researching, analyzing, and criticizing this book. Jeff's impressive knowledge of the Beach Boys and of popular music has been invaluable in constructing both an accurate history of the group and a discography of their work.

Finally, I must thank Mike, Brian, Carl, Alan, and Dennis for permitting me the opportunity to explore their lives and their songs and to produce a visual interpretation of some of the sweetest and most beautiful music to emerge from a turbulent and challenging time.

Surf's up!

—Byron Preiss
New York City
Summer 1978

THE BEACH BOYS

CAPITOL RECORDING ARTISTS

For Your Entertainment Pleasure

BRIAN WILSON, LEADER
Bus. OR 8-6054
Res. OS 5-6566

TEENAGE HOPS
TV, RADIO AND
STAGE APPEARANCES

THE BEACH BOYS

SUMMER DAYS AND SUMMER NIGHTS 1961-1965

It all started in 1961, when Dennis, then 17 and a surffiend since 13, began to slingo the surfing lingo around the family pad in Hawthorne, a green grass town near enough to the ocean to see the bikini'd beach bunnies on a clear day. Brother Brian and Cousin Mike perked their ears to the fab vocab and began tinkering it to music and rhyme.
———*from "Swinging the Surfin' Scene"*

    The first thing you saw was the blue sky. Then the sun. The sand. The water.
    Woodies were cool to drive. People lived in pads.
    Big wooden surfboards plastered with decals were boss.
    If you were a gremmie, with a big brother who surfed, you hung out on the beach and spit in the sand.
    At night, no matter if you came from Balboa or Pasadena, you parked by the highway and forced your way through hundreds of other suntanned kids to dance to the music of Dick Dale and his band.

It just came out of me. One day I started picking faster and faster like a locomotive. I wanted it to sound hard and powerful. There wasn't anybody who influenced it actually. I mean, there is nothing to influence you once you create a style and stick to that style. ———*Dick Dale*

    It just started coming out. On impulse. On feeling. It was the style of the surf. Freedom and youth. The energy and the hope. Southern California, 1962.
    "America" was still intact, the assassin's bullet had not struck, the cities simmered but did not burn, and the generation gap, that mythical hole between youth and adult, had not yet widened to encompass an entire country.
    Liberation still meant having fun, having a *good time,* and in Southern California, the sunniest, richest, most leisure-oriented showplace in the Western world, a *good time* was always waiting right outside the door.
    Suburban California 1962 was a world of high-school sports, one-family houses, drive-ins, cherry-flavored Sludge, cruisin' for chicks, miniature golf, cuttin' classes, hot rods, sunbathing, necking and listening to the radio. If you were a teenager, style and speed were the standards. *Could you do it fast? Could you do it fast and well?*
    The pressures were social. You were smart if you were *cool.* *Cool* was often superficial: You had to wear the right clothes, have the best car, use the right words, have the best body and best friends. Needless to say, guys were cool. Girls could be cool too, but the guys were the focus of attention. They told you what was cool—and the way they told you, well, that had to be cool too.

    Cool meant keeping a lid on your feelings, not losing the "upper hand." *Cool* meant saying the smartest (funniest) thing or delivering the best put-down to your best friend on a Saturday night. *Cool* meant picking up on the newest fad before anybody else did first. *Cool* was cultural. In California, it covered surfin', cruisin', and rock and roll.

The genesis of a distinctly California rock style can be traced to the Letterman's supercasual, harmony-laden "Come Back Silly Girl," or the Four Preps' "Down By The Station," whose clean-cut white vocals prefigured standard surf music maneuvers. But the real antecedents in the specific sense were, of course, the two West L.A. blonds with the two-track and the empty garage. Jan and Dean's "Baby Talk" (1959) and "Heart and Soul" (1961) once and for all set the standards for California rock and roll; brisk, lightweight, sparse or Spectorian, always white and pop.
———*Gene Sculatti, "A California Saga"*

    Always white, always light, always pop. Like the surf, rock and roll music embodied freedom, celebrated it, fought for it and triumphed. It had harmony and drive, and it established a language for an entire generation. Rock and roll was *our* music, *our* expression, and nobody else could legitimately share in its meaning—whether they wanted to or not.

Brian, Mike, Dennis, Carl, David

"Rock Around the Clock" shocked me. I mean, I was so electrified by the experience. Some of my friends came over and said I had to hear this new record, so we went out and bought it and took it home and put it on. We were really screaming, that song was really it.

——Brian Wilson

Before rock, the kids had pop, and before pop, Sinatra. Sinatra, the movies and the war.

My mom and her brother Murry Wilson came to California in the middle of a depression, 'cause, you know, they couldn't make it in Kansas. The first place they lived was on the beach in Huntington, because they had no money to live anywhere.

——Mike Love

In California, Murry Wilson met Audree Neva Karthof and found they shared a love of music. They married and took a modest apartment at 8012 South Harvard Boulevard in Los Angeles. Murry was a hard worker, religious and somewhat strict. His wife Audree took life less seriously; she enjoyed having fun and loved to play the piano.

They were a young couple in wartime America, struggling against bigger business and a difficult time in history to establish a heavy machinery enterprise in Southern California. Murry sold big lathes, imported from England, objects that seemed totally incongruous in the land of the Pacific.

We had never heard the word smog. It was beautiful. You could see the mountains.

——Audree Wilson

On June 20, 1942, Audree and Murry Wilson had their first son, Brian Douglas. By the time their third, Carl, was born, on December 21, 1946, Audree and Murry had already made the jump from Los Angeles to a comfortable suburban home on West 119th Street in the South Bay community of Hawthorne. It was suburban, not rural, but still quiet at night. As Brian would say, "It was really weird. We'd mow down the lawn and the lawn would taper into the street."

In those four years, from 1942 to 1946 the American recording industry had grown 1000 percent. RCA and Decca Records were selling close to 100 million sides per year and through the jukebox, 5 billion nickels were being spent to hear the likes of Tommy Dorsey, Frank Sinatra, and Doris Day. Television had not yet come into vogue. Music still had an important place as entertainment for the entire *family*. Radio, phonographs, and (traditionally) churches had made singing a major diversion in the American home. The Wilson household was no exception. Murry, a songwriter of the Lawrence Welk school, would frequently entertain his wife and guests with songs and a bottle of beer. Audree would play the piano. It was corny but fun. By 1943, the Wilson duet turned into a trio.

This is the truth, you may not believe it—when Brian was born, I was one of those young, frightened fathers, you know? But I just fell in love with him and in three weeks he cooed back at me, responded...and when he was eleven and a half months—it was just at World War II—I would carry Brian on my shoulders with his little hands up above and I would sing, "Caissons Go Rolling Along" and he could hum the whole song. He was very clever and quick.

——Murry Wilson

He was more than quick. He was sensitive.

Brian started singing when he was just a little bitty guy, three years old. He'd sing right on key. He loved to hear me play the piano, he loved the chords and he'd say, "Play that chord again."...

Brian took accordion lessons on one of those little, baby accordions for six

weeks. And the teacher said, "I don't think he's reading. He hears it just once and plays the whole thing perfectly."

——Audree

This, despite the fact that Brian was deaf in one ear because of a damaged nerve. Nobody is sure how the defect occurred.

By the time Brian was nine, the Wilson trio was a full-fledged quintet. Seven-year-old brother Dennis, already athletic and prone to trouble, would join in singing with five-year-old Carl, a pleasant, blue-eyed, and slightly shy boy.

sunporch outside where we could sit out and look all over the city. We used to sleep in the bunks and I'd have a transistor radio on under the covers so we could listen to the late-night R and B on KGFJ and KDAY.

——*Mike*

Brian, Carl, friend and Dennis, Hawthorne 1950

Dennis age 10

Carl age 8

At gatherings of the wider Wilson family, Emily Love, Murry Wilson's sister, would bring along her son Michael, Brian's elder by six months. Both boys loved music. When Emily decided to give a small "concert" in honor of her brother's songs, little Mike came up with one of his own. It was called "The Old Soldier." Murry Wilson loved it and rewrote it into a hymn. At the "concert," Brian did both Mike's and Murry's version. He brought the house down (how could he miss?) and unwittingly began a lifelong collaboration between himself and his cousin Mike Love.

The friendship of the brothers and cousin grew as they moved through elementary school to the higher grades. The boys had three common all-American interests, and all three became more and more important as they got older:

Sports, girls, and music.

I can remember that around '57–'58, I guess it was, Brian had an old Rambler, and he used to come over to my house a lot and hang out and sing. I was living on the corner of Mt. Vernon and Fairway in the View Park/Baldwin Hills section of Los Angeles at the time… My bedroom upstairs had a fantastic view. We had knotty pine bunkbeds built into the wall and we had a

Brian and Mike heard the music that was electrifying teenagers across the country. Deep, sensual vocals. Stomping percussion. Music that seemed to move at the speed of sound. Cutting bass guitar. Chuck Berry. Rhythm and blues. Rock and roll.

Every record had something you'd listen to—every record had some kind of twist in it that gave you the feeling that says, "Oh man!" You'd go to the piano, you'd say, "How'd they do that?" Start learning about it. It's an education! Anybody with a good ear is gonna pick up on those songs and go to the piano.

——*Brian*

They listened to everything. Sweet vocals. Airy arrangements. Soft harmonies. *The Four Freshman.*

They learned the words, picked up on the pacing, knew by memory where the guitar came in and the voice went out. They loved it. Rock and roll.

Mike's dad would kick us out, so we sang in the car.

——*Brian*

It was 1957. The Malibu Hosiery Company on Santa Monica and Vine had just gone out of business, and Stan Ross and Dave Gold were making plans for expansion into its quarters. Their small but popular Goldstar Recording facilities next door were well-known as "the" place to cut demos in L.A. Now Gold wanted to add an "A" studio, an acoustically deep and geometrically balanced echo chamber that would be known for its reverb and balance. A sixteen-year-old Bronx expatriate, Phil Spector, lived down the street from Goldstar. He had never been inside a recording studio, but he was working on a rock act with his friend Marshall Leib for a high-school talent show.

Farther south, in Hawthorne, Brian Wilson locked himself in his room and made up a studio of his own. Straining his fifteen-year-old voice, he'd spend hours duplicating the falsetto harmonies of the Four

Freshman. When he was satisfied with the results he'd bring his brothers into the music. It was a little bit like a bedtime routine they had a few years earlier.

We used to harmonize in bed. "Come Down, Come Down From Your Ivory Tower," that was the special one we'd sing. We developed a little blend for that.

————Brian

While John F. Kennedy spoke about a "new frontier," the easygoing Wilsons and Love were busy living it. Mike was a cross-country runner at Dorsey High. Dennis, handsome and tan, already had a philosophy that would last him a lifetime. ("Let the good times roll ....everyone have a good time....I love everything there is to do.") The least-patient Wilson when it came to singing, he was the first to get into trouble.

A real nature boy. He'd get up in the morning and go searching for trashcans...He just liked to open up the lid and see—he liked to see.

————Brian

Carl, soft-spoken and pudgy, shared many of his brothers' qualities. Though sensitive, he refused to let others push him around. Developing an interest in music, he'd sing a lot with Brian and study arrangements of popular folk songs. More significantly, he showed a serious interest in learning how to play guitar.

Older brother Brian was an enigma. At one moment he could be the prankster, dreaming up every trick in the book.

We'd be driving down the street going to school when we were kids. Brian would be drinking a carton of milk. He'd stop and open the door and pretend he was throwing up by emptying the whole milk carton! He totally let go and whatever could happen, he'd let happen.

————Dennis

Yet ten minutes later, he could retreat behind a pair of soft, wistful eyes.

He's very very vulnerable. He would lay down his life for a butterfly....He's had a very tragic life emotionally. I remember in sixth grade. Brian used to sing in school. He sang very high and all his buddies that he'd hang out with laughed at him. He ran home from school, and I chased after him. It broke my heart to see him emotionally involved in the music at such an early age and have his friends laugh at him, call him a girl or something. But every time he's ever stuck it out, put it out for people to see, to share it with people, a lot of time he's been hurt. Or maybe people just didn't understand him.

————Dennis

Brian could be different things at different times. Extremely competitive. Sensitive. Funny. Introspective. Fred Morgan, his music teacher at Hawthorne High, remembered him as "quiet....a nice boy and a good student." Another acquaintance, watching from the Hawthorne forty-five-yard line, would recall a top athlete, quarterback for the Cougars and centerfielder for the varsity baseball team.

At sixteen, riding around in a car was a big deal. Going out to the hot night-spots at six o'clock at night. The hamburger joint. The streets of Los Angeles were bumper-to-bumper with kids. We'd always been a little political. When you're seventeen, you know, a very political thing would be getting out of the house for a wild weekend.

————Dennis

Through it all was the music. In the car. In bed, transistorized, under the pillow. Youth night at the Angeles Mesa Presbyterian Church was a showcase for their harmonizing—Brian, Mike, Carl, and

Dennis doing sweet, youthful cover versions (new renditions—usually faithful) of the latest Everly Brothers' and Four Preps' tunes. By the time Brian was a senior in high school, he was a veteran at making new, more complex arrangements of their hits. He even took things a step farther and taped his family singing two parts of a four-part harmony. Then, as the tape played back, he'd have them sing the other two. It was Brian's first 'recording' experience.

His first real studio participation, however, had almost occurred years earlier, aided and abetted by his father.

We knew Audree and Murry....He used to come to us when the boys were little kids....He was a very good songwriter. We published some of his songs.

Art Lebow of Original Sound—he was also a DJ in L.A.—had a song called "Chapel of Love," not the one that was a big success, but another. He was looking for a singer. We talked to Murry. We had honestly forgotten about his kids. He said Brian was turning into a pretty good singer....He sent Brian over. We auditioned Brian with Art. We thought Brian was pretty great, but Art turned him down for a kid named Rodney....He was on "Chapel of Love." I think it would have been a big hit if they had used Brian.

————Dorinda Morgan, Guild Music Publishing Co.

Carl

Brian

Dennis

Mike

In the winter of 1959–1960, the boys' interest in sports and music intersected for the first of two crucial times.

Fumbling a pass from quarterback Brian, Hawthorne Cougar Alan Jardine fell and injured his leg. Jardine and Brian were both students at Hawthorne High. A soft-spoken, easygoing native of Lima, Ohio, Al shared Brian's enthusiasm for music. The two began a lasting friendship. They had the same circle of acquaintances and often found time to get together alone and sing. Al played bass and loved the folk sound of groups like the Kingston Trio.

It was early 1961 when Mike Love and Al Jardine were coming over to the house and Brian was teaching them songs with Carl....So it was eight months before the record "Surfin'" of December 8, 1961, when the Beach Boys really started.

———Murry

After high school, Brian and Al took different directions. Jardine headed East, with plans for a career in dentistry. Brian stayed close to Hawthorne, attending college at El Cerrito, with one ear glued firmly to a three-inch AM radio speaker. At home, with Carl and Mike, he'd continue to do cover versions of various top-ten hits.

Throughout this time, Murry kept after Brian to sing some of the songs he had written for Hite and Dorinda Morgan's small but successful Guild Music Publishing Company in Los Angeles.

Murry was fed up with Brian because he didn't want to do any of his songs. ...He thought Murry's were too square, which is understandable.
———Dorinda Morgan

Brian stuck with Chuck Berry and the Four Freshman. Then, one day that following spring, Alan Jardine returned home for vacation. He began hanging out at Brian's school.

I bumped into Brian on campus one day. Smash-o. We crossed paths. Literally. I said, "Brian, this is it. We have to get together." So we went into the music room between classes and sang Four Freshman songs. When we got kicked out of the music room we'd finish up in the nurses' quarters. Then he told me more about his brothers ... "Carl, he's about twelve and he really sings good and he plays the guitar too." So I met the Wilson boys and Mike Love.

———Alan

Al also met Murry Wilson, who was impressed by the boy's interest in music. Like Wilson's own sons, Al had a warm sense of humor and innate musical talent. He was a proficient guitar player and an expert on contemporary folk. Murry sent him to see the Morgans.

Alan came to us with another group first. Two other boys...I forget what they were called. They were older, very good, they had a much slicker sound, but they didn't have any original material. They were doing the Kingston Trio sort of thing. They could do the Four Freshman. Professional, but not original. We turned them down.
———Dorinda Morgan

It was the latter half of 1961. Over at Herb Wallach's Music City on Sunset Boulevard, top-ten charts went up and down with the regularity of the sun. There were only two rock albums in the top fifty, but for singles' action, there was everything from Dion's "Runaround Sue" to Neil Sedaka's "Happy Birthday Sweet Sixteen." In Detroit, an enterprising Berry Gordy, Jr., was planning the first release for his fledgling Motown Record Company. Half a world away, manager Brian Epstein wooed a young group of Liverpool musicians called The Beatles.

Rock music was young, Brian was young, Al was young. Murry Wilson was disgusted. He just couldn't understand why Brian would not sing even one of his songs. Brian, as always, was a stubborn kid.

Murry called us up and said, "See if you can do something with him.... Audree and I are going to Mexico City."
———Dorinda Morgan

It's so bizarre how this happened....Brian's father gave me the number of a studio to record at, so I took Brian and the guys down to do a folk song. I wanted to sing—anything. I forget what song we were supposed to sing that day.

———Alan

The Wilsons and Mike Love, like any other healthy, musically oriented fans of rock and roll, had visions of their own rock band. They had tossed around the name The Pendletons, but did little more than sing with each other at home. Now, with Alan, they rushed over to Guild in L.A.

Alan came over with the Beach Boys....Of course, they weren't called that then. Brian said, "I bet you don't remember me"—and honestly, I didn't. He had grown so much since he was a little boy....

They had several things....They weren't as smooth as the other group Alan had brought, but knowing Murry and whatnot, we figured Brian had talent as a songwriter. We asked them if they had any original material and they said they did not....They were doing top ten—I think, "Duke of Earl." We asked Brian what his favorite songs were and he said they were top ten.
———Dorinda Morgan

For the first time in their lives, Mike, Carl, Dennis, and Brian were faced with someone who was really interested in knowing whether or not they had any music of their own. They didn't have any songs but they did have their dreams. For the second time, sports and music met to play a crucial role in the group's career.

I wouldn't go out....I was scared, scared of the water. It really scared me.
———Brian

Brother Dennis loved to surf. He'd come home and rave about the feeling of being free on the water. He wanted Brian to try it.

I watched.

———Brian

Surfing was so popular on the West Coast that it had its own language, even its own music, but oddly, there had not been any major combination of the two.

So we were in our office on Melrose. Dennis said, "Why doesn't somebody write a song about surfin'?" Well, surfin' didn't mean a thing to us but I said, "We have nothing to lose." Then Dennis told us that every morning they have surfing news on the radio. You know, they tell you the best places to surf.

I had Dennis write down a page of surfing words and suggested that they write the song then and there.

In the office right **then and there** *they started!*

It came quite quickly. They picked up the harmony on it. I think Alan brought a guitar.

They took what they had home and improved it. After just a couple of days, they came back all excited. They had it in good shape.
———Dorinda Morgan

The song was called "Surfin'." It was three-chord rock with a beat out of *Billboard's* California backlist and a parcel of bom-dip phrases, but it had style and it had youth and it said "Surf!"

Brian and Mike wrote the final version and were aching to record it. The money Murry and Audree had left the boys for provisions during their Mexico jaunt was quickly diverted.

When we left, the refrigerator was completely stocked and we gave the boys enough money to buy whatever else they needed. We came back and here

they had gone out and rented a bass, a big standup, as tall as Al for sure, and drums and a microphone. They had used every bit of their food money. They said, "We want to play something for you." They were very excited about it and we thought the song was darling.

——Audree

The boys made arrangements with the Morgans for a recording session. Time was booked at Keen Recording Studios in Beverly Hills.

Brian was very engaging, over-tall, ambitious, but at the same time diffident, a little belligerent toward Dennis....Dennis was the surfer, very physical....Carl was the peacemaker. ...Mike and Alan seemed older; more mature.

——Dorinda Morgan

With Hite Morgan producing, Brian, Alan, Mike, Dennis, and Carl performed "Surfin'."

It was really incredible....It started off, we went into a room and sang and it got on the air. It was wonderful....

——Carl

We sang in a loose structure, we sang around a piano; we didn't have any plans to become big rock and roll singers.

——Mike

For the flip side of a surfin' single, Dorinda Morgan pulled out a composition by her son Bruce. The five sang "Luau," simply, as she tells it, "because we wanted to do originals."

Although it was not as slick or professional as other products of the period, Brian and Mike's "Surfin'" impressed the Morgans as a genuinely infectious and youthful song. Hite Morgan began to look for ways to get it released.

I think he'd gone to some other people and they'd turned him down, but Herb Newman wanted to bring it out immediately. At this time, they were not known as the Beach Boys. They wanted to be called The Pendletons...they figured Pendleton shirts would give them free jackets or something. We never told them but they were very cute. Several other groups had come to us wanting to use that name....The name The Beach Boys was picked out of Herb Newman's office by my husband, Joe Saraceno, and Herb Newman.

——Dorinda Morgan

Newman owned a small label called Candix, and his distribution ties in the L.A. area would be sufficient to back up a local hit.

Joe Saraceno at that time had an instrumental group called the Surfaris and

he thought the boys were just great...They threw around names like Surf-airs, but Joe thought that was too corny—you know, a lot of Beach names.

——Dorinda Morgan

The men finally agreed on "The Beach Boys" and the group accepted. Newman pressed "Surfin'." With support from Russ Regan, KFWB librarian Bill Angel, and Brian-come-lately Art Lebow, The Beach Boys made a surprising debut on the L.A. charts.

SURFIN'   *(Original version)*   *by Brian Wilson and Mike Love*

Well, I woke up this morning, turned on the radio
I was checkin' out the surfin' scene to see if I would go
And when the DJ tells me that the surf is fine,
That's when I know my babe and I will have a good time

Surfin', surfin', surfin', surfin', surfin',
Surfin' is the only life, the only way for me
Surf, surf, with me
Well, from early morning to the middle of the night,
Any time the surf is up the time is right

And when the surf is down, to take its place,
We'll do the surfer stomp, it's the latest dance craze...

Well, now the dawn is breaking and we really gotta go,
But we'll be back there early, boys, and that you better know
Well, my surfin' knots are rising and my board is losing wax
But that won't stop me 'cause you know I'm coming back.

Chorus
Bom-bom di-dip-dip-dip.

Copyright 1961, 1962 by Guild Music Co., BMI

We didn't even know we were The Beach Boys until the song came out. It was that kind of thing. We could have said, "No, we're not going to be The Beach Boys," but it sounded pretty far out.

——Mike

Murry Wilson didn't really like the song, but from Torrence to Manhattan Beach it was a smash.

They were looking for a label that they thought would catch on....They thought the "X" was a clever idea.

——Dorinda Morgan

"Surfin'" came out on two Newman-owned labels, X and Candix. It won a three-way popularity contest, became a local sensation, then rose to seventy-five on the national charts.

I remember when Carl, Brian, and I, and David Marks were driving in Brian's fifty-seven Ford down Hawthorne Boulevard and we heard that our first record, "Surfin'," might be played that day—and the moment we heard that record on radio, that was the biggest high ever. Nothing will ever top the expression on Brian's face. Ever.

——Dennis

It was played on three stations in L.A. every hour, twenty-four hours a day. ...Then after "Surfin'," the boys were off the air and they couldn't get back on the air. No one wanted them, they thought they were a one-shot record.

——Murry

I made a dollar a day sweeping a laundry out. Then we made a record that was number two in Los Angeles. We got so excited hearing it on radio that Carl threw up. I ran down the street screaming: "Listen! We're on the radio." It was really funky. That started it. The minute you are on the radio...

——Dennis

Plans were made for the group's first real public appearance—with the legendary Dick Dale at the Balboa Ballroom.

They were delighted with the single, but they were scared stiff of performing live. The only boys who weren't were Mike and Alan—and probably Carl because Carl is basically a musician. He gets so involved in his music that he forgets about the crowd. Brian and Dennis had a little stage fright.

Brian was a little perturbed by the crowd. The Beach Boys were not a smash there, but they weren't badly accepted, but they thought they were, especially Brian. Brian had thought that this first shot was going to be big.

———Dorinda Morgan

Although they were uneasy about appearing before an audience, the boys prepared for another, more significant date on December 31, 1961—New Year's Eve. A big rock and roll show was scheduled as a memorial to Richie Valens, a forceful pop singer who had been killed with Buddy Holly and the Big Bopper almost two years earlier in an airplane crash over a snowy field in Iowa.

The reception for the Beach Boys improved. With a sympathetic audience at the Long Beach Auditorium, the group did a quick set of three songs, highlighted by "Surfin'."

On February 8, 1962, the group returned to Keen Studios. Brian had four new songs, none longer than 2:12.

We cut "Surfer Girl," "Surfin' Safari," "Judy," and "Karate," otherwise known as the "Beach Boys' Stomp." They were follow-ups to "Surfin'." We did them at union sessions. In addition to Dennis, Brian brought along a drummer he thought was a hot-shot...but I didn't—too much drum. He was a hillbilly Gene Krupa. We paid him and sent him away.

———Dorinda Morgan

These songs were cut by the group with the understanding that they would probably be new releases on Herb Newman's Candix, Era, or as Dorinda Morgan put it, "whatever other label they were calling themselves at the time." Herb Newman, however, seemed unenthusiastic about their follow-up songs.

In contrast, super-salesman Murry Wilson was anxious to get a good deal for his boys. If Candix was foolish enough to pass up his family, then he'd pay a visit to the majors with them himself.

While Murry made his plans, the "group" continued to develop their skills. Carl had a jump on the rest. Heavily influenced by Chuck Berry and a student of John Maus (who went on to fame with the Walker Brothers in England) Carl and his Fender guitar became an early symbol of the Beach Boys' sound.

Dean Brownel was a very technical musician....He used to say of a chord, "Oh, that's a G-flat third, augmented by a fifth...." We were amused by that, but I was very impressed by his playing. He left his guitar at our house and I learned a few bar chords. From that point on, I'd get a real thrill seeing a Fender guitar in the music-store window....After a bit, John Maus began giving me lessons, and that went on for a few years.

———Carl

Brian, in the meantime, wrote songs. His third composition, "Surfer Girl," proved that he could write a ballad as well as an up-tempo rocker. His material was ingenuous and melodic. Without formal training in music composition, Brian was free to interpret rock and roll from the cultural standpoint of a South Bay college sophomore.

Gary Usher picked up on the Beach Boys' sound. After he introduced himself to Brian, the two quickly became friends. The night they met, Brian and Usher penned "The Lonely Sea" over hot fudge sundaes. Gary was a catalyst. He and Brian turned out thirty songs in a few months, songs focusing heavily on girls, cars, and the California surf.

He kind of showed me the spirit of competition...sorta showed me how to write songs. He just knew our next-door neighbor. He came by and said "Hi." He was very creative.

———Brian

I can still remember being outside the Wilson house in Hawthorne. It was like two A.M., and here we got a tape recorder out on the lawn and peeling rubber, just dragging down the street, was this "409." O-boy! Neighbors

calling up and coming out yelling, "Shut up!" It was a trip. We needed the sounds, y'know.

———Mike

"409" was an ode to a Chevy engine that had been put out by GM to rival the superstock Dodge. Usher owned one of these engines, a California status item.

Murry took "409" and three of the cuts from the last Keen session and went with Usher and the group to record more polished versions at Western Recorders under the supervision of veteran engineer Chuck Britz.

They called and wanted to book a session on a Sunday. We did several tunes including "Surfin' Safari," "Surfer Girl," and "409." They weren't even signed to anybody. Their mother was with them, and their father too. They just wanted to do songs, and I guess they wanted to experiment with a different studio. They heard we had done good work, even though we weren't as modern as some of the other studios....

Murry, Audrey, and myself were in Studio 3's control room: The booth had been built but the studio wasn't completed yet. So they were in a big studio across the hall and I talked to them on an intercom. As far as producing, indirectly Brian was producing everything even at that early stage.... As far as I'm concerned the total commitment of producing was from him. He was beautiful—an all-American kid who knew what he wanted and was pretty sure of himself. Gary Usher was with him.... He sang on one of the tunes.

———Chuck Britz, Engineer, Western Recorders

With "409" and the three versions of Brian's songs in hand, Murry hit Liberty, Dot, and whoever else would listen to the tapes.

We did those four tunes, and I didn't see them for a few months. They ran in here with their father, and they were thrilled. They had been signed with Capitol....

———Chuck Britz

Finally Nick Venet at Capitol recognized the potential of the band. Nick was a young producer, closer to the "scene" than many of his staid counterparts, but he lacked the authority to sign the group.

Venet...was responsible for having the big shot at Capitol, Voyle Gilmore, hear the song "Surfin' Safari." Nick acted real cool. He says, "You come back in an hour and we'll let you know if we want you to be Capitol recording artists."

He didn't act like he was too excited....So we walked out of there and I said, "Brian, let's make them wait five minutes. You know, let's don't act too eager."

This is the truth. We got back in an hour and five minutes. In the meantime (we found out later) Nick Venet rushed across the tower, burst in on Gilmore and said, "Boss, I've got a double-sided smash for Capitol."

———Murry

Middle-aged Gilmore was prepared to take a chance with the group. Before signing formally with Capitol, the Beach Boys made one final set of recordings for the Morgans.

We put their voices on pre-recorded instrumental tracks of "Barbie" and "What a Young Girl Is Made Of"—both written by my son, Bruce. We had wanted some more sides of them and Murry agreed that they owed us a couple....

Dennis didn't come to those sessions, but Audree did. Audree is singing on those....We had recorded the tracks for another singer. Apparently Brian didn't mind....Mike didn't come in. Alan and Carl did.

———Dorinda Morgan

Murry successfully signed the group with Capitol Records, leaving Hite and Dorinda Morgan with two cuts by a band who would

RANDY
RECORDS

Guild Music Co.
B.M.I.

Time 2:20
(422-B)

WHAT IS A YOUNG GIRL MADE OF
(B. Morgan)

KENNY
and THE CADETS

422

soon be appearing on another label. Not wishing to antagonize either the group or its new company, the Morgans decided to release "Barbie" under another name. Playing off the name of the boyfriend of the popular "Barbie" doll, Dorinda Morgan came up with the name "Kenny" and then added "The Cadets" (Ken was a marine). The single "Barbie" by Kenny and the Cadets came out in early '62.

I had to make a decision to sign with Capitol Records and drop my professional ideals, or stay in school. I decided to stay in school....At that time we were doing a lot of Chubby Checker tunes. They were cute, you know, but I didn't enjoy singing them that much....Then Brian sneaks in all these great songs after I decide to leave the group!

——*Alan*

With their conscientious rhythm guitarist off on a rendezvous with a spit sink (a pre-dental program), the Beach Boys drafted neighbor David Marks (a capable young guitarist with a freshly scrubbed, boy-next-door look) as replacement.

For Capitol, Gilmore and Venet picked the Wilson-Usher "409" as the first single. Reasoning that surfin' was a local phenomenon, with little appeal in the arid midwest, they put their money on a love song to an engine. To play it safe, however, Brian's "Surfin'," follow-up was used on the flip side. In June, "409"/"Surfin' Safari," Capitol 4777, debuted.

To support the single and make a name for the group, Murry booked gigs across the West, sometimes taking rock where, so to speak, it had never gone before.

We played at halls for men who were all over sixty. It went down all right. When you're playing you think it's fantastic. I don't know whether the people liked it because they'd never seen anything like it before. They all walked out, all twelve of them. But we kept on playing and we got ten dollars between us.

——*Dennis*

Their three "featured" songs, "409," "Surfin'," and "Surfin' Safari," shared a breezy, good-natured style. From the start, the Beach Boys displayed a refreshing sense of humor and harmony. Mike's fast, nasal lead was ideal for both sides of the "409"/"Surfin' Safari" single.

We'll do a thing, a giddy-up, giddy-up, meaning horses for horsepower. We were just kidding around. We came back and put it to three simple chords and it became a million-dollar craze.

——*Usher*

If "409" was worth a million, "Surfin' Safari" was worth

three. In Arizona, of all places, the intended flip took off, and by the time the new "A" side hit fourteen on the national charts, surfing bands were singing it in the cities where the nearest ocean might as well have been on the moon. Together with Jan and Dean, Dick Dale, and the new wave of West Coast bands, the Beach Boys' music turned America into Southern California in the course of one (1962) summer. By the time Labor Day had come around, the airy, impulsive beat of the Pacific was sharing the focus of rock and roll with Phil Spector's driving, impenetrable, melodic, urban wall of sound.

The most memorable thing was when we were doing ballrooms in the Midwest. That was our first touring experience and we drove like eight-hundred miles from one place to the next. We set up our own equipment and played on existing P.A. systems, which were really horrible. "Surfin' Safari" had just come out. We played in Lake Minnetoka outside of Minneapolis, Minnesota....one station wagon and a U-Haul. We played Hatfield, Minn. It was literally a barn, converted into a dance hall, and there was a stage that was so narrow...I was standing on the front of the stage and there were two mikes. A drunk sat down on my foot.

——*Mike*

America went to the beach, whether it was there or not. In Colorado, the Astronauts sang of woodies; in industrial Michigan, the Rivieras did odes to the summer; and in frigid Minnesota, the lyrically distinctive Trashman professed a love for swimming, surfing, and ninety-nine days of vacation.

It was an extraordinary musical event. The two-sided single carried a regional lifestyle to an entire country. Rock went beyond its usual role. "Surfin' Safari" spoke to kids who had seen only waves on the top of their heads.

The Beach Boys had exploded not one trend but *two*, and in doing so, sent shock waves through the recording industry. "409" was the biggest car song since "Maybelline," with none of the lyrical ambiguity of the Chuck Berry classic. The distinctive voice of Mike Love, blaring from hundreds of thousands of transistor radios that summer, sung forcefully (with-tongue-in-cheek) about displacement figures in cubic inches. Mike's "Surfin' Safari," fast, funky, and authoritative, with percolating background vocals and infectious pacing, gave the news on America's biggest craze—"Surfin's getting bigger from Hawaii to the shores of Peru."

We had no preconception that we'd be big and famous...but the first time we thought we might be onto something was for me in that barn in Minnesota. We had just played our second set of four, and we stopped outside to get some air. It was totally sold out....We saw cars down the road for a mile and a half trying to get up—so I knew something was happening.

——*Mike*

Hot for a single, hot for an album, hot for exposure, Capitol pushed their plans for the Beach Boys by targeting an album for late 1962. The deadline pressured the group. In one thirteen-hour session, Brian, Dennis, Carl, Mike, Jardine's replacement, David Marks, cut

Dennis, David, friend, Mike, Carl

Carl, Mike, Brian, Alan, Dennis

Brian, Mike, Alan and Carl two years later in Paris on tour

the bulk of *Surfin' Safari*. Under the supervision of Murry Wilson, Nick Venet, and Brian himself, the album showcased the two-sided hit ("409"/"Surfin' Safari"); a standard surfin' instrumental ("Moon Dawg"); and the catchy "Ten Little Indians," a variation on the old nursery rhyme, which became the group's next single.

When they signed with Capitol, Nick Venet wanted to do an album with "Ten Little Indians"...and that was the only bomb I know they had.
——*Chuck Britz*

To their credit, Brian and the group stuck primarily to originals for the rest of the record. With the exception of "Summertime Blues," a Dick Dale-influenced cover of the driving classic, and "Little Miss America," a standard teen-dream melody co-authored by Herb Alpert, the balance of *Surfin' Safari* celebrated the small pleasures of a South Bay existence.

Instrumentally bare, with stock musical gestures from the early sixties' repertoire (*ooh-aahs*, guitar solo, simple fading tags), songs such as "Country Fair" ("I had to win a stuffed doggie or break her heart in two"), "Chug-a-lug" (with an absurd root-beer drinking contest), and "The Shift" (the dress, not the automotive part) were notable primarily for their sense of humor and vocal promise.

They'd give that extra burst of energy and do it beautifully...I drove the Beach Boys up a wall. You see, a manager and a father can be pretty rough.
——*Murry*

By the time *Surfin' U.S.A.* was released in March 1963, the Beach Boys had made a fuller transition from local fame to national success. From December 17, 1962, to January 1, 1963, they grossed $26,000 for five nights' work. The income was staggering, the popularity unexpected. They had spent hundreds of hours listening to music and now people were listening to them. Suddenly, *they* were the music. *They* were the trend that others were imitating. They were five healthy, talented young men tossed into the musical spotlight. It excited them, it wore them down; it challenged them, it scared them. Like so much of rock and roll, it was an instant, a peak high, soaring with no destination and no constant thought of coming down again.

I'll tell you something, every song we ever did, I never heard one song that didn't make me feel mellow inside because of the beautiful way they did it.
——*Chuck Britz*

With a hit album under their belts and the support of Capitol Records growing with each new wave of the surfin' phenomenon, Brian Wilson began to exercise what would prove to be a dazzlingly accurate ear for the musical tastes of sixties America.

If everybody had an ocean across the U.S.A.
Then everybody'd be surfin' like Californiyay!

The music was Chuck Berry's "Sweet Little 16." Brian, student of rock, was humming the tune. As Chuck Berry's vocal worked its way through his head, it occurred to Brian that the song was ideal for another purpose. If all the places mentioned in Berry's tune (St. Louis, New Orleans, etc.) were replaced by the names of surfin' towns and all references to sweet sixteen changed to talk about surfin', wouldn't it be fantastic. Wouldn't it be *a gas* if they could get *every* possible surfin' hangout into the song.

"Surfin' U.S.A.," like so many other Beach Boys' classics, was a totally accessible sound. Carl's electrifying riff kept the opening appeal of Berry's original. The song just grabbed out. It was music like glass—shiny, clear—you could see right through it to the environment it described. *"Inside-Outside U.S.A.!"* There was no pretense. It

expressed the enthusiasm of youth—and it was immersed harmonically in the positive California style of life. Brian gave the rights to his lyrics to Berry's publishing company in exchange for use of the music.

I think for Alan it was the Four Freshman, the Kingston Trio. For my little brother Carl, it was Chuck Berry. For myself it was groups who sang ballads, love songs. Richie Valens used to wipe me out. At that time I was interested in music—but not like Brian and Mike. I suppose I was really just into being popular.
——*Dennis*

"Surfin' U.S.A." was a monster hit and, coupled with its "cool" hot-rod flip "Shut Down," it stayed on the charts for months. It gave kids all across the country direct contact with a world beyond their reach. Whereas most rock trends dealt with experience that could happen anywhere (you could be at the hop in any town in America and everybody had his own heartbreak hotel), the Beach Boys' surfin' tunes delivered a fantasy—a distant nirvana of warmth, water, and fun.

It is for this reason, perhaps, that even the rocking, upbeat Beach Boys' tunes such as "Surfin' U.S.A." still evoke a subtle sense of loss. There is for most of us a sense of never having been there, never knowing the California experience. In reality, it was special—but it was also filled with as much anxiety, affection, and disappointment as any other part of the U.S. But the Beach Boys, through their relentless harmony and youthful spirit, made it sound like a near-perfect world. They sang about—and were part of—the California dream.

A year after I dropped out of the group, "Surfin' U.S.A." and "Shut Down" had just come out. I got a call from Brian and he says, "How'd you like to go on tour with the group again?"
——*Alan*

Although David Marks was to appear on some of the group's then-unreleased tunes, Brian wanted a return to the original Beach Boys. After the group's first big tour (a forty-day midwestern bus trip), David left the group and Al Jardine returned from the East Coast.

He went from playing rhythm guitar for us to Dave Marks and the Marksmen, a small band in Southern California, then he went east to Boston to study at the conservatory of music.
——*Mike*

When the group followed "Surfin' U.S.A." with a re-cut version of "Surfer Girl," every love-starved fourteen-year-old knew exactly what she looked like—and in the realm of teenage fantasy, that could be any one of a thousand shapes and faces.

"Surfer Girl" is probably one of the sweetest intros to a song you're ever going to hear. It's what you call a sweet little ballad. It had a Paris Sisters' sort of sweetness. They were one of my favorites....We did it without knowing how. It was the first time we ever did a song like that. ... It was an innocent try—our first innocent recording experience.

——Brian

SURFER GIRL   *by Brian Wilson*

Little surfer, Little one
Made my heart come all undone
Do you love me, do you Surfer Girl,
Surfer Girl, my little Surfer Girl.
I have watched you on the shore
Standing by the ocean's roar
Do you love me, do you Surfer Girl,
Surfer Girl, Surfer Girl OOH
We could ride the surf together

While our love would grow
In my woodie I would take you
Everywhere I go
So I say from me to you
I will make your dreams come true
Do you love me, do you Surfer Girl,
Surfer Girl, my little Surfer Girl.

Copyright 1963 by Guild Music Co.

The song bore resemblance to Phil Spector's "I Love How You Love Me" hit. Both had an up-and-down harmony that flowed softly, taking you with it. Like earlier Beach Boys' singles, it had a direct emotional appeal reinforced by their "all live" method of recording. The harmony, though super-sweet, is sincere.

Simple. There's this guy and he loves this girl who hangs out at the beach and he wants to be with her. It was the first Beach Boys' ballad to hit nationally, and it showed off Brian Wilson's skill in taking a seemingly light-hearted fantasy of adolescent yearning and turning it into a full-fledged emotional plea. He dignified the teenage response, without losing its innocence, and put it on a par with any other "adult" emotion. It was as if he were answering some unnamed parent—explaining that it didn't matter that he was a "kid"; that his feelings were just as important as those of anybody else. "Don't tell me I'm going to outgrow it! This is how I feel now!"

The music told you that there were other guys and girls out there feeling the same things. This was one of the special properties of early rock and roll. Brian did this type of song so well because the Wilsons were so much like any other American family. He had really gone through the things he wrote about in his songs.

The lyrics just popped into my head. I'd be going "I just heard something that made me jealous!" Or "I'm uptight about that!" Then—all of a sudden—zap! I'd be right back there trying to answer it.

——Brian

I think there was always a special kind of relationship between Brian and Mike. They were a tight family. Dennis was Dennis, what more can you say? A happy-go-lucky guy. Carl was pretty young and very naive. He played excellent guitar.

——Chuck Britz

Brian moved to Hollywood not too long after "Surfin' Safari." The change in him was not a very apparent one. It was gradual. Brian was never frustrated in the studio in those days. He was easy, in control.

——Marilyn Wilson

With a string of hits developing, the early insecurities and shyness of the group began to fade. The Beach Boys' stage act took form, with Dennis on drums, Mike at the mike, Brian on bass, Al on rhythm guitar, and young Carl on dazzling lead guitar. The music elicited a wild audience response—a combination of adolescent excitement, teenage sexuality, and sheer delight at the simple, singalong quality of the Beach Boys' tunes.

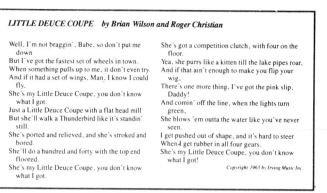

LITTLE DEUCE COUPE   *by Brian Wilson and Roger Christian*

Well, I'm not braggin', Babe, so don't put me down
But I've got the fastest set of wheels in town.
When something pulls up to me, it don't even try.
And if it had a set of wings, Man, I know I could fly.
She's my Little Deuce Coupe, you don't know what I got.
Just a Little Deuce Coupe with a flat head mill
But she'll walk a Thunderbird like it's standin' still.
She's ported and relieved, and she's stroked and bored.
She'll do a hundred and forty with the top end floored.
She's my Little Deuce Coupe, you don't know what I got.

She's got a competition clutch, with four on the floor.
Yea, she purrs like a kitten till the lake pipes roar.
And if that ain't enough to make you flip your wig,
There's one more thing, I've got the pink slip, Daddy!
And comin' off the line, when the lights turn green,
She blows 'em outta the water like you've never seen.
I get pushed out of shape, and it's hard to steer
When I get rubber in all four gears.
She's my Little Deuce Coupe, you don't know what I got!

Copyright 1963 by Irving Music Inc.

Filled with more car lingo, the flip side of "Surfer Girl," "Little Deuce Coupe," sped right out of the radio with a chorus as high and as catchy as anything else that summer. It was ideal screaming from the back seat of a convertible.

Like Brian's "Cherry, Cherry, Coupe" ("chopped nose and decked with louvers on the hood"), "Little Deuce Coupe" had lyrics by Roger Christian. Christian was part of what had emerged as the California rock music scene, a loose fraternity of studio musicians, songwriters, vocalists, and producers. Most had grown up in Southern California, and all were working the same section of Sunset Boulevard. Many had sprung from L.A. High, and their names, later read like a roster of celebrities: Lou Adler, Herb Alpert, Jan and Dean, and Bruce Johnston. Johnston, a singer/composer/producer, teamed up with his friend and Columbia Records producer Terry Melcher to forge an old group, The Rip Chords, into a Beach Boys' style car combo. By going so far as to sing along on some mixes, Johnston and Melcher turned out two pleasant hits with the group, "Hey Little Cobra" and "Three Window Coupe." As "Bruce and Terry" they had a big hit of their own, "Summer Means Fun."

"Summer Means Fun" and dozens of other songs of the period were the work of P. F. Sloan and Steve Barri, a songwriting team whose ability to turn out catchy two-minute hooks resulted in separate but highly successful rock careers over the next decade. Together with producer Lou Adler, Sloan and Barri were partially responsible for the success of Jan Berry and Dean Torrence—*Jan and Dean.*

The immediacy of rock is quite apparent in the relationship between Jan and Dean and the Beach Boys. It must have seemed like yesterday to Mike Love when he first heard "Heart and Soul" on KRLA. Yet a few years later, the Beach Boys were jamming with Jan and Dean on a set of *their* songs *and* at a concert near Hawthorne!

We were headlining and they were an opening act. When they got through, we came out, did our set, and then everybody wanted to hear more and in those days, nobody knew more than about six songs, y'know? Especially when you had a pickup band. We were usually at the mercy of whatever band the promoter linked you with to open....When the Beach Boys played the two or three songs we did, those were all the songs we'd rehearsed together. So we said, since we did all of our songs, let's do all of your songs again. They kind of looked at us as if to say, "You'd do our songs with us and let us stand in front?" They thought they had to stand in the back. They were really amazed. We were able to add in two more vocal parts—a nice amount of parts—and at that point they realized two more voices were more valid and so did we. So we started thinking in those terms. Sometime after that was our first time in the studio together...on our album. They cut "Surfin'" and "Surfin' Safari" for us.

——Dean Torrence, Jan and Dean

A friendship developed quickly in the months that followed. Jan, Dean, and Lou Adler all thought the surfin' craze was the way to go and from that time on, the groups filled in on each other's sessions. The most famous Beach Boys/Jan and Dean story concerns the making of

"Surf City." Brian had recently composed "Surfin' U.S.A." and was at a piano to play it. Jan and Dean loved the song and suggested to Brian that they do it as a single. "No," Brian said, "that's for the Beach Boys—but I've got some others. How about this?" Whereupon the eldest Wilson pounded out an opening, chorus, and a verse for "Surf City." Jan and Dean quickly cut the tune, surpassed the Beach Boys' current hit and made the top spot on the charts. Much to Capitol's chagrin—they threatened to sue the Beach Boys over Brian's vocal on "Surf City"—both groups continued to overlap audibly during the next two and a half years. You can even hear "Thanks, Dean" at the end of "Barbara Ann" on *Beach Boys' Party*.

As Brian's themes for the Beach Boys' music moved beyond Chevy engines and sand-flecked woodies, the surfing and car genres were unofficially bequeathed to Jan and Dean, who turned out such Berry-Torrence-Wilson singles as "Drag City" and "Ride the Wild Surf." The duo's own classics including "Little Old Lady From Pasadena" ("Go, Granny, Go!") kept them in the spotlight until the mid-sixties.

Over three quarters of the car-song lyrics of the period passed through the hands of disc jockey Roger Christian. A fountain of drag-strip phrases, Christian's words lent an accurate and oddly poetic backdrop to the automotive output of the L.A. rock scene. Even Brian's dazzling "Don't Worry, Baby" profited from Christian's lyrics, weaving a drag-race premise for the song with Brian's musical theme of insecurity.

We had a lot of musicians supporting the Beach Boys, including a lot of Phil Spector's musicians—and Phil Spector had the best. There was no doubt about that. He was the best—and is the best.... We went to at least ten—I preferred Western Recorders at 5000 Sunset Boulevard. It seemed to have the best echo chamber for what we liked to do vocally. It had good balanced echo, a really fat echo. RCA had a good studio too, and Sunset Sound was great.

———*Brian*

Brian did a song that Phil was gonna record with the Ronettes called "Please Don't Hurt My Little Sister." Brian wrote the song and came to the session, and I thought it was a good session, but Phil never released that one because he didn't...share in it, the writing. During that date Leon Russell couldn't play anymore...Phil had to ask him to stop playing piano, so Brian played it.

———*Jack Nietzche*

Once we got past a certain period, we usually ended up with four sax, maybe four or five guitars, a couple of drummers and maybe sometimes four basses.

———*Chuck Britz*

In the four-chamber "A" studio of Goldstar Recording, pop wunderkind Phil Spector was transforming the nature of the rock-and-roll single. By making the *production* the star of any given recording, he made a revolutionary statement about the potential of rock. With properly produced instrumental and vocal tracks, Spector theorized, he could make almost any song a hit. A remarkable string of tunes on his own Phillies label, from "He's a Rebel" to "Zip-a-Dee-Doo-Dah," was Spector's way of proving the theory. That echo system at Goldstar, coupled with a collection of L.A.'s finest studio musicians and arranger Jack Nietzche, resulted in the Spectorian "wall of sound"—a driving, melodic musical effect, filled with percussion and symphonic in scope. This textured, complex, orchestral rock sound established a standard for Brian Wilson to meet in producing any new Beach Boys' record.

Dennis, Mike, Alan, Brian, Carl

SURFIN' DOWN THE SWANEE RIVER
SHOOT THE CURL

THE HONEYS

Following Spector's lesson, Brian gathered such talented session men as Leon Russell, Glen Campbell, Carol Kaye, and Hal Blaine for instrumental work on Beach Boys' background tracks.

I first met Spector in sixty-three.

———Brian

By this time the subtle shift of California from film capital to rock capital of the world was getting underway. Scores of singers and musicians in L.A. were earning a living as background performers on other people's records. Brian's collaborator, Gary Usher, was familiar with this scene. Young groups were hoping to "make it" by first working with established stars. Usher's friend Ginger Blake had a "girl group" with her cousins Marilyn and Diane Rovell. They called themselves the Honeys—the surfers' *girls.*

My cousin Ginger was dating Gary Usher and he was friends with Brian, and he came over one night and said, "I want to take you to see this group called the Beach Boys." They were at a place called Pandora's Box in Hollywood.

———Diane Rovell

During the performance, Brian noticed one of the Honeys, fifteen-year-old Marilyn Rovell, in the audience. Asking for a sip of the hot chocolate on her table, Brian proceeded to spill it (accidentally, of course) on her blouse. That same night they were formally introduced by Gary Usher. A friendship was born. Marilyn found Brian to be hysterically funny—and formed an immediate romantic attachment. At the time, Brian was engaged to an attractive blonde named Judy Bolles, about whom he had written the song "Judy" in early '62. During the next year and a half, that relationship fell apart and the friendship between Brian and Marilyn grew.

I was about fifteen at the time. Brian would take me home after being out with me, you know? Then at two in the morning he would all of a sudden call me up and say, "Please, you gotta come over here, I can't do without you!" He'd beg me—and naturally anything he said I just did, you know? I'd go over there on a Honda motorscooter. I'd get bundled up in hat and gloves....the whole bit. My parents thought I was really nuts.

———Marilyn

Brian was going through changes. The people he had begun to socialize with in Los Angeles were often different from his old friends in Hawthorne.

He was totally naive. Because of his talent, he was taken to the best studios in town.... the hip part of the industry. He was impressed. It was exciting. It was like a kid growing....grabbing everything he could. He was going "Oh, that's great! I want to use that! I want to get to know that!" He took it all in ....He just admired others' work more than his own.

———Marilyn

Marilyn, her sister Diane, and cousin Ginger became the focus of Brian's first major production effort outside the group. Having cut an obscure single on Dot in the fall of '62 with a group called Rachel and the Revolvers ("The Revolution"/"Number One"), Brian was now set to prove that his success did not begin and end with the Beach Boys. Working on the first Honeys' single, "Surfin' Down the Swanee River"/"Shoot the Curl" (the "A" side was an arrangement of the Stephen Foster classic) in the spring of '63, he followed up with two Spectorian "girl group" melodies, both heavy with percussion, in the next six months.

We never got a hit...cute little sound.

———Brian

Capitol pushed Marilyn, Ginger, and Diane as a "Beach Girls" group, posing them with short skirts, teased hair, and the traditional surfboard-in-arms. They were no Ronettes.

Both "Pray for the Surf" and "The One You Can't Have" sank despite lively productions. Perhaps there were just too many girl groups already.

Undaunted, Brian turned his attention to a streak of musical unknowns, putting out a pair of singles for Mike Love's friend Sharon Marie (11/63 and 6/64) and "Poorest Boy in Town" for *The Donna Reed Show* TV star Paul Peterson (3/64). It took the single, "Pamela Jean," cut by the Wilsons under the name "The Survivors" (1/64), to convince Brian, if only marginally, that his efforts were best-received commercially under the Beach Boys' name.

The rock world was exploding and the Beach Boys were at the center of the action. The year 1963 found them surrounded by Frankie Valli's falsetto on "Walk Like A Man"; Spector's pulsating "Be My Baby" and "Baby, I Love You"; Dion DiMucci's yearning rock style (which Dennis would later cop affectionately for "The Wanderer") on "Ruby Baby" and "Donna the Prima Donna"; Jimmy Gilmer's sweet guitar licks on "Sugar Shack"; Peter, Paul, and Mary's cover of "Blowin' in the Wind" and the incredible R & B of Smokey Robinson, Curtis Mayfield, Sam Cooke, and Martha Reeves. The group absorbed the music with a mixture of admiration and competitiveness.

He was excited about being able to use Phil Spector's people...being able to use those people to play his music. Brian and Phil were very good...well, I can't say good, but they were friends. I know they have a mutual admiration. Brian couldn't understand that Spector even thought about him. Phil had been in the business for a while.

———Marilyn

It was late '63 and rock was still raw and unpretentious, lacking the corporate sheen that would sterilize later sounds. Martin Luther King was marching. Kennedy was alive. The Beach Boys were *seeing* America.

Touring heavily, the group was greeted by a huge female fandom from Sacramento to the Midwest. Mike Love, "the ladies' man" of the group, had emerged as energetic "emcee" for the concert act, and his lead vocals as well as visual presence set a loose and humorous tone for the group's on-stage behavior. Dennis, laid-back, muscular, and tan, became the "sex symbol." Al and Carl, on Fender guitars, came off as "good time" people, seemingly as at home on the stage as the crowd was in their seats. Brian loved to sing. In concert, he was extremely alert to the band's vocal performance.

Two new songs were added to the concert repertoire by late 1963. Drawing on his Hawthorne background, Brian came up with another two-sided hit, "Be True to Your School" and "In My Room." The former was a call to arms for school spirit, a still-negotiable commodity in the pre-cynical sixties. Whatever might have been growing in the classrooms of 1963, it still vanished when somebody across the tracks said their school was better.

Now what's the matter, buddy? Ain't you heard of my school? It's the number one in the state!

The opening line cleverly covered every high school in the country. Brian backed the lyrics with an AAH-AAH vocal and sax opening, then put in a RAH-RAH-RAH-RAH-SIS-BOOM-BAH chorus to reflect the "school" theme. The single version even had the Honeys doing a cheerleader chorus ("Push 'em back! Push 'em back! Way back!"). It was a smash, rising into the top ten at the height of the football season.

You're not afraid when you're in your room. It may be dark, the lights may be out, your folks might say, "Okay, it's time for bed." And you go in there, you say to yourself, it's dark and I'm alone, but I won't be afraid in my room.
——*Brian*

"In My Room," the popular flip, revealed Brian's more personal side, and replaced the usual bouncy group spirit with a prayerlike harmony. Backed by a violin track, the song never went higher than a middle "B" and the low-key, lonely effect was ideal for playing under your pillow at night. It was the Beach Boys' first major attempt at showing the private side of teenage life, and in its own way "In My Room" was more universal than any of their earlier hits.

The last Beach Boys' single of the year was a holiday song. "Little St. Nick" was a short, bouncing tune that gave the impression Santa hung out at National Speedway in his spare time. It was part of a mini-genre taken to later heights by Phil Spector, Motown, and the Beach Boys themselves.

In addition to heavy touring, 45-rpm hits, collaborative production efforts, and some songwriting ("The Humpty Dumpty," "Back Home") with an old college friend Bob Norberg (Bob Norman) Brian and the Beach Boys found time to cut three uneven, yet exuberant albums for Capitol in 1963.

The discs, *Surfin' U.S.A.*, *Surfer Girl*, and *Little Deuce Coupe*, mixed their popular singles, cover versions of surfing instru-

Alan, Carl, Brian

mentals, rock standards, and new surfer/teen/car/tunes. They further revealed the Beach Boys' influences to the national audience and continued the popularization of the Southern California sound.

Everything was done on a four-track basis; the first sessions were done on a three-track. Everything was mono as far as the music was concerned. We did all the vocals live and dubbed them. Everybody sang at one time.
——*Chuck Britz*

Surfin' U.S.A., released in the spring of '63, had five instrumental cuts and showed the strain that time (and Capitol) put on the group for material. The Dick Dale influence was apparent. His standards "Miserlou" and "Let's Go Trippin'" were covered competently as was "Honky Tonk." More pervasive were the doses of Chuck Berry and the Four Freshman harmonic blend. Brian and Gary Usher's "The Lonely Sea" lulled the listener with a sweet, repetitive ballad, especially notable for its evocation of a natural environment. The approach and the subject—the water—would continue to appear throughout the group's career. "Farmer's Daughter" showcased a smoother, seductive falsetto. "Shut Down," a more thematically grandiose successor to "409," featured Mike's nasal lead on the story of a Sting Ray vs. a 413 Dodge. Both foreshadowed the leap in production values as Brian took control.

On a U-47 mike I might have Carl, Dennis, and Al, and Brian would be right by them on a 545 singing lead, and then Mike was on a U-47 across to my right. They were all in a line and that is how we did those vocals. Everything was done live. All the tracks were done live. In the booth we'd have four or five instruments, like a couple basses and three or four guitars. Everybody else would be out in the studio and we'd do all of this live with just earphones.
——*Chuck Britz*

Surfer Girl hit the stores in October '63 and firmly established Brian's reputation as a creative producer/composer. It also formalized the Beach Boys' existence as a modern rock-and-roll *group*. In the studio and on stage, they could function as a self-sufficient entity. They played all their own instruments, did arrangements, composed their own music, sang all the vocals, and supervised production. Within the restrictions of Capitol's commercial values and his own preoccupation with the Berry/Four Freshman/Spectorian styles, Brian was able to develop a fuller, more consistent and sophisticated teenage sound. He was starting to approach the cuts on an album with the same creative attitude that Phil Spector had reserved for the "A" sides of his singles.

Clockwise from left to right: Mike, Carl, Alan, Brian, Dennis

This attitude grew partly out of Brian's perfectionist nature but was also colored by genuine love of music and the competitive drive of an extraordinarily talented young man. Brian wanted things done his way. By getting Capitol's acquiescence in the development of the Beach Boys sound (if only because of their hit-making track record) and by assuming the responsibility of producing that sound from composition to acetate, Brian established a clear creative independence for himself and the group. From *Surfer Girl* on, the Beach Boys' studio work was to epitomize the modern production relationship between a musically successful rock-and-roll artist and his recording company, a standard for the future of the art form.

Brian was the first guy to do it until it was right ... then he gave them the record. He took his chances. A lot of us would get chicken after four hours and say, "We'd better get off that tune." Brian would hang in there for nine hours no matter what the cost. I used to think he was crazy, but he was right.
——*Nick Venet*

While Brian may not have been the first practitioner of musical integrity in rock and roll, he set a high standard. He had a musical vision and he honored it, working with both the group and contracted studio musicians until the sound merited release. The money wasn't important; the sound and the success were. Brian wanted the singles to be as good as they could be, and he also wanted to see them at the top of the charts. Album cuts benefited from these demanding ideals also.

As an lp, *Surfer Girl* excelled in its evocation of the surf and car era. Chauvinistic surfing tunes such as "Catch a Wave" and "Surfer's Rule" were the epitome of the group's fad-oriented music. "Wave" featured a luscious group harmony and more lyrical humor ("They'll eat their words with a fork and spoon, and watch 'em, They'll hit the road and all be surfin' soon.") "Surfer's Rule" put down greasers and landlocked Joe Cools and delivered a falsetto rock rank-out at its tag, with the Beach Boys telling Frankie Valli, "Four Seasons, you better believe it!" Side two echoed the boys' sentiment for the world of teenage cruisin'. "Our Car Club" featured a poised Mike Love defending an imaginary East L.A. clique, complete with requisite "grown-up" sponsor.

"Hawaii" offered another spectacular Brian Wilson falsetto and opened the door to a parade of South Sea knock-offs. "In My Room," already a teen anthem, summed up the creative advances of the album, a beautiful harmonic brushstroke with a sophisticated production and simple, flowing musical base.

The money was never very important. We were never into the money. ... It was funny.
——*Marilyn*

If Brian was content to hang out, have fun, and let others take care of the financial end, Capitol was just as eager to make the most of the group's impact.

Little Deuce Coupe arrived only two months after *Surfer Girl,* just in time to cash in on holiday sales. With the exception of "A Young Man Is Gone," a sweet, full-bodied version of "Their Hearts Were Full of Spring" with lyrics about James Dean, and "Be True to Your School" (minus the Honeys), all of the songs focused on cars—*Coupe* was a glossy forerunner of the "concept album" in rock. There were four reissued cuts ("Coupe," "Shut Down," "409," and "Our Car Club"), a nervy feat by Capitol, who had just put out an anthology of car songs—*Shut Down* with B.B. tunes—before *Surfer Girl.*

A floating, high-pitched "Spirit of America" ("The border, the Southland, had seen some strange things/But the strangest thing yet was a jet without wings") by Brian and Roger Christian was one of the most beautiful pieces on the album, and its salute to Craig Breedlove, the race-car driver, put his race just a step below the World Series. It was the softest of the Beach Boys' car-oriented songs, a change from the rousing and progressively intricate melodies that filled out the album.

On November 21, 1963, at home with Mike Love, Brian wrote a haunting melody so beautiful that, as Mike explains, he could only think of lyrics for it in terms of a sense of loss.

We went to sleep maybe at three in the morning. We got up at maybe nine, awakened by the radio saying Kennedy had been shot in Dallas. ... It was kind of a shock because we felt so melancholy ... but we didn't go into the studio and express it. It was more feeling. We always felt that the Beach Boys as a group, if we're going to be making music, that it should be some-

Dennis, Brian, Carl, Alan, Mike

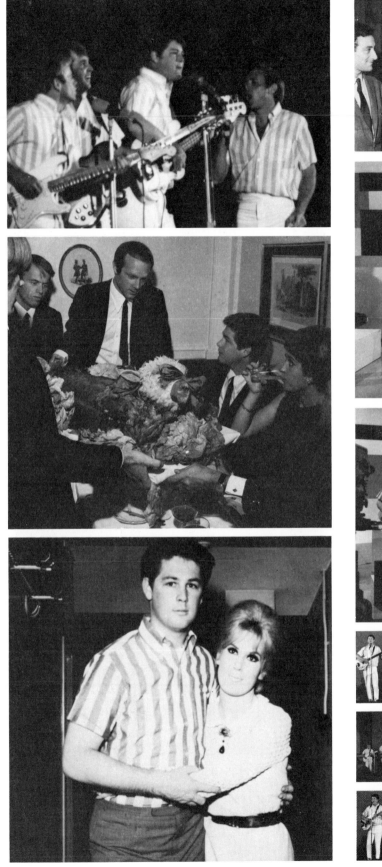

*thing positive — harmonies. Even if it was something negative ... we could
turn it into a positive thing.*

——Mike

The song was called "The Warmth of the Sun." The lines
Mike wrote were a departure from his usual lyrics, and the music itself
capsulized the mood of the country in the context of young romance. A
gentle sound was exuded in the Beach Boys' rendition, a lush evolution
of the "Surfer Girl" sound.

*What good is the dawn that grows into the day?
The sunset at night or living this way?*

Nineteen sixty-four came quickly with a new President, new
dissent, new talk of war. For the Beach Boys, it was a period of extensive, exhausting touring. Their fame had taken on international dimen-
sions and they were scheduled for tours of England, Europe, and Australia, and much of the U.S.

*We were in a cab going from the Holiday Inn in Salt Lake City to the airport
...I got an idea to do a song about a girl who borrows the car from her father
and instead of going to the library like she tells him, goes cruisin' to see and
be seen by all the boys. Her father finds out she didn't go to the library; she
went to the hamburger stand. Yet when he takes the car keys away, the guy
says, "Well, that's okay because now we'll have fun, fun, fun, now that
daddy took the T-Bird away."*

——Mike

"Fun, Fun, Fun," the first Beach Boys' single of 1964,
opened with a "Johnny B. Goode" riff and quickly segued into Mike's
nasal story of cruisin' in California. The tempo of the song was as fast as
anything the boys had done and its popularity was reflected on the
charts. Soaring from start to finish with flashy overlapping falsetto, it
reached number five, the highest outing of their careers.

FUN, FUN, FUN   *by Brian Wilson and Mike Love*

Well, she got her daddy's car and she cruised
   thru the hamburger stand now
Seems she forgot all about the library like she
   told her old man now
And with her radio blastin' goes cruisin' just as
   fast as she can now
And she'll have fun, fun, fun till her daddy takes
   her T-Bird away
Well, the girls can't stand her 'cause she walks,
   looks and drives like an ace now
She makes the Indy 500 look like a Roman
   chariot race now
A lotta guys try to catch her but she leads 'em on
   a wild goose chase now

And she'll have fun, fun, fun till her daddy takes
   her T-Bird away
A-well you knew all along your dad was gettin'
   wise to you now
And since he took your set of keys you've been
   thinkin' that your fun is all thru now
But you can come along with me 'cause we gotta
   lotta things to do now
And you'll have FUN, FUN, FUN now that
   daddy took the T-Bird away
And you'll have fun, fun, fun now that
   daddy took the T-Bird away.

Copyright 1964, 1976 by Irving Music Co.

---

*When I sit down at the piano and play a new song, the others can visualize
the whole arrangement right away. We take the melody apart and work it out
phrase by phrase. If they don't like my approach, they suggest another. If
Carl doesn't dig my idea, I'll change it immediately because Carl has
exquisite musical taste. I trust it completely.*

——Brian 1965

Brian Wilson was quickly expanding his range as one of
rock's most innovative producers and the group's formidable vocal talents were keeping pace. The closing section of "Fun, Fun, Fun" reveals
just how intricate Brian's plans were for each song. As Mike's line
"took the T-Bird away" fades out, the Boys' chorus of "fun, fun, fun"
builds, and Brian comes in with a separate, high *"a-wooooooo"* melody. This piece quickly fades out as the chorus comes in again, then it
returns, rises to join the chorus, and both fade out together. Across
America, a hundred thousand orange-and-yellow discs swirled to the
syncopated harmony of the group.

If "Fun, Fun, Fun" soared, the next Beach Boys' single flew
up like a rocket. Complex, airy, fast, "I Get Around" was a gem of
California cruising rock.

I GET AROUND   *by Brian Wilson*

Chorus
I get around—from town to town
I'm a real cool head I'm makin' real good bread.

I'm gettin' bugged, drivin' up and down the same
   old strip
I gotta find a new place where the kids are hip
My buddies and me are gettin' real well known,
Yeah, the bad guys know us and they leave us
   alone.

(Repeat chorus)
We always take my car 'cause it's never been beat
And we've never missed yet with the girls we
   meet.
None of the guys go steady 'cause it wouldn't be
   right
To leave your best girl home on a Saturday night.

(Repeat chorus)

Copyright 1964 by Irving Music Inc.

Brian's high voice curves over the opening chorus, arcing a
bass riff to introduce Mike's driving nasal solo. The boys sing a sweet
background harmony, and a walking bass guitar drops in and out for
punctuation with a surfing twang. The listener doesn't even get a chance
to catch his breath. There's so much to hear!

*I remember when "Fun, Fun, Fun" came out. He wasn't interested in the
money, but wanted a top-ten record. He wanted to know how the song would
do against the Beatles and if KFWB would play it. But I never saw Brian as a
competitor.*

——Phil Spector

*"Fun, Fun, Fun" was fun, fun, fun. In the earlier days, when we were
doing just the group basically, we did more than one take, but we never really
did a lot of takes — maybe four, five, six....Most of our tracks came off very
smooth and easy. We rehearsed a lot. Brian would sit down and talk to each
of them before we ever rolled the tape. There were never any scores; maybe
just chord structures.*

——Chuck Britz

The fast, raucous style of "Surfin' U.S.A." had been trans-
formed into a sophisticated but still youthful sound. Like a kinetic
sculpture, the song functioned as a whole, yet it was filled at the same
time with smaller, independently exciting elements. Hand-clapping,
rim-tapping, and guitar combined for a driving interlude that expressed
Brian's musical concept of the "cruisin'" feeling.

The song came out in May '64. By June it was the anthem for
summer vacation.

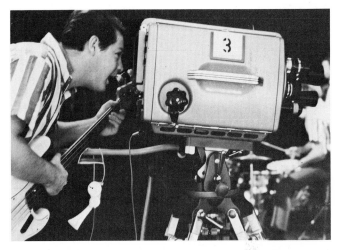

In his mind, Brian had established rock and roll as a form equal to and no less respectable than any other "serious" music. With rock as his form of expression, he began to focus on the way people felt rather than what they did. Songs about cars and surfin' began to fade. In his quest to bring both the composition and production of rock to higher levels, Brian slowly changed the focus of the Beach Boys' music.

As studio time took more and more priority in his life, Brian became more serious, but no less enthusiastic, about his work. He would often want the group in the studio at odd hours of the day and night.

When I hear really fabulous material by other groups I feel as small as the dot over the i in nit. Then I just have to create a new song to bring me up on top....That's probably my most compelling motive for writing new songs—the urge to overcome an inferiority feeling...I've never written one note or word of music simply because I think it will make money. My ideas for the group are to combine music that strikes a deep emotional response among listeners and still maintains a somewhat untrained and teenage sound. I depend upon harmonics more than before and fuse it with a 1964–1965 approach in production.

——*Brian, 1965*

American rock music and production in 1964 was a silver mine. The Four Seasons returned with "Rag Doll" and "Dawn." Motown/Holland-Dozier-Holland turned out "Baby Love" for the

Supremes and "Baby, I Need Your Loving" for the 4 Tops. Spector handled the Righteous Brothers "You've Lost That Loving Feeling," and Johnny Rivers cut "Memphis." Beyond that, it was the year of the invasion.

The Kinks, the Zombies, the Animals, the Dave Clark Five, the Rolling Stones. The Beatles. In five months British rock swept the American charts. McCartney-penned tunes held down the first five slots in *Billboard's* Hot 100. A driving English beat earned rock's respect and shifted the focus of music and fashion from America to London. "She Loves You," "Glad All Over," "She's Not There," "You Really Got Me," and a dozen other hits launched a craze and brought a tough, rocking style. Pendleton shirts were out, long hair was in.

We were very threatened by the whole thing.

——*Brian*

At the height of Beatlemania, "I Get Around" was number one. I think it challenged Brian's creativity.

——*Mike*

The Beach Boys' "I Get Around" rode the top of the charts for a month. The British may have known rock and roll, but Brian knew America. While the Burdon/Price "House of the Rising Sun" may have sent a chill out of the three-inch speaker, "I Get Around" fit the teenage milieu like a shake and fries. The flip went straight for the heart.

DON'T WORRY BABY *by Brian Wilson and Roger Christian*

Well, it's been building up inside of me for I
   don't know how long
I don't know why but I keep thinkin' something's
   bound to go wrong
But she looks in my eye
And makes me realize
When she says, "Don't worry baby, everything
   will work out all right"
I guess I should have kept my mouth shut
When I started to brag about my car
But I can't back down now.

Because I pushed the other guys too far
She makes me come alive and makes me want to

drive
When she says, "Don't worry baby everything
   will come out all right"
Oooo—ooo
She told me baby
When ya race today just take along my love with you

And if you know how much I love you
Nothing could go wrong with you

Oh what she does to me when she makes love
   to me
And she says, "Don't worry baby everything will
   work out all right."

Copyright 1964 by Irving Music Co., BMI

"Don't Worry, Baby" was a staggering, textured tour de force of harmony, dramatic falsetto, and revolving melody. As an expression of teenage yearning and emotional insecurity, it was unsurpassed in the history of rock. If "I Get Around" made you want to jump, "Don't Worry, Baby" made you want to cry. If you were crying already, listening to it helped you feel like you weren't alone.

The song was a youthful plea for love and understanding, expressed through Brian's dramatic use of harmony. With "Don't Worry, Baby," the Beach Boys elevated their use of the voice as a musical instrument to new heights, transcending both the drag-race motif of Roger Christian's lyrics and the current standards of the popular ballad. The song was a classic for both its indomitable romantic spirit and vocal strength.

*You know, Brian was frustrated a **lot**, just because of his mind. He was so sharp, and he would always get into things more....The music business used to get him down. You know—this guy did this and this guy did that....*

I used to say to him, "Don't worry, baby."

——*Marilyn*

The song's opening was washed by the surfing sound. The Beach Boys' sweet chorus *("ahh-ahh")* blanketed the lyrics, and a rhythm guitar sent out a choking chord that hurt in the same place as romance. Then a wall of sound took a walk by the sea. The song's sense of loss was lightened only by its reassuring harmony and spirit.

As he went along, he went further and further into more aesthetics in the studio.... A lot of it was attempting to prove he wasn't just a beach group.

——*Chuck Britz*

The Fun/Worry single—an apt description for two prevalent Brian Wilson moods—was the cornerstone of their forthcoming album, *Shut Down Volume 2*.

Side one featured "Fun," "Worry," "The Warmth of the Sun," and one new Wilson-Love car tune, the funky "This Car of Mine," with Dennis's raspy vocal debut and a rolling display of early Beach Boy counterpoint. Closing the side was a beautiful, airy, and instrumentally textured remake of "Why Do Fools Fall in Love?"

Side two revealed the album's schizophrenic nature. An uninspired version of "Louie, Louie" was coupled with two modest Wilson/Love originals, "Pom Pom Playgirl" and "Keep an Eye on Summer" (again co-written with Brian's ex-college roommate Bob Norberg [Norman]). Carl contributed the title track and Dennis cut a meandering percussion filler, "Denny's Drums." The whole side seemed rushed. Among the most interesting pieces was a cut that wasn't a song at all.

Predating the Monkee's TV patter and such off-the-cuff rock humor as *A Hard Day's Night*, "Cassius Love vs. Sonny Wilson" was a rank-out contest between Mike Love and Brian. Unpretentious, affectionately critical, and often funny—Brian on Mike's singing: "At least my nose doesn't sound like it's on the critical list!"—the cut, which was Mike Love's concept, previewed later studio antics.

"I Get Around" opened (perhaps *kicked-off* would be a more fitting statement) the next disc, *All Summer Long*. The record was their first album released in the summer and it went top five before the season was out.

I remember when we did "Little Honda," Brian wanted to get this real distorted guitar sound, real fuzzy. "This guitar sounds like shit," I said and he goes, "Just do it."

When I heard it, I felt like an asshole. It sounded really hot. That was before fuzz became a big deal.

——*Carl*

All Summer Long contained four hits and a respectable mix of other Brian Wilson originals. It helped launch one minicraze and wrote a closing tune for another. "Little Honda" (the hit single was cut by the Hondells) played to the public's enthusiasm for Honda's new mini-motorcycle, a precursor of the moped. The Beach Boys' version had a fuzzy, ambiguous percussion track and high-pitched vocal. A super-nasal Mike shouted:

First gear —It's all right!
Faster! It's all right!
It's not a big motorcycle —just a little motorbike!

"Don't Back Down," which fittingly closed the album, was a high-pitched farewell to the surfing scene. Their last surfin' period song possessed an upbeat, anthemlike quality mirrored in a light backbeat and sweet falsetto blend ("gotta be a little nuts...show 'em now who's got guts").

"Wendy," also on side two, was a love-hungry ballad with heartbreaking lyrics and an exceptional Brian Wilson falsetto. "Hushabye," a super lush harmonic version of the Mystics hit, continued Brian's tradition of cutting his favorite classics.

"Our Favorite Recording Sessions" continued the "Sonny Wilson" tradition with another off-the-cuff routine. The sound it parodied, "All Summer Long," was never released as a single, but its evocation of suburban summer—complete with its famous polychromatic opening—was so innocent and wistful that years later Director George Lucas would select it as the coda for his film *American Graffiti*, even though the events in the movie took place two years before the song's release. A stunning collage of harmony and summer reflections, it stood out next to the other teenage/suburban songs on the album.

"Drive In" was a mini-spectacular, a funny salute to suburbia's teenage passion pits. Backed by an *oo-wah* Beach Boy chorus, Mike's tongue-in-cheek lead was ideal for Brian's lyrics. You can almost see him putting in every possible drive-in story from the Hawthorne experience ("If the windows get fogged you'll have to take a breath down at the drive-in"). With the "We love the drive-in" falsetto chorus, bell-tree, and racing melody line, the song was a fitting caveat about front-seat romance.

Mike Love with Annette Funicello

A clever "Do You Remember" was Brian's fractured history lesson—a questionable ode to rock-and-roll roots ("Little Richard sang it and Dick Clark brought it to life") that succeeded more for its background innovations and vocal arrangement than anything else. The group's voices percolated in good-natured frenzy with Brian's characteristically smooth lead over a light series of narrative choruses (*oos, aahs,* and *dodiwadahs*) that underscored the lyrics along with Carl's synchronized Chuck Berry riffs.

"Girls on the Beach," a sweet reprise of the melody of the "Surfer Girl" melody, did double time as title track for a *Girls on the Beach* movie, in which the group played other songs from the album. The Beach Boys also showed up in a Walt Disney–Annette Funicello epic, *The Monkey's Uncle,* for which Brian wrote and produced the title track. A rock concert movie, *The T.A.M.I. Show,* wrapped up the group's film career for 1964.

In August of '64, one month after the release of *All Summer Long,* the new single "When I Grow Up to Be a Man" debuted. By this time, Beatlemania was the rage and London-influenced "mod" go-go clubs had sprung up from L.A. to New York. The Jerk, the Monkey, the Bird, and a score of other dances were being stomped out to a British beat.

Amid the noise, Brian's fragile, childlike song was lost. "When I Grow Up to Be a Man" came in like a playground tune. Brian called it, "A projection song." A harpsichord played off the melody and a chorus counted off the years of life. Brian, his voice reaching lower as the numbers climbed higher, sings about the basic anxieties of growing up and the single evoked a picture of a little boy looking up at his father.

Neither "When I Grow Up" nor its successor, a four-cut ELP mini-album of "Wendy"/"Little Honda"/"Don't Back Down"/

Alan, Mike, Carl, Brian at the Hollywood Bowl

"Hushabye," had the commercial impact of their 1964 predecessors. Brian was getting more experimental, more complex in his work. They were touring constantly, becoming seasoned performers—and nervous wrecks.

WHEN I GROW UP (TO BE A MAN) *by Brian Wilson*

When I grow up to be a man
Will I dig the same things that turn me on as a kid?
Will I look back and say that I wish I hadn't done what I did?
Will I joke around, and still dig those sounds,
When I grow up to be a man?
Will I look for the same things in a woman that I did in a girl?
Will I settle down fast or will I first wanna travel the world?

Now I'm young and free, but how will it be,
When I grow up to be a man? Oh, Oh, Oh.
Will my kids be proud or think their old man is really a square?
When they're out havin' fun yea, will I still wanna have my share?
Will I love my wife, for the rest of my life,
When I grow up to be a man? What will I be,
When I grow up to be a man?
Won't last forever.

Copyright 1964 & 1975 by Irving Music Inc.

I'd call up the guys and say, "You guys think the last one was good? Well, wait till you hear this one...." I was a better-better-better type. What's that called?... I was glued to that aspect. I thought that was the way—and that is the way. The way to think is that what you're doing now is the best.

——Brian

Al Jardine was a married man. After a year and a half, twenty-two-year-old Brian was about to tie the knot with sixteen-year-old Marilyn Rovell. Dennis was cruising in his Sting Ray 85. Carl, eighteen, was dating a series of cute Beach Boys fans. Mike Love was the prototype for the L.A. bachelor—suave, selective, and sociable at twenty-two.

Yet all five were no longer part of a normal world. They were doing thirty-city tours, spending their summers not in the warmth of the sun but in the polyester confines of jet planes.

The group really didn't have any reason not to listen to Brian....They were making a lot of money and also building up confidence in what they did.... Mike was always older than the rest of them, more mature than the other brothers. Brian and Mike agreed on almost everything.

——Chuck Britz

When they weren't at concert dates, Capitol was waiting for new product. The strain was pulling Brian to the edge, but the pressure for new work did not let up. Picking up on the dance craze, he wrote "Dance, Dance, Dance." Backed with "The Warmth of the Sun," it made the top ten by November.

We didn't do that much touring until 1963. We did a little bit in 1963—started to tour in 1963. By the end of 1963 we were really into a touring bag. Then in 1964, we really started working.... Used to go up and do the hits, do like forty-five minutes, all the records, one after another, like a jukebox. That was it and the girls screaming and yellin' and stuff. It was fun but I dig playing a lot more now.

——Carl

Still not satisfied with the Beach Boys' output, Capitol recorded a performance in Sacramento and released *Beach Boys Concert*—an upbeat, sometimes funny version of their youthful stage show. As an album, it was a grabbag, with everything from the standard "Let's Go Trippin'" instrumental to Brian's soft "In My Room" to Carl's sizzling guitar on "Johnny B. Goode." Mike Love had a chance to get his greenfaced version of "Monster Mash" on vinyl and the Boys did a bouncing cover of Jan and Dean's "Little Old Lady From Pasadena." Topping it off was a high-wire act on "Graduation Day," soaring harmony with an innocent edge. The co-stars on the album, however, were the girls in the crowd whose high-decibel enthusiasm summed up the Beach Boys' reception by teenage America. Five singles, four albums, and extensive touring in one year would seem to be enough for any group. There was more.

"The Man With All the Toys" became Brian's new single for the holiday season. It joined four new compositions (including last year's "Little St. Nick") and seven standards to form *The Beach Boys' Christmas Album*. For a mellow and expansive sound, Brian teamed with Dick Taylor and his forty-piece orchestra.

Glen Campbell, Carl, Dennis, Alan

Alan, Carl, Mike

The recording experience gave Brian a direct and creative exposure to the components of a full symphonic sound.

Backed by Taylor's rich arrangements, the group's harmonies soared. Brian's crooning solo on "Blue" was a delight, warm and innocent yet with more vocal sophistication than usual. Together with Phil Spector's all-star 1964 Phillies album, the Beach Boys made 1964 the most memorable year for "holiday songs" in the annals of rock and roll history.

I was very close to Brian....I was with him the day he couldn't continue any longer. I was with him in the morning and I knew that it wasn't just that he was copping out — he couldn't take it any longer....

——Carl

Nobody knew what was going on. I wouldn't talk. I just put my head down and wouldn't even look at anyone. That night the road manager took me back to L.A. and I didn't what to see anybody except my mother...it's a kind of security to be able to talk to your mother as I can talk to Audree.

——Brian

It was Christmas time 1964, the first night of a two-week tour. The boys were in Houston, Texas. The year was about to take its toll on Brian. He was under pressure from his father to share the same touring responsibilities as Al, Carl, Dennis, and Mike. He was under pressure from Capitol for new product. More than anything, he was under pressure from himself to stay on top, to meet the musical competition and extend the range of rock and roll. He felt threatened by the British invasion. Despite the Beach Boys' continued popularity, their last two singles, "When I Grow Up" and "Dance," did not have the impact of "I Get Around." Al Jardine remembers: "Brian decided to give up touring because he wasn't writing like he should have been."

The pressure had been building up slowly. Audree Wilson noticed her son was spending more and more time alone. Then he began complaining of stomachaches, headaches, fatigue. When Brian made an early return from the Houston dates, it was obvious that he needed a change. Mike, Carl, Al, and Dennis finished the Texas tour without him. When they returned, things were just not the same.

Carl, Mike, Alan, Dennis, Glen Campbell

I told them I foresee a beautiful future for the Beach Boys' group but the only way we could achieve it was if they did their job and I did mine. They would have to get a replacement for me....I didn't say "they." I said "we" because it isn't they and me, it's us.

———*Brian*

Touring without Brian, their teacher, brother, composer, and friend, was a shock. There had been reason to suspect that Brian would make a quick "recovery" from his fatigue and go back out on the road. He had begun work on a solid new album, *The Beach Boys Today,* and there was every indication that it would be up to the level of their earlier work. Yet in Brian's mind there was no turning back. He had to commit himself to the studio. It became level-headed Carl's responsibility to keep the group together. Brian would have to be replaced on the road.

I usually played rhythm on their sessions....When it came to being one of the Beach Boys, they called me. They said, "We got a gig in Dallas day after tomorrow. You want to play with us?"

"You mean open the show for you?" I asked.

"No, Brian's sick and can't make it. We need somebody to play bass and sing the high parts."

"Yeah, sure." I didn't know all the lyrics. It was fun — an experience. I stayed with them six months after that.

———*Glen Campbell*

Glen Campbell became the seventh Beach Boy. A talented blond-haired guitarist, he was an adequate Beach Boy, not really the visual or vocal substitute the group might have picked if there had been enough time before the tour. No matter, it gave Brian a chance to do what he wanted to do musically.

His changing revolved around the fact that in the earlier days everything was much more relaxed and more fun, but when he got into the heavier sounds, the making of something more aesthetic to him, he developed more of a sense of responsibility and he'd be more critical, not frustrated, but unsure.

———*Chuck Britz*

Brian put the finishing touches on *Today.* In February 1965, Capitol released the album's "Do You Wanna Dance" as a single, another response to the go-go scene across the country. It went to number twelve.

More than any earlier album, *The Beach Boys Today* reflected Brian's personal feelings and innate musical talent. He was alone more often now, spending time in the studio while the group was on the road. Full Spectorian instrumentals were the norm for each cut. With the help of seasoned session men, Brian spun a romantic, slow-paced wall of sound for the album's second side.

He'd come in with nothing — no sheet music. He'd just book a session and he'd come in with all the guys. Easy. At one time I used to be the contractor for that stuff and I'd call him and I'd say, "Do you want everybody?" He'd say, "Always." So we'd have everybody here and we'd usually start out with the bass or percussion and he'd tell them exactly what he'd want them to play and he'd go through every section just like that. They would write down the music. He'd have it all in his head. Maybe after five or six hours we'd do a take. He didn't have to break down the vocal parts. They'd been singing together since they were kids. They knew exactly what he wanted. They had their parts worked out exactly in advance, before they came into the studio. They didn't sing them, but after he'd have all the instrumental tracks done, they could get right on the mike and basically sing the four- or five-part harmony, they just knew each other so well.

———*Chuck Britz*

The lovely and yearning "Please Let Me Wonder" featured mellow m.o.r. falsetto by both Mike and Brian; "I'm So Young" ("so young ... can't marry no one") was another of Brian's elaborate

remakes, punctuated by a fancy guitar and fading chorus tag; "Kiss Me, Baby," a real *love* song, gushed vocally, but made up for the schmaltz with a fascinating instrumental track. "She Knows Me Too Well" presaged the intense personal nature of *Pet Sounds.* Brian's lead vocal and the intricate compartmentalized group chorus (based on the title) highlighted another beautiful melody. Less impressive was "In the Back of My Mind," an instrumental throwback to a fifties movie soundtrack, rescued by an ingenious orchestral tag.

The balance of *Today* was vintage '64– '65 Beach Boys — impeccable production of exuberant pop music, polished to a high gloss and filled out by Brian's textured, symphonic rock sound. There was the light, romantic "Good to My Baby." "Don't Hurt My Little Sister," the cut planned for a Phil Spector session, clearly showed its roots. Another comedy session, this time with writer-photographer Earl Leaf, featured dialogue about kosher pickles, french fries, french bread, and English TV — a reflection of their recent European tour.

It was "Rhonda" I had difficulty with....It was the second song I sang lead on. I was used to singing background. It was a whole different thing ... quite complex....It seems quite simple now but it's something called timing meter, and rhythm. It was a matter of getting your mind-body concentration together....Finally it came together real well. The way we cut the first version was different than the way we sang the second....When Gary Usher

Bruce Johnston

decided he might want to cover it, we decided to get a version out first. So Brian raced in and said, "Let's do it again."

———*Al*

"Help Me Rhonda," the Beach Boys' next single and a rousing number one on the charts, was also featured on *Today,* but the more diffuse album version was longer (by 22 seconds), more laid-back ("easier" vocals), and sweeter (a harmonica rounds out the sound and tambourine, echo, and ukelele contribute to a less focused, softer backing). The single release in April was shorter (2:45), faster (sharper bass lines), and more exuberant (the vocals are pushed up front in a tighter mix, ukelele is dropped, and saxophone added).

HELP ME RHONDA   *by Brian Wilson*

Since she put me down I've been out doin'
In my head,
Come in late at night and in the mornin'
I just lay in bed;
Well, Rhonda you look so fine,
And I know it wouldn't take much time,
For you to help me, Rhonda,
Help me get her out of my heart.

Chorus
Help me, Rhonda! Help, help me Rhonda!
Help me, Rhonda! Help, help me Rhonda!

(Repeat chorus)

Help me, Rhonda! Help, help me Rhonda!

She was gonna be my wife and I was gonna
Be her man,
But she let another guy come between us
And it ruined our plans;
Well, Rhonda you caught my eye,
And I'll give you lots of reasons why,
You gotta help me, Rhonda,
Help me get her out of my heart.

(Repeat chorus)

Copyright 1965 by Irving Music Inc.

The single version surfaced on their next album, *Summer Days and Summer Nights,* about the same time Bruce Johnston surfaced as the eighth Beach Boy.

Bruce Johnston is very clever, very healthy, very ambitious and very rich.... None of these ingredients he parades, except his health, which glows relentlessly through the worst hangover or the longest city-to-city tour...His brain he inherited and he sharpens it by contact with the abrasive group wit of the Beach Boys....Bruce Johnston is an adaptable man. This is how he gained complete acceptance with the Beach Boys.

———*from their concert booklet, 1966*

He understands.

———*Brian*

The performing of Bruce Johnston and Terry Melcher (Bruce and Terry) had been losing speed as the Beach Boys-inspired car and surfing trends were replaced by other sounds. Melcher was moving on to a successful role as producer for Paul Revere and the Raiders and one of the early L.A. folk-rock bands, The Byrds. Johnston's falsetto blended comfortably with the sound of the Beach Boys. When Mike Love called with an offer for him to join the group as a last-minute replacement for an ailing Glen Campbell, Bruce Johnston accepted. In New Orleans, on April 9, 1965, he became the eighth official Beach Boy.

His relationship with the group was already comfortable, as they shared friends from the L.A. recording scene. Bruce also had a soft, fun-loving appearance that fit in with the Beach Boys' own. His experience as a musician-singer went right to their roots.

I even used to be in a band with Phil Spector. It didn't have a name, we played high school dances together, though not for long. But I knew he had it together, 'cause he was playing on demos.

He asked the drummer of the band if I would come and play on a demo and I didn't 'cause I was busy that night—had a date or something, and I wasn't old enough to drive, so I had to be driven wherever I had to go. So I didn't make the session, and it turned out to be his first hit with the Teddy Bears, "To Know Him Is to Love Him."

I'm not that old, but I've been doing it for so long. I used to back Richie Valens up when he was very big in the States, and that drummer Sandy Nelson. He asked me to go on the road with the Big Bopper, Buddy Holly, and Richie Valens, you know where they had the fatal plane crash?

My ma wouldn't let me go on tours. I was too young...Of course, nothing would have happened to me, 'cause I wouldn't have been on that plane. So that night after they died, Bobby Valino (Vee) stood in for Holly and that's when he got his start. A year later I played his show.

———*Bruce Johnston*

The Beach Boys were part of an increasingly sophisticated rock scene. Bob Dylan, whom Brian regarded with a mixture of admiration and concern—a genius who could threaten rock and roll—electrified his sound and (backed by the band), cut the driving "Like A Rolling Stone." Simon and Garfunkel emerged with *Wednesday Morning, 3 A.M.,* an introspective, gentle style of rock. The Lovin' Spoonful provided a soft East Coast echo to the Beach Boys' sound. The Beatles launched "Eight Days a Week," "Ticket to Ride," "Help," "Yesterday," "We Can Work It Out," and *Rubber Soul,* an album that helped motivate the production of *Pet Sounds.*

Brian was really sort of the first one to get into the album thing as an art, you know? I think that **Summer Days and Summer Nights** *was the first indication of it.*

——*Carl*

The enormous output of quality from London, Detroit, New York, and even nearby L.A. challenged Brian. He returned to the studio and began production of what was to become a classic sound of the sixties.

It kind of represents California living. It's so centered on California. It has to do with my interest in girls. There's nothing greater than a girl....Well, a kid, your daughter, but that's a girl, too. It reflects my philosophy. It's kind of a high point of Mike Love's career....It features Mike Love as a great rock-and-roll singer...not to mention that it has some good harmony, plus a good background track. If you listen, you'll hear that the instruments are playing really nice. We had a lot of musicians supporting the Beach Boys, including a lot of Phil Spector's musicians.

——*Humble Ol' Brian, 1976*

The song was "California Girls," cornerstone of their new album, *Summer Days and Summer Nights.* Its keyboard opening is one of the most famous in rock and roll. The lyrics and music painted an innocent picture of girls stretching from one end of the world to the other—all beautiful, and all good to their men. They were cute, they were warm, they were hip, they were stylish, they were sexy. What a sixties dream. It fondly summed up the touring preoccupation of the band—*girls.* Even today, the memory of one line from the song triggers another.

CALIFORNIA GIRLS   *by Brian Wilson*

Well, East Coast girls are hip
I really dig those styles they wear
And the Southern girls with the way they talk
They knock me out when I'm down there
The Midwest farmers' daughters really make you
   feel all right
And the Northern girls with the way they kiss
They keep their boyfriends warm at night
I wish they all could be California
Wish they all could be California,
I wish they all could be California girls

The West Coast has the sunshine and the girls all

get so tan
I dig a French bikini on Hawaiian island's dolls
   by a palm tree in the sand
I been around this great big world and I've seen
   all kinds of girls
But I couldn't wait to get back to the States, back
   to the cutest girls in the world
I wish they all could be California
I wish they all could be California
I wish they all could be California
I wish they all could be California girls.

Copyright 1965 by Irving Music Co., BMI

It had number one written all over it and provided their concerts with an incredible closing number.

Basically the first thing we did with a "big band" was "California Girls." They did the tracks at Goldstar and we did the vocals. They did one more song like that over there. They didn't think Western was big enough for an orchestra that size....I finally said to Brian, "Why the hell didn't you give us a chance to do it?" Brian said he didn't think we were big enough to do it and I said, "We can do it!" Once we started, then we did all of them.

——*Chuck Britz*

The balance of *Summer Days and Summer Nights* was light and carefree, with some impressive instrumental backing. Some cuts seem overly casual; Brian was under pressure to complete the album for the summer season.

"Then I Kissed Her," with Al Jardine's lead vocal, once again justified the use of a Spector-Greenwich-Barry original. It became a hit single in England when the label was short on new material from the band.

"Girl Don't Tell Me" was Carl's turn to sing lead, and the uncomplicated melody was a delightful variation on the McCartney-style uptempo love song common to mid-sixties rock. Brian backed it with a rich guitar track and vibes.

"Salt Lake City" rambled pleasantly, using sax and vibes for an instrumental bridge. Strong harmonies within a playfully intricate arrangement gave the song an absurd edge, taken even further by the lyrics. As with so many of the Beach Boys' songs, the group seemed to be having as much (or more) fun singing as you did listening. By this time, fans could often visualize the group's performance. In addition to their concert tours, the Beach Boys had made numerous television appearances, including *The Ed Sullivan Show,* Dick Clark's *American Bandstand, Tonight,* and others.

Both "Amusement Parks U.S.A." and "I'm Bugged at My Old Man" were thematic throwbacks to the *Surfin' Safari* days. "Bugged" in particular was a bizarre inventory of parent-teenage hassles, with Brian (noted on the jacket credits as "TOO EMBARRASSED") singing lyrics like "I wish I could see outside but he tacked up boards on my window" and "I wish I could do some homework but I got suspended from school" and the group good-naturedly chiming in with a chorus of *"Blew his cool."* In contrast, there was "And Your Dream Comes True," smooth a cappella cut in the Four Freshman style.

The real gem of the album, however, was "Let Him Run Wild," an elaborate instrumental track as sophisticated as anything Brian had done to date. The song was both exuberant and sentimental, a romantic suite of soft, pleading vocals, falsetto exhortations, rousing syncopated chorus, and choking "Don't Worry, Baby" guitar. In 2:21 seconds Brian pulled bass, hand-clapping, woodblock, vibes, mellow trumpets, tambourine, and drums into a cascading wall of California sound that foreshadowed the musical direction of the group.

THE BEACH BOYS
GIRL DON'T TELL ME
BARBARA ANN

5561 Capitol RECORDS

PRINTED IN U.S.A.

A beautiful circular teaser, a pause after "Look out!" a high searching vocal tinted with the sound of the tambourine, guitar, and a single key on vibes all contributed to the Beach Boys' next record, "The Little Girl I Once Knew."

Somebody said, "Let's take a four-beat pause." I said, "Fine."

——Brian

Issued in November, it was their most noncommercial single, a complex arrangement with unusual pauses throughout the song. Brian was experimenting further, this time using the group's single as a showcase for subtle musical changes. It did not catch on as quickly as the usual Beach Boys' release. And Capitol quickly wiped it under the carpet and issued another single in January.

The Beach Boys were down the hall in the next studio cutting the Beach Boys Party album. I walked into the Beach Boys session or—oops, should I say party (hope I didn't spoil any illusions about a swinging party at the Wilsons' house) and they were all sitting around trying to think of another song to do. So they asked me what I wanted to sing. I said "Barbara Ann" for what reason I don't remember. We sang "Barbara Ann." Two months later it was number one almost everywhere.

——Dean Torrence

Get this: an album complete with pictures of a wood-paneled den, Brian and Marilyn, Al and Lynda, Mike and potato chips, a bottle of Orange Crush, Carl and Annie, and Dennis with a suitably tanned California girl.

A party—an extemporaneous record of a party at the Wilsons' house! The Beach Boys at home.

Not quite. *Beach Boys Party,* their last album of 1965 was a hoax.

We all got together at Mike's house....We got together and sang. We actually had a party....We got into it. Then it was done in the studio, too. Some songs were from the party and some songs were from the party at the studio....We actually did have a party there, too. We'd go across the street and get some

hamburgers and come back with them. Yeah!

——Marilyn

I doubt if much of it was done at Mike's....We did it at Studio Two and we had a kind of P.A. deal and everybody just sat down out there and started playing and singing. Everybody was joining in as they walked into the studio, Diane and Marilyn were there. Carl and his wife-to-be. They weren't married at the time. Dean, Phil Sloan, Jan Berry. There was none of that animosity between groups. People would just walk in and have a good time. It was all done live. In that day and age a lot of things just happened. We did a lot of gimmick things. We did the bottle popping—a lot of things for experimental purposes.

——Chuck Britz

Under Brian's eye, the Beach Boys consciously kept an extemporaneous party atmosphere, singing loose, often hysterically funny versions of their hit songs and others.

Beach Boys Party was a put-on within a put-on, an album hyped as casual and unrehearsed when it actually had been produced as a whole by Brian Wilson. He went so far as to tape noise tracks for possible use in the final mix..

The session was scheduled to start at 5 P.M. Mike Love was there at 5, but the last of the group didn't show 'til 6. The first delay came in getting the necessary instruments and amplifiers into the studio. Ron Swallow, their band boy, had lost the key to the inner sanctum where these items were kept....

While waiting for the group to arrive, Brian thumped on the piano, and Mike Love and Bruce Johnston tried on new stage pants. Dennis Wilson put in an appearance, but he was suffering from bronchitis (caused by skindiving with a bad cold) and was sent home. Hal Blaine did drum duty for the group.

Mike Love brought in four suits which he had ordered from New York and began trying them on, using one of the microphones for a coat rack....

By now it was 7 P.M. and the drummer was scheduled to leave at 8. Panic. They began running through three songs — "Hully Gully," "I Should Have Known Better," and "Tell Me Why"...they had obviously been over the songs during the previous session; everyone seemed to know the timing. It was only a question of getting the right balance of voices and instruments.

Rather than take one song at a time, Brian chose to go through all three in a row for a rough idea. They made it by eight, at which time they adjourned to the control room to listen to the play-back—and take in some more food.

——Teen Set

Although there were real "parties" for *Beach Boys Party,* the record was fully embellished and coordinated in studio sessions. Brian was a perfectionist, but he could adopt an even more relaxed, less pressured style than usual when he wanted that musical effect. The *Party* album was fun to do and easier to complete than his recent orchestral classics. He had been playing volleyball and had come up with the concept for the party album. The record had a truly "live" feeling, spontaneous and very funny.

Mike sang "Alley Oop." Brian and Mike sang "PapaOmm-MowMow" with full acoustical bass sound and appropriately tinny vocals. A surprisingly full "Devoted To You" had Brian and Mike in Everly Brothers ("Cleverly Brothers") style. Two Beatles tunes were featured including a creaky "You've Got To Hide Your Love Away" and delightful "Hey!" chorus from the party group. "I Get Around" had Brian parodying the lyrics ("We never get turned down by the girls we pick up on") and the party responding "not much." "Little Deuce Coupe," had Carl on nice light box guitar and a disastrous party vocal. It was all genuinely humorous—and in the instance of "The Times They Are A-Changing," mildly satirical, too.

As Al Jardine sang out a folky "Times They Are A-Changing," the party shouted out "Right" or "Wrong" at the end of each chorus. It made a shambles of the lyrics—and turned the rendition into a good-natured criticism of "serious" rock.

Closing the album, with Dean Torrence, was "Barbara Ann." High-spirited and remarkably harmonic, the familiar "Ba-ba-ba" swept into a full party chorus—laughter, noise, and fuzziness intact. Cut to 2:05 from the 2:53 album version, the Beach Boys' rendition of the old Regents song was a smash, topping the more highly produced rock singles of the day.

1965 closed on an up note, Brian was happier, confident, eager to expand. Bruce Johnston had been well-received as his replacement on the road. The Beach Boys' earnings put them at the top echelon of an expanding business. "Barbara Ann" was solidly entrenched in the top ten. More than any other pop group in America, they had outlasted the British invasion.

Evolving from its fifties roots, sixties rock and roll had revealed three major, overlapping themes in its expression of modern youth—*political* (protest rock with folk roots), as evidenced in Dylan's early work; *teenage blues* (earnest, sexually charged, frustration rock with R&B roots), epitomized by Mick Jagger and the Rolling Stones; and *pop* (innocent and romantic rock that kept its white upbeat roots and spoke about life in the teenage generation).

Pop had been refined, explored, and taken to new limits by the Beach Boys. Their songs went beyond rock's musical impact and was in effect a social force—the true test of classic rock and roll. Chuck Berry had done it; so had Elvis. The Beach Boys' songs about cars and surfin' reflected a local phenomenon but their impact was such that they turned a local phenomenon into something international. Kids headed out to the dream of California after hearing the music; and the music was developed from the California dream itself.

Brian's most personal work was more subtle in its impact, but was nonetheless important. His musical innovations—the synthesis of harmony, R&B, and full production—influenced the entire field. His ability to express teenage frustration and insecurity in lyrical, emotionally accurate songs affected young rock and roll peers such as Peter Townshend of the Who, Paul McCartney and John Lennon of the Beatles, and even Jerry Garcia of the Grateful Dead.

McCartney and the Beatles were friends of theirs....One of them said to me, "We're doing the same thing basically as the Beach Boys are doing as far as vocal parts are concerned, and instrumentals are basically the same. It's the relationship of the vocal to the instrumental where the change occurs. If you go back and listen to some of the stuff that the Beach Boys did and that the Beatles did, you will hear that the structure of the vocals is basically like the Beach Boys. The instrumentation is basically the same but the Beach Boys, they had their vocals further out and the instrumental track was back. Now if you blend the Beach Boys' vocals back into the track, you'll have something similar to the Beatles' sound."
———*Jim Lockhart*

Of rock's three overlapping preoccupations—protest, teenage blues, and romantic pop, perhaps the latter was the most timeless and most identifiable. It focused on the traditionally paramount preoccupation of teenage life: *love*. Its influence was most direct in that it was emotional; Brian's innocent and romantic pop dealt more with how you felt than with what you thought. At the same time it was rock and roll.

Between 1961 and 1965 events had happened so quickly and with such impact that American society had hardly had a chance to look back. Rock had blossomed into a cultural phenomenon unlike anything in recent time. "Beatle haircuts," for example, seemed at first to be a funny fashion. Yet their impact on America was to be political, sexual, and sociological in scope. Unisex had its roots in the moptop look. "Long" hair became a matter of individual freedom, and court battles were initiated on the right to attend school with hair over your collar. "Long" hair became a symbol of youthful independence and discontent. It visually set a kid apart from his family, the first step in a growing separation of generations and values which would not be reconciled until the end of the decade.

The impact of the Beach Boys' music was not divisive. Its roots were with the Wilson family and the concepts of family, friends, and home. There was a security in their harmonic sound. Yet Brian and the group were far from conservative. In 1961 they were seeking out whatever was *new*. At that time it meant surfin' and cars. In 1966, things were more intellectual. What was *new* was self-discovery and the exploration of new ideas.

In the fifties and early sixties, as Dennis recalled, going away for a weekend was a political act. It *was* because at the time cruisin', dancin', having fun or feeling frustrated were the only "accepted" channels for youthful expression. Political action, with the exception of traditional voting, was still on the perimeter of most kids' experience.

Rock and roll was an alternative. People could hear and say things about life in rock and roll that weren't being expressed anyplace else. Rock was like a coded message that teenagers could understand. Rock dealt with the frustrations of youth. It was also often the first expression of something young and new.

Since the Beach Boys' music had consistently expressed their life experiences, it had simultaneously expressed some of the things that were "new" for American youth. Now with Brian growing older and a bit more worldly, he was starting to look past his own preconceptions. Keeping the perspective of a tenaciously romantic and innocent young man, he sought out new experiences. In doing this, he would expand the thematic concerns of the Beach Boys' music.

The Beach Boys were America's premier rock and roll band. Soon they would be recognized as *artists*.

Bruce, Dennis, Mike, Brian, Alan, and Carl

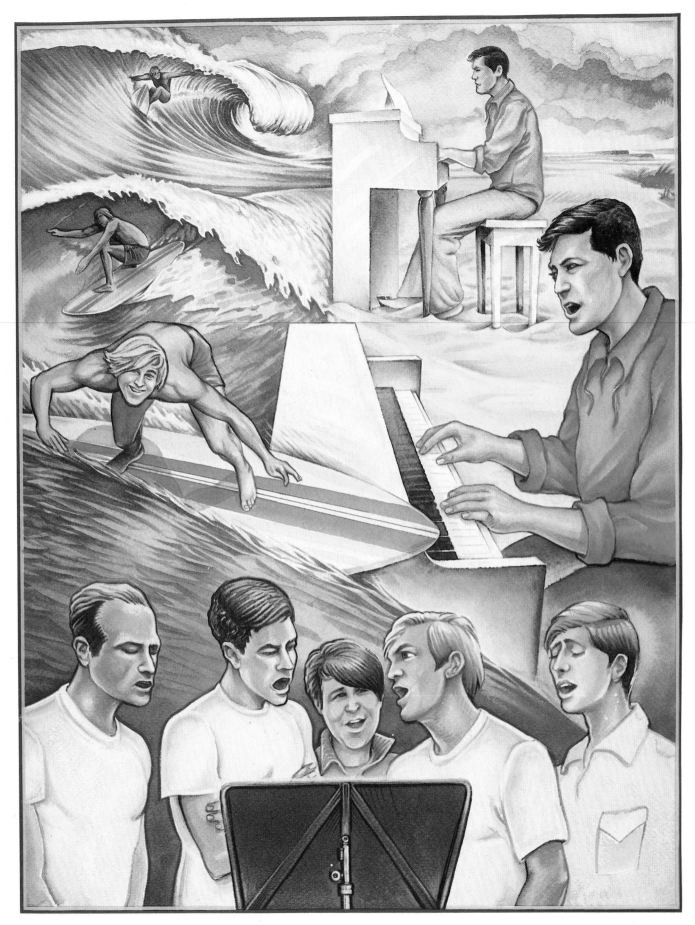

SURFIN'

Painting by Arnie Sawyer/Original design by Michael Pilla

Top: Mike, David Marks, Brian, Dennis, Carl

Above left: Dennis, David, Carl, Mike, Brian

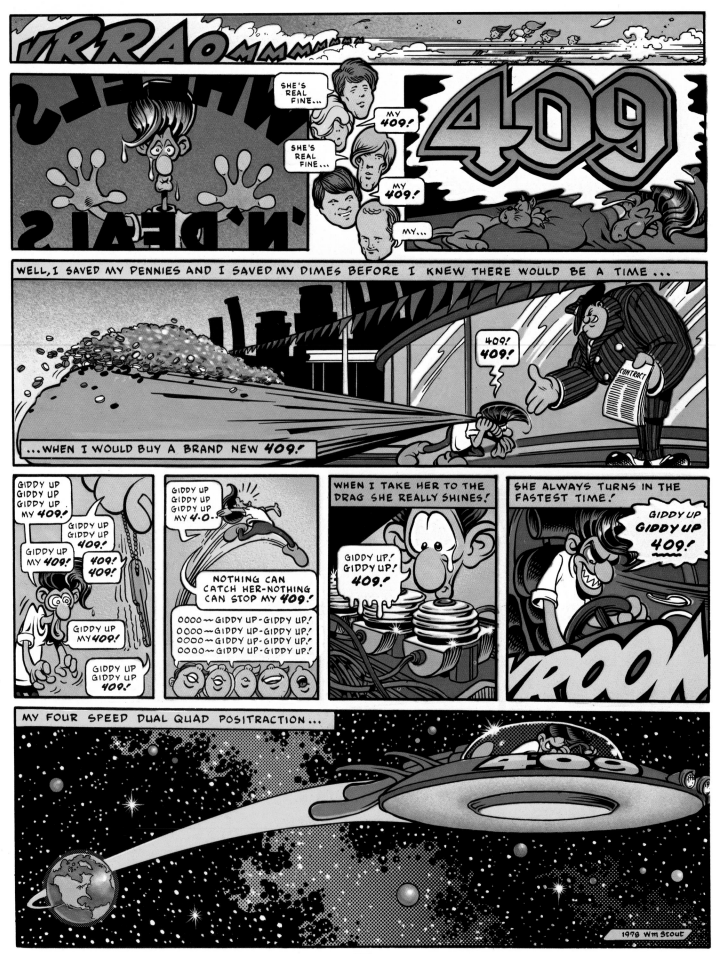

LITTLE DEUCE COUPE
Mac Evans • The Workshop

Top: Carl, Mike (standing), Dennis, Brian (standing), Alan

Above: Carl, Mike, Dennis, Al, Brian
Left: Dennis, Carl, Al, Brian, Mike

SURFER GIRL
Michael Kanarek

DON'T WORRY BABY
Ralph Reese

IN MY ROOM

Christof Blumrich

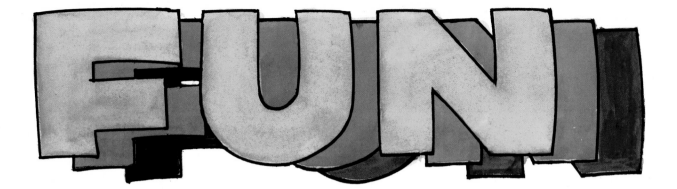

FUN, FUN, FUN
Harvey Kurtzman

Above: Alan, Brian, Dennis, Carl, Mike

Above: Alan, Carl, Mike, Brian, Dennis

HELP ME RHONDA

Alex Jay

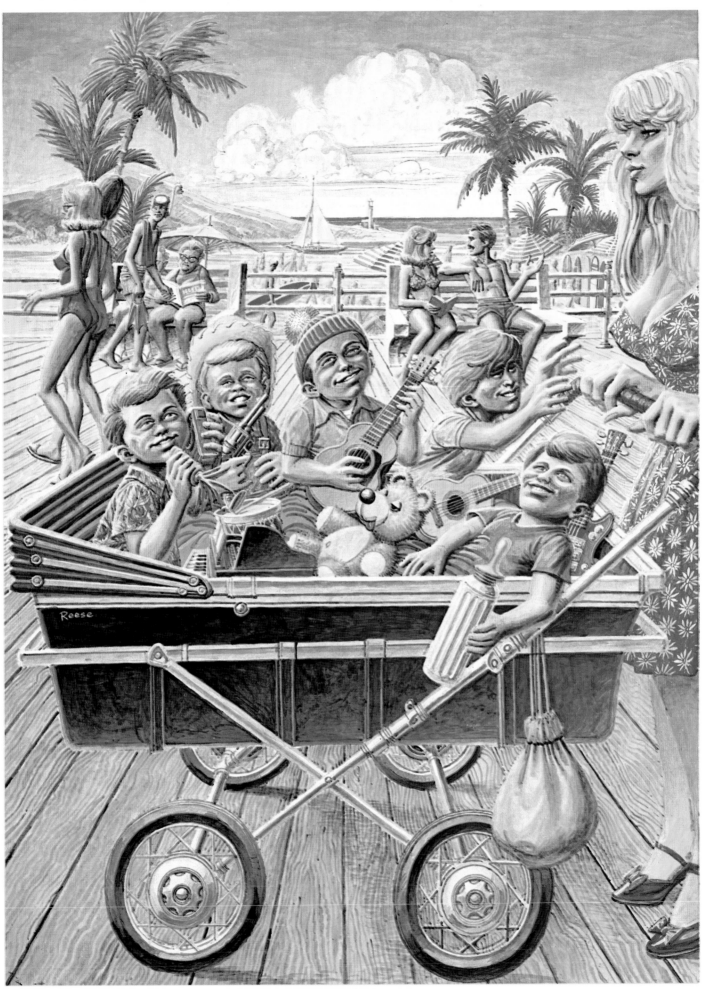

WHEN I GROW UP TO BE A MAN
Ralph Reese

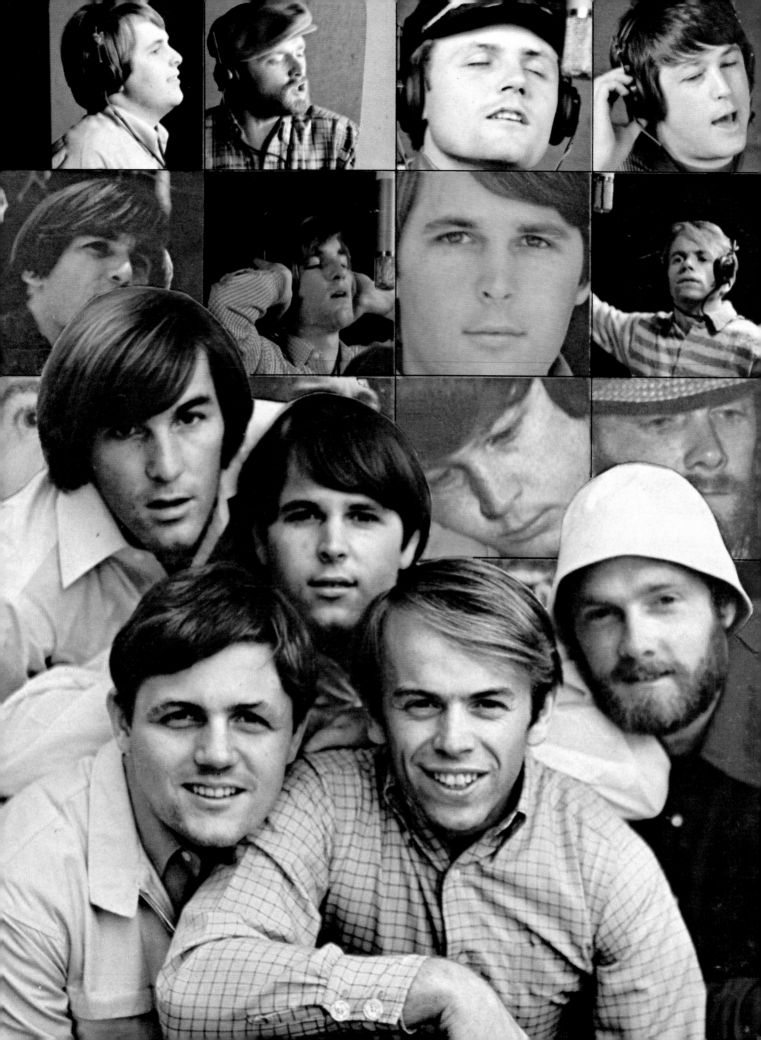

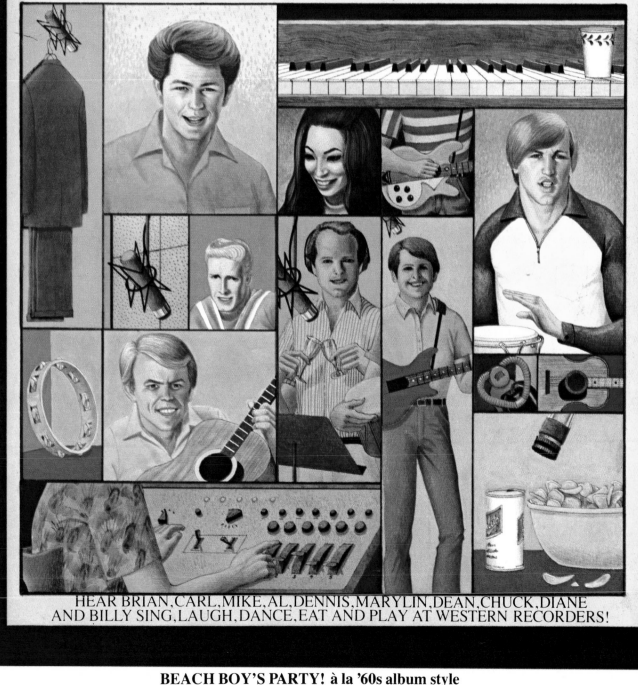

BEACH BOY'S PARTY! à la '60s album style

Sean Earley

I JUST WASN'T MADE FOR THESE TIMES
1965-1967

Dennis was in the studio and there was a lot of that closet talk you hear from bands who have known each other for years and years and Brian played me a new cut called "Wouldn't It Be Nice" and another called "I Just Wasn't Made for These Times" and he said, "Wait until you hear the one we're planning. It's called 'Good Vibrations'...and all of what we're doing represents a new plateau."

———Derek Taylor, former publicist, the Beach Boys

Early 1966. The Pacific was as blue as ever, but the heavy surfing days had faded. People were sitting on the beach listening to a more sophisticated style of rock and roll. The rap was still about last night's date, but more and more there was talk of peace and love. The sound of "Ba-ba-ba Ba-barbara Ann" was as familiar as the pop of a freshly opened Coke.

For Brian Wilson, it was the most musically creative time he had ever experienced. The influential sounds of early rock were joined by the conceptual breakthroughs of the Beatles' classic *Revolver*. In Brian's mind they had replaced Phil Spector as the main competition.

From the kitchen, den and living room there are city lights spread out as far as you can see...all the way to the ocean immediately south....We first went into the den...it had a jukebox and a soda fountain set-up as well as a very impressive heavy Spanish table and chairs....
———from "At Home with Brian Wilson," Teen Set, 1966

From his mansion in Beverly Hills, Brian and his young wife Marilyn were undergoing the trials of early married life. So were other members of the group; unknown to their fans, all the Beach Boys had been married once by early '66.

Having played to audiences from the Santa Monica Civic auditorium to the Parisian Olympia Music Hall, the Beach Boys had grown from a local rock band to internationally acclaimed performers. While Brian had established their reputation on vinyl, Mike Love substantiated their talent on the road.

It's 1 A.M. and the lights of the American Airlines jet are dimmed. The Beach Boys are tired....Nobody talks. Some try to sleep. Suddenly they are interrupted. It's Dennis Wilson, wide awake.

"Hey, fellas. Interested in some fishing? They'll just be biting about 4:30 A.M. We could pick up my boat when we land and be at the ocean by then.... Or maybe Lake Arrowhead....Or—"

Before he can go any further, Al Jardine and Mike Love are saying in unison, "WE DON'T LIKE FISHING, DENNIS! We've been through all this before and most of all we're tired!"

They smile at each other as Dennis huffily stalks off to his seat. They know he's tried everyone else.

He'll go fishing just the same. On his own.

———Rave magazine, 1966

Alan

Brian

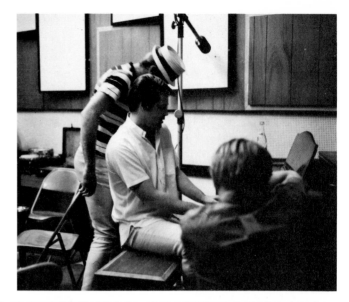

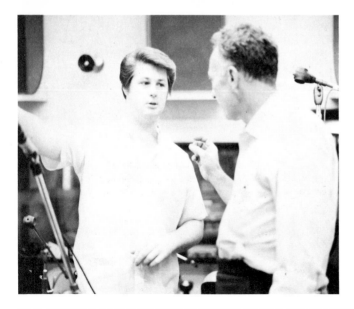

I JUST WASN'T MADE FOR THESE TIMES 1966–1967

The pressures of touring continued. Terry Sachen traveled with the group, having become road manager after Brian's breakdown. With Bruce Johnston, the Beach Boys went to Japan, Honolulu, and Hong Kong for a wildly successful tour. When they returned, they found Brian hard at work on the most ambitious album of his career.

The absence of the Beach Boys' "family" during concert tours pushed Brian to seek another circle of friends. Rumblings of America's counterculture were first being heard (intellectualism, peace, pop philosophy, pot, and social freedom)—and as something new, youthful, and experimental, Brian sought it out still maintaining his own ingenuous and perceptive qualities. He befriended pseudointellectuals and members of the L.A. music scene.

Brian gets into something so intensely and then he's out of it and he goes into a new thing and if you personally can't get into the new thing, then either you have to go by yourself or then make it known on a very non-uptight level that you're just not fitting in.
——David Anderle, former manager, Brothers Records

Capitol Records, as usual, was eager to keep the momentum rolling. They pressed for new "product" and another single.

Innocence—his own and that of America's youth—had always been at the center of Brian's work. For the new music of the Beach Boys, he wanted to address this feeling directly, both in the music and lyrics. Brian played with a tune called "In My Childhood" and cut a wistful track with bicycle bells and horns.

It's fair to say that the general tenor of the lyrics was always his and the

actual choice of words was usually mine. I was really just his interpreter.
——Tony Asher

To expedite matters and assist in the writing of lyrics for the next record, Brian contacted a passing acquaintance named Tony Asher. An advertising copywriter and composer for an L.A. agency, Asher had briefly known Brian from the local studio scene.

Taking a leave of absence from his job, Asher accepted Brian's offer and began an arduous, day-to-day collaboration with him at the piano. Brian had not done much recording to this point. He played Asher an instrumental track for a remake of an old Kingston Trio number, the folk standard "Sloop John B."

The final version of "Sloop John B." appeared in March 1966. Al Jardine had suggested the cut as far back as the "Wendy" days—"I played some chords. He came back and arranged an entire symphony around it"—but now, as Capitol waited for something new from the group, it formed an ideal response to the "laid-back" and "folk" influences in rock. If "Sloop" was a concession to the music of the Byrds and Dylan, it was a concession expressed in the Beach Boys idiom. It had the sweet energy of their early hits and a lighter, more progressive feeling. Mike and Brian's solos rose over a rolling combination of glockenspiel, bass guitar, and drums. It was a happy, oddly Spectorian sound. You could feel yourself standing on the deck of a single-mast ship. If you were a girl, you were probably next to Dennis.

"Sloop John B." soared to the top five. The production was as sophisticated as anything Brian had done, but even at that, "Sloop" was only a glimpse of the music in the group's near future. Brian had reached a plateau in music composition that rivaled his skill as a producer. His personal life was filled with the emotional conflicts of a sensitive, intellectually growing young adult. His feelings were further compounded by his ambitions, his competitiveness, pressures from his father, and the responsibility of producing music for one of the most popular bands in the history of rock and roll.

Brian was still very much a native of suburban Hawthorne, but he was *growing* in his understanding of himself and the world. He wanted to compose an album that would capture the feelings of change—of emotions lost and gained and even those not fully understood. He wanted his emotions—and those of a quickly fading teenage America—to be the focus of his music.

In the studio Brian assembled L.A.'s finest studio musicians. His songs would evolve more slowly than usual this time; the feelings he wanted to express were more complex. He started to produce interlocking compositions with dazzling combinations of instruments uncommon to rock and roll.

In March 1966, the same month as "Sloop John B.," the first of Brian's personal symphonies emerged as a single under the title, "Caroline, No." It was a counterpoise to the group's own hit, moody, filled with a sense of loss and undeniable beauty. Brian's high, crying voice was so full of love, pain, and uncompromising innocence that it hurt just to listen to it.

That song was directly about Brian himself and the death of a quality within him that was so vital. His innocence. He knows it, too.
——Bruce Johnston

Whether the song itself or simply the absence of the B.B. cachet was responsible, "Caroline, No" did not share the commercial success of "Sloop John B." It hit number thirty-two on the charts. Brian continued working on the album.

The first thing Brian will come up with is a concept, an album concept; generally he wants to do a thing. I say a "thing" because it's ...you don't really know what it is, he throws out a whole bunch of one-liners and words and half phrases.

He would get a musical idea. He would then extend off that musical idea. In

---

doing that extension, something else would pop up. So he would stop the first thing and take off on the second thing. He would develop the new concept that hit his head until he came to another concept. He would then abandon for a while that second thing and start off on the third, so that what he was doing was building, like with blocks or a web, that's why there was the beautiful consistency within, musically.

... then the lyrics started happening, at the same time, he may get into a feeling on one thing. He'll play, he'll hear a track, and he'll say, "Gee, this track is a beautiful thing to express a feeling between this and this." Then he'll start to do the words on it. Then it becomes a song and then it gets a title.

———*David Anderle*

The early months of 1966 were a rewarding time for Brian. He had set out to top himself, to top an entire industry, and he felt as if he was actually going to do it.

When he got into the **Pet Sounds** *we did pretty intricate things, but those were* live *things. The cellos—everything from the time he graduated from the five- and six-piece thing to the point of* **Pet Sounds** *was live recording. All the instruments at the same time....It was amazing. You'd have to see the size of the studio to understand. He had his planning so well that nothing fought. He worked with these people as he went along. He worked with each section so they'd understand what he wanted.*

———*Chuck Britz*

With studio musicians such as Hal Blaine, Steve Douglas, Larry Knechtal, Don Randy, Mike Rabini, Ray Pullman, Billy Strange, and Jim Horn, he laid down track after track of groundbreaking rock and roll.

Brian had to do **Pet Sounds**, *whether it was going to be a hit or not. Brian was probably saying to himself, "It's something I have to do for my own consciousness." I knew it was going to be a hit. It was one of the finest pieces of work I had heard at the time.*

———*Chuck Britz*

The musicians were great. There were times they would go, "Hey, it's not the money that's important, it's the opportunity to work with Brian...." All of our sessions they enjoyed working on. Everybody was having fun...a great rapport...the people we worked with in the studio were incredible...I can't remember a time they did not let Brian be at ease at the board.

———*Diane Rovell*

The group also contributed; Dennis on drums and Carl on memorable rhythm and electric guitar.

Carl was receptive, but he was learning, he was learning but Brian already had it. Dennis was cooperative, he played what Brian requested him to play, sang what Brian requested him to sing—his part. So did Mike and Alan.

———*Jim Lockhart, Beach Boys' engineer*

Brian's style of recording and composition was extraordinary. He was able to weave a complex musical piece through direct communication with his artists. He would actually sit down with each group of musicians and tell or play them what he wanted to be done. The songs had an immediacy and special emotional depth, qualities that were reinforced by the musicians' own contribution to the tracks. Brian would produce and record the complex instrumentals live—all at one time— the fruition of hours of work with melodic ideas that reflected the traumas of romance and growing up.

Quite a few of the times he came in and got a piece of paper and wrote out what he wanted the guy to play. He had a great knack for coming up at the

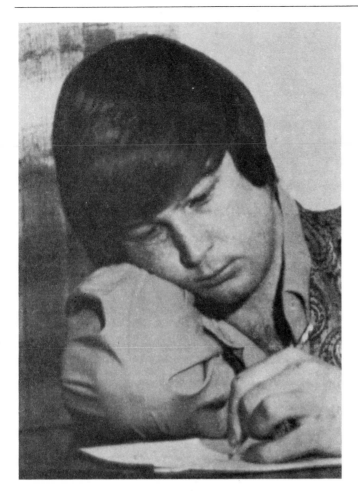

last minute with **changes** *that he had suddenly decided to try which ninety-nine times out of a hundred were an improvement over what they originally thought they were going to do.*

———*Jim Lockhart*

Brian's music received much support in the studio. His talented sister-in-law, Diane Rovell, was responsible for assembling the various musicians needed for each session. Chuck Britz, Jim Lockhart, and Phil Kaye functioned as a seasoned team of engineers at Western Recorders; Britz in particular was responsible for the majority of sessions.

The eldest Wilson pushed Western to its limits. Something *special* was happening with this young musician. His grandiose plans were a learning experience—immediate, emotional, and fun.

It always started with the basic tracks. He always knew what he had in mind. We'd cut the basic tracks during the day from like 1 P.M. to 6 P.M. Sometimes he had a regular session and he wanted to play also. We'd put on sweeteners later in the evening—horns, violins—it got to the point where Brian could go in and play them what he wanted and they would write out their own charts. A lot of times Brian would sit down and write out the charts for six or eight instruments....He writes great charts.

———*Diane Rovell*

The one thing that used to gripe me is that if one person said it was wrong he'd do it over again even if they didn't know what they were talking about... he'd just listen. Some people would say things that they had no right to say. He was the kind of person who would do it over but when it was over we'd usually wind up using the first take we did.

———*Chuck Britz*

While this went on, the other Beach Boys continued their Asian tour. Often Brian would grow impatient for the group's return, and he'd go in and cut rough vocal tracks just to see how the final production would sound.

He could have in his mind the four different parts....He'd have four- and five-part chords in his mind and he'd dish them out to all of us. Then he'd take the top, which is the melody....It never ceased to blow my mind that he could know those notes and retain them.

———*Mike*

When the group came back to the studio, Brian would be waiting with a tight, preconceived notion of what he wanted their voices to do.

It was a pain in the ass because Brian was a taskmaster. I loved "Wouldn't It Be Nice" and "God Only Knows."

———*Mike*

He was producer, writer, arranger at the time. He told the group how things should be. Very little discussion. Sometimes there was discussion about why he wanted to do this, that, and the other, and sometimes they would change to what they wanted rather than what he wanted, but most of the time they came back to what he wanted because when they heard their way and his way, why it just made as much difference as daylight and darkness.

———*Jim Lockhart*

The live instrumental tracks were elaborate. The songs were miniature symphonies, huge arrangements with the most delicate placement of sax, tambourine, cello, bell-tree, and other evocative sounds. Most of Brian's work on *Today* and *Summer Nights* paled by comparison. This new music was so full that it sounded as if it could explode.

We'd be in the studio and we'd be crying, it was so beautiful. We'd say, "How'd you write that?" There wasn't one person in the group who could come close to Brian.

———*Dennis*

There was a natural creative progression with Brian.... Recording techniques evolved which allowed us to stretch out even more in terms of sound textures. Brian took advantage of that and pioneered his way through. He blended symphonic arrangements with rock music in **Pet Sounds.**

———*Mike*

Brian's *Pet Sounds* was a private puzzle—introspective, wistful, painfully honest, innocent, yet filled with a sense of loss. There wasn't a Deuce Coupe or laughing long-haired blonde to be seen. The Beach Boys' formula had been put through Brian's heart and had changed. The music was still warm and spirited, but it was also distant and melancholy. The emotional hunger, heartbreak, and insecurity of "In My Room" and "Don't Worry, Baby" were now the focus of attention.

This was *not* the sort of music that Capitol Records would expect. It was the evolution of the Beach Boys. Under Brian's supervision, the group cut and recut dozens of complex vocal tracks, performing some of the most impressive harmonies in the history of rock and roll.

I've always been insecure about my lyrics. I always felt that what I wanted to say was never imparted in my lyrics...that the message just wasn't there.

———*Brian*

Brian knew he could have written the lyrics for the new album. Yet in the face of Dylan, Lennon-McCartney, and other mid-sixties songwriters, he felt uncomfortable. Tony Asher was different.

More sophisticated. He seemed to genuinely respond to the beauty of Brian's music and he was capable of expressing its meaning in a more eloquent, but still natural, fashion.

I can vividly remember the first time he played me his finished track for "Don't Talk (Put Your Head on My Shoulder)." I was literally speechless. Let's just say it was a great joy making music with him but that any other relationship with Brian was a great chore.

——— *Tony Asher*

Together they composed the lyrics for nine songs, including "Let's Go Away for a While," which Brian later decided to keep as an instrumental. In addition to "Sloop," at least three other cuts were planned. "Hang onto Your Ego" dealt with defensiveness, but the title and lyrics proved a bit much for a Beach Boys' song. The title was replaced by "I Know There's an Answer" and new lyrics were contributed by Terry Sachen. Mike Love added his romantic style to "I'm Waiting for the Day."

Remember the dogs? That was the whole idea...calling it Pet Sounds *after the dogs.*

——— *Brian*

By the end of winter, all the vocal tracks had been recorded. The epic instrumental core of the new album was already a topic of conversation around the L.A. studio scene. Capitol was anxious for the new work; its production had already exceeded the boundaries of 'normal' recording time, especially for a Beach Boys album. Management was anxious. "Caroline, No," for all its beauty, had not been a financial success.

In the hallway of Western Recorders — we had just finished doing a cut — I gave Brian the name Pet Sounds.

——— *Mike*

Capitol was reluctant to support a new and less popular direction. Yet there was little choice. The Beach Boys were proud of *Pet Sounds*. Arrangements were made to shoot cover photos at the San Diego Zoo. A series of shots from their Japanese tour would be used for the back cover slick. Although he had contributed to the *Pet Sounds* sessions, Bruce Johnston was still under contract to CBS. Under an agreement with the Beach Boys, he did not appear on the front jacket. A pressing was scheduled for the longest album in the group's career.

The record that was released in May of 1966 was rock's first major-concept album, a virtuoso production years ahead of the "pop" norm. The cute boys in surfer shirts were gone. So were the tunes you could play at a dance.

From the exterior, *Pet Sounds* looked like any other Beach Boys' album. The usual silly and "fun-loving" photos adorned the sleeve. There was no big hype. Suddenly the album was in the stores. Not even a new single graced the airwaves. There was just *Pet Sounds*.

Saying "just *Pet Sounds*" is like saying "just a sunrise." The new record was more than music; it was an *experience*.

Beautiful elements from the Beach Boys' earlier work blossomed across thirteen new songs. Brian's experimentation with sound was apparent in *every* cut. Cello, drawling sax, clarinets, chimes, tambourines, even the thudding of an inverted plastic soda waterbottle with a drumstick meshed into a musical dream.

He was very happy with Pet Sounds. *Extremely happy with that album, thought that he had done something very important, and was very unhappy that it didn't do well commercially. For the first time he was aware of that. But he'd experimented himself and succeeded.*

——— *David Anderle*

Success had always been of a single nature to the Beach Boys. It meant popular acceptance with a smattering of critical support. Their work had sold millions internationally. There had never been a "rock press" to tell the group whether or not their music had been important. It *was* important because it had affected so many people in a positive way.

Now with *Pet Sounds*, the nature of their music and its acceptance was about to undergo a major change. A handful of magazines had begun to take rock and roll seriously. In Europe, where American popular culture was treated with more respect than at home, *Pet Sounds* was met with open arms. In England, the group would be mentioned with the same critical respect as the Beatles.

Brian put his heart and soul into his music in the hope that others could respond to what he was feeling. A teenager listening to *Pet Sounds* knew he was not alone. The emotions of a new love and the lonely, painful process of growing up were deeply imbedded in the music. The Spectorian backbeat made everything seem important—an accurate mirror to the trauma of teenage love. *Pet Sounds* was a *whole* album, an artistic expression with a special symmetry and balance. The elements played off each other lyrically, thematically, and musically. There was a special sense of change—an emotional as well as musical use of counterpoint. The group vocals beautifully expressed this warm quality. Hope echoed despair. Love answered rejection. The melodies questioned each other. There was a natural ebb-and-flow relationship in the music.

I don't remember doing any piecework with Brian. The tracks were all done "live"—instrumentals and vocals. We usually didn't do the vocals and instrumentals the same day. Usually within a day or two we'd have the vocals. "Sloop John B." was done live, "Caroline, No" live, "I Just Wasn't Made for These Times" live.

——— *Chuck Britz*

The music Brian had recorded over the past months had coalesced into thirteen emotionally and instrumentally related songs. Only "Sloop John B." stood apart. Its conception and lyrics had been arrived at earlier, but the production and innocence of the music enabled it to fit in comfortably with the rest.

The general idea is clear: larger sections can be divided and subdivided until one discovers the germ motives out of which music is made. Conversely, we may begin with small motives and arrive at phrases, periods, or double-periods.

——*George Thaddeus Jones,*
Music Theory

Pet Sounds drifts in and out as a chronicle of romance. It opens with "Wouldn't It Be Nice." A simple series of guitar chords set up the optimistic cornerstone for the album, an attitude that is answered by "Caroline, No" at the end of side two. Throughout "Wouldn't It Be Nice," Brian's high vocal surges over a carousel of thudding bass, sax, vibes, triangle, and tambourine.

"You Still Believe in Me," the next cut, has a rich hymnlike quality. Brian's harmony reinforces the lyrics—a lover's amazement over his partner's faithfulness and understanding. His use of horn and bells (actually retrieved from the discarded "In My Childhood" tapes) maintains a sense of innocence. The Beach Boys' subtly shifting chorus floats you away. "You Still Believe in Me" lends a comforting feeling like that of "Don't Talk (Put Your Head on My Shoulder)," the mellow love song that follows.

I think "That's Not Me" from **Pet Sounds** *reveals a lot about myself...just the idea that you're going to look at yourself and say, "Hey, that's not me." You're going to get your identity clear, kind of square off with yourself, say this is me, that's not me. That explains it.*

——*Brian*

"That's Not Me" and "I'm Waiting for the Day" are emotionally charged songs, filled with positive youthful energy and an optimism that love and honesty will triumph. The lead vocals take the same confident male posture of their early hits and give it a different edge. Both songs are helplessly defiant. The singer knows what he wants, but now he also knows that he may have to wait for it. There is an emotional change here, a recognition of the needs of another person in a relationship, and the more basic recognition of the *need* for other people. Behind it all is Brian's throbbing wall of sound, punctuated by bass guitar, tambourines, thudding drums, and chorus.

On **Pet Sounds,** *he worked on each section to get it together until he got the song done.*

——*Jim Lockhart*

The instrumental "Let's Go Away for a While" settles into a period of quiet anticipation, a sweet mixture of vibes, strings, horns, woodblock, surfing guitar, and drums.

"Sloop John B." closes the side.

I think "God Only Knows" explains a lot about me in that I believe in God, and I am humble enough to say God knows what I would be without whoever I was talking about....But it just goes to show feelings. When you believe in something you reflect it in your songs, you say how you feel, and songs don't lie. Songs are the most honest form of human expression there is—there's nothing that lies about a song.

——*Brian*

"God Only Knows," the first rock song to use God in its title, opens the second side with a full-bodied romantic orchestration of French horn, flute, tambourine, cello, violin, hollow plastic bottle, and bell-tree.

"God Only Knows" is one of the purest love songs in rock. The words, simple and poetic, are ideal for the composition. The music and lyrics are major examples of the album's symmetry. The tentative nature of one line of the song ("I may not always love you") is answered in the affirmative nature of the next ("But long as there are stars above you"). Drum and piano answer piano; then drum, piano, and French horn answer piano and drum. The music is constantly echoing itself, rising in beautiful orchestrations, then receding only to rise again.

Carl's vocals are exquisite. There is an emotional and melodic resonance to the entire song.

"I Know There's an Answer" explodes with the use of sax, drum, tambourine, and organ. A set of aching vocals once again deals with the problems of becoming an adult. The raucous intensity of the instruments echoes the theme of the music—the struggle of growing up. There is a release only when Mike does his *"doo bee doo bee"* tag and the music fades into a final duet of tambourine and organ.

"Here Today," with its haunting keyboard progression, is just as effective. A taut bass guitar rises over the organ. Then percussion—the instruments cascade down behind the lyrics—drum, tambourine, guitar, tuba, and sax streak through Brian's lead vocal and a complex chorus. Again the lyrics echo the yin-yang structure of the music—a crashing, cohesive sound when "love is here" and a fading, gentler arrangement when "it's gone."

"I Just Wasn't Made for These Times" is the most personal song on the album. Over a whining chorus, Brian sings about his own feelings of alienation. A strong percussion line punctuates the song, and the music is as melancholy and emotional as the vocals. Toward the tag, a high "aooo" solo gives the piece a surreal echo and foreshadows Brian's further use of the voice as a separate musical instrument.

The closing line (and chorus), "Sometimes I feel very sad," sums up Brian's pain and makes a lyrical resignation sound like a protest. "I don't want to be sad, dammit!" seems just below the surface.

"Pet Sounds" was one of the early tracks. He knew what he wanted to do.... Sometimes we had to experiment around—when you have it in your mind and nothing's written down you have to make sure you get the right people to understand what you want and sometimes the vibrations themselves have to be right.

——*Chuck Britz*

"Pet Sounds" follows. It is a rolling and mellow instrumental and, in the context of the album, a reprise of earlier themes. Recorded in the earlier days of the album, it enables us to hear some of the musical ideas from which later parts of *Pet Sounds* were generated.

"Caroline, No" is the last song on *Pet Sounds*. Brian's painful remembrance of fading youth and less complicated days is expressed through the longing for an old girl friend.

"Where did your long hair go?/Where is the girl I used to know?" An awareness of time and change permeates the entire cut and is symbolized by the thudding, solitary sound of the drumstick hitting an empty bottle.

To close the album, Brian delivers a nonmusical coda: the barking of Brian's two dogs (Banana and Louie), a clanging train, and the silence of night.

I wanted moodiness...something moody.

——*Brian*

The roar of the railroad fades, leaving us with the barking dogs and then silence. Brian achieves the emotional effect without music. At the end of *Pet Sounds* all is peaceful. Broken affairs, emotions, and memories fade but *never disappear*. Comfort is to be found in the simple things. The silence at the end of the cut becomes an integral part of the album.

Pet Sounds was an inspiration for hundreds of musicians. Al Kooper, Elton John, Paul McCartney, and scores of other professionals cite it as one of the most important records they have ever heard.

Yet, in 1966, *Pet Sounds* did not suit the traditional rock marketplace. Who could dance to "I Just Wasn't Made for These Times"?

I'm so proud to have been able to sing on that album.

——*Bruce*

I JUST WASN'T MADE FOR THESE TIMES 1966–1967

Soon everyone was saying "genius" and the beauty of it, as with the beauty of anything, was that it was true.

——*Derek Taylor*

Although the relatively poor commercial reception for *Pet Sounds* was to hurt Brian emotionally, his enthusiasm for experimentation with music continued to grow. Intellectual and extemporaneous experiences were flying through him at an incredible rate. The experiences had a revolutionary effect on his concepts for music. Each new personal discovery was a jumping-off point for a new musical expression. There was a creative balance in Brian's existence much like the balance in *Pet Sounds*. So much of Brian's music was his life; so much of Brian's life was his music. There was one particular song that became the focus of his work. It was to be the ultimate Beach Boys' single—a revolutionary production that would, once and for all, establish the group's reputation as rock-and-roll artists.

There was an era where songs would be written in twenty minutes—a half-hour.... "Good Vibrations" took a couple of days.

——*Brian*

Brian Wilson had a reputation for doing things quickly, for wanting immediate gratification in the development of his music. Unlike his mentor Phil Spector, who would put on a "performance" for those in attendance at his recording sessions, Brian worked seriously. If strange things were going on in the studio, they were usually connected to the music being made.

He walked in and I saw this instrument, I didn't know what the hell it was.... I'd worked with theremins before but I never worked with this unit. The sound was so weird. It was just fun to watch. He just walked in and said, "I have this new sound for you."...I think he must have heard the sound somewhere and loved it and built a song around it....

——*Chuck Britz*

When the Wilson boys were young, Audree's mother would tell them about *vibrations*—feelings that animals would receive from people and other animals that could not be seen or heard. Invisible feelings. Brian remembered the concept and developed it musically—to get the feelings of "good vibrations" into song.

I only looked in her eyes
Then I picked up something I just can't explain
It's weird how she comes in so strong
and I wonder what she's picking up from me
——unreleased lyrics, "Good Vibrations"

Brian was excited. He had a new sound—good-natured and eerie—an electronic instrument called the theremin which had been used primarily for movie soundtracks in the 1940s. He also had a new concept. The song and approach were presented to his trusted studio musicians and the group.

The first session for "Good Vibrations" was done at Western...totally live... the whole thing. To me it was the same as when he finished it seventeen tracks—seventeen sessions later. Dennis wasn't there for the first session, Carl and Al played bass. Mike was in and out. We had a slew of musicians. Hal Blaine, Al DeLaurie, Don Randy on organ, Brian usually played piano. Brian sang on everything. He had a lot of fun. The first session, everything just jelled. Again, I think he tried and tried to please everybody. Then when he was all done he went back to the first sound because it was the best of them all.

——*Chuck Britz*

After producing a spectacular version of his new song "live," Brian decided to experiment with it further. Traveling from Western

The album reached the top ten, but it took significantly longer and sold significantly fewer copies than earlier Beach Boys' records. Capitol's dissatisfaction hurt sales, and lower sales reinforced the company's conviction that they had been correct about the album from the start. Hard-pressed for new Beach Boys' material, however, Capitol issued "Wouldn't It Be Nice" and "God Only Knows" as a two-sided single in July. Both became monster hits; "Wouldn't It Be Nice" went to number eight in the U.S. and "God Only Knows" hit the two spot in Britain. There was no way Capitol could deny their impact, but artistic relations with the company did not noticeably improve.

Under the wing of publicist Derek Taylor, the group set out to rectify their image without the company's help. The group wanted to be seen for what they were.

Brian took me into another room and said that the Beach Boys were a strange group; he said they had neglected many things, like artwork and pictures and press, but that now things had a shape and form and direction he could recognize and describe, he didn't want things to get away from them. He wanted everything to come together....We decided to have new pix taken, simple things in fields—without the striped shirts—and we decided not to beat around the bush about anything anymore at all....

I lived in Hollywood then, but my British links were strong and with **Pet Sounds** *out and the Beatles increasingly flattering about the Beach Boys (Beatle praise was real power in those days—I guess it still is) and with "Good Vibrations" on the way, we started to pump information into England about this tremendous band, with their new plateau....*

Brian and Mike

THE BEACH BOYS
GOOD VIBRATIONS

Recorders, to RCA, to Goldstar, to Columbia, and then back again to Western, Brian used the peculiar acoustics of each studio to get different sounds.

He *knew* "Good Vibrations" was spectacular. Either tomorrow or six months from tomorrow, a single record with all the care and attention of the *Pet Sounds* album would be a classic.

We wanted to do something that was R and B but had a taste of modern, avant-garde R and B to it. "Good Vibrations" was advanced rhythm-and-blues music.

——Brian

He had taken his process of developing musical themes a step further. Rather than settle for the "live" sound of musicians playing in one studio at the same time, he'd have dozens of musicians playing at different times in different studios. When he was finished, he'd sort through all these tapes and select the music from each session that he'd want for the final song.

"Good Vibrations" was done in a bunch of studios in Los Angeles. I went over once to Columbia with him. He had a feel for what he wanted. He was trying to get across his feeling to the guys and the musicians. It was an idea that he knew would really come off good if he could get off his ideas to the guys that were performing. I think the problem was that they were swapping from one place to another to get a different sound, a different feel and a different performance, using different engineers, different musicians, and different places....I think that's one reason why it took so long. He had an idea that if he could imply sections of this thing....Brian was a guy who would do songs by sections. He would write the song out completely, words and music in his mind or on a piece of paper, but when it got to a recording stage, he'd want a certain section verse to be a certain feel and he'd want a chorus to be a certain feel. Then he would keep working on those sections regardless of the time it took, until he felt it was the way he wanted the thing....

He had already made up his mind how it was going to go together.

——Jim Lockhart

It took six months, four studios, ninety hours of tape, and up to twenty different versions before Brian would settle on a "Good Vibrations" for release. Mike provided the final lyrics.

"Good Vibrations" was to be the most spectacular collage in the history of rock and roll. The theremin would play a major role; Brian had a way to use the sound for an upbeat musical representation of

"vibrations." A cello would be mixed up front. Anything went. Discarded tracks piled up quickly. Early mixes of the song were more immediate, less polished. Fuzz bass and organ were teamed for a funky track. A full wall of Spectorian sound was dropped. An organ and clarinet arrangement provided an easy forties beat. It didn't quite fit. The vocals went from soft lullaby to exuberant shout. If there was an end to Brian's musical experimentation in sight, most people didn't see it. "Good Vibrations" just continued.

When I first heard the "Good Vibrations" track it really zonked me out. We heard it on playback at Western Recorders. We were just playing it for Russ Regan, a guy in the record industry out there....It was a very heavy R and B track. The first track Brian kept was so R and B it sounded like Wilson Pickett would be recording it. It was so far out. Then he did another which wasn't as heavily R-and-B flavored but it still had that element to it. Then we did sections of track, and finally we were satisfied with enough sections, you know, a cappella things and harmony things with the tracks, and it culminated in what came out, the edited single version of "GV." There's a track laying around somewhere that would be far out to hear someone like James Brown do. You know, with those freaky horn things they do and some girl singers in the back.

——Mike

There was a lot of "Oh, you can't do this, that's too modern" or "That's going to be too long a record." I said, "No, it's not going to be too long a record, it's going to be just right."

——Brian

At one stage, Brian removed himself from the production of the record. Disenchanted, he almost sold the song to Warner Brothers as a vehicle for one of their R-&-B groups. When his friend David Anderle got word of the events, he made an effort to get "Good Vibrations" for Danny Hutton, a client who would go on to later fame with Three Dog Night.

I proposed, made a proposal to him, which I don't think caused him to decide to finish but maybe...it gave him a different perspective.

——David Anderle

We went and fixed it up. Changed it, altered it.

——Brian

In May 1966 Phil Spector released his opus, "River Deep, Mountain High." It was the culmination of his work as a producer, and it did what Brian was setting out to do—take a special "sound" toward its musical limits. Spector did it with Tina Turner and the "wall of sound." Brian was doing it with his trusted studio corps and the harmony of Al, Carl, Mike, and Dennis. The lack of acceptance of "River Deep" in America bothered Brian, as he says, "a little," but he confidently pressed forward on the production of "Good Vibrations." The song went through four "final" versions before Brian was satisfied. A "third" mix, breezier and less energetic, was almost given to Capitol, but Brian pulled it back at the last minute. To anybody else, "Good Vibrations #3" may have sounded like a smash, but to Brian, the single still needed work.

I remember the time we had it...I remember I had it right in the sack. I could just feel it when I dubbed it down to mono. It was a rush—a feeling of... artistic beauty.

——Brian

To Chuck Britz, the final mix-down of "Good Vibrations" seemed familiar. He remembered the original version of "Good Vibrations" as very close to the final release. Brian had effectively combined a variety of musical sounds without losing a "live feeling" in the track as a whole.

"Good Vibrations"—you have three pieces totally...two edits in there. He did the opening at Goldstar for the drum sound, then RCA for a few bars, and then back to Western all the way through....You have two edits in there because I made them for Brian. Everything was mixed at Western.
——*Chuck Britz*

Released in October 1966, "Good Vibrations" was the biggest production in the history of rock. It shot straight up to number one around the world and gave the Beach Boys the largest response of their careers. It sold 400,000 copies in four days. When sales passed one million Capitol's prior resistance to the "new" Beach Boys could be easily dismissed.

It had a lot of riff changes...movements....It was a pocket symphony— changes, changes, changes, building harmonies here, drop this voice out, this comes in, bring this echo in, put the theremin here, bring the cello up a little louder here....It was the biggest production of our lives!
——*Brian*

If, without pretension, the word "rainbow" could be saved for any rock-and-roll song, "Good Vibrations" would deserve it. The subtle musical changes in the song were exquisite—tonal shifts in mood and expression. There is a feeling of every sound being exactly where it should be. The punctuation by drum and tambourine fell meticulously into place. Brian's use of organ and tambourine harked back to "The Little Girl I Once Knew" and "Here Today," with a more ephemeral effect.

"Good Vibrations" changed spectacularly from hymn, to white soul, to California rock, to surrealistic chorale, and then back again to joyful rock in a dazzling three minutes and thirty-five seconds. Backed by one of the most complex instrumental tracks in rock history, it initiated a critical explosion.

GOOD VIBRATIONS **by Brian Wilson and Mike Love**

I, I love the colorful clothes she wears,
And the way the sunlight plays upon her hair.
I hear the sound of a gentle word,
On the wind that lifts her perfume through the air.

Chorus
I'm picking up GOOD VIBRATIONS, she's
  giving me excitations
(Repeat chorus)

Close my eyes, she's somehow closer now,
Softly smile, I know she must be kind

Then I look in her eyes,
She goes with me to a blossom world.

(Repeat chorus)

I don't know where but she sends me there
Oh my my, what a sensation
Gotta keep those lovin' GOOD VIBRATIONS
A-happenin' with her.

(Repeat chorus)

Copyright 1966 by Irving Music Inc.

"Good Vibrations" was climbing up the charts to be their first million-selling single. They had conquered England—we were getting daily phone calls with stories about the three hundred photographers at EMI, the **New Musical Express**, *they were the number one group, they'd overtaken the Beatles, the first act to do that. The meetings between Brian and Lennon and McCartney and all those things were going on, the first recognition of Brian from the critics, from the hippies. It was all very beautiful, a very happy time.*
——*David Anderle*

It was an incredible period for the group. Wherever they toured, the Beach Boys were on top. Nonrock heavies such as Leonard Bernstein gave their blessing. The *Saturday Evening Post* wanted an article. CBS made plans to include Brian in a prestigious prime-time rock-and-roll special. Rock music had replaced the movies as the most talked-about form of popular culture, and the most talked-about group in the most talked-about form of American popular culture was the Beach Boys.

There was more than enough reason for Brian Wilson to smile.

Brian Wilson's energy and ambition were at their peak. His spontaneous enthusiasm extended from his music to his life. He not only wanted to change the face of rock and roll, he wanted to affect the entire music industry. Brian was turned off by the AM radio he was hearing. He spoke of a different type of programming—progressive, lighter, with more personality and less garbage. He was interested in experimenting with video and film—musical movies. He wanted to do a health-food album—an esoteric concept reflecting his active interest in nutrition and natural foods. Like many other plans, the proposal made little sense to anybody but Brian, yet his enthusiasm for the idea was such that his friends were anxious to see him pull it off.

We were down at the studio and Brian didn't feel like putting down a track. We were just lying around and he said, "Come out here, everyone." So we all went out...and he had us making animal noises, incredible noises...and then he just drove us into it. We went into the studio and listened to it; he put it with music; we listened to it again and walked out knowing once again Brian had done it.
——*David Anderle*

Brian loved to experiment—not just with music, but with the things around him. He put his piano in a sandbox so his feet could feel the beach as he composed. Whoever came into his life was a new source of information and excitement.

David Anderle was one of the most important people to come into Brian's circle at this time. David was both artist and talented young manager with impressive record-company connections. He brought a variety of intellectuals and rock enthusiasts to Brian, including Mike Vossi and Paul Robbins. Mike Vossi would visit Brian's house and, like many other guests, was quickly put to "work."

Brian sent me out with a tape recorder to tape water sounds—all kinds of water. He wanted to do a thing with natural sounds. He had me go out and get the sounds of sports—basketballs bouncing....Somewhere there are two **huge** *stacks of tape.*

—*Mike Vossi*

It was June 1966. Brian was working hard on developing the final version of "Good Vibrations." The Beach Boys were more independent of each other now, and more involved with their own personal lives. More significantly, they were frequently on tour. Brian's circle of friends provided him with some of the camaraderie and encouragement that had come from his family in the past. In addition to Anderle and Vossi, Brian associated with Paul Robbins, *Saturday Evening Post* writer Jules Siegel, Lauren Schwartz, and a young poet and composer who looked about as different from a Beach Boy as a California immigrant could.

Van Dyke Parks was a student of classical music who had come to Hollywood at the age of thirteen. He had been a child actor and later, a writer for MGM record-label rock groups such as Harper's Bizarre. He was also a client of David Anderle.

I met Brian during **Pet Sounds** *when the inclusion of the cello—which I recall was my idea—was important to the development of that sound on record. Brian generously did everything he could to help me along—so I became, as it were, an exercising lyricist. I just started writing the words for him.*

—*Van Dyke Parks*

I met him at Terry Melcher's house. Listening to that guy talk, I said, "That guy's articulate, I'll bet he'll make a good lyric writer"...and he **was.**

—*Brian*

Van Dyke's friendship and working relationship with Brian developed quickly. They admired each other. Brian was open and innocent in his work. Van Dyke was intellectual. Yet in many ways, they were both reaching for the same thing. Brian used music to produce spectacular pocket symphonies—epic fragments filled with sounds and feelings. Van Dyke used words the same way. His poetry was filled with grandiose pictures and ideas. Van Dyke's concerns were more literary than Brian's; Brian's were more traditionally romantic than Van Dyke's. Yet both were concerned with the process of capturing emotions. They shared a love for comedy. Brian's simple Hawthorne humor was the counterpart of Van Dyke's sophisticated wordplay. The two men may have differed in their styles and approach, but both Brian and Van Dyke were creative showmen who loved innovation.

I think Van Dyke is one of the few, very few people that Brian looked on as an equal, or maybe that's a little presumptuous to say. Van Dyke blew Brian's mind and I haven't seen anyone else do that.

—*David Anderle*

We just started working a few weeks after we met. We just wrote songs.

—*Brian*

As he had done with "Good Vibrations," Brian used "Heroes and Villains" as an opportunity to produce a wide range of musical experiences—diverse combinations of vocal and instrumental effects to play out the songs' varied expressions. With "Good Vibrations" the concept of developing new songs in fragments had gone a step further. Starting with "Heroes and Villains," it was a process he could apply to an entire concept album.

Brian dubbed his next effort *Dumb Angel*, an allusion to the humorous and spiritual themes in the music. The title was quickly changed.

[Dumb Angel] was just a passing title. **Smile** *was more cheery, so we used the more cheery title.*

—*Brian*

You see, where I had always seen a musical cooperation going on was in the studio, and particularly when they were cutting tracks. In the studio, they had a happy relationship going.

—*Mike Vossi*

In the intimacy of the whole thing there was this impressive innocence.

—*David Anderle*

They worked at the house in Beverly Hills, or at the recording studio, or out by Brian's pool. Brian enjoyed the collaboration. Van Dyke had so many *ideas*.

"Surf's Up"—Van Dyke and I really thought we had something special done when we finished that.

—*Brian*

Written in one night, the shimmering, euphoric, and quietly apocalyptic "Surf's Up" was a major piece of songwriting. Composed at the piano, it symbolized Brian's growth as a composer and put the Beach Boys' relationship with the sea on a metaphysical level. The melody of "Surf's Up" was gorgeous, a precious series of chords that in its beauty was reminiscent of the first steps of a child. It became a lullaby and then a prayer.

Out in the farmyard the cook is chopping lumber...
Out in the barnyard the chickens do their number.

—*from "Barnyard"*

The Barnyard Suite, that was going to be four songs—In four short pieces—combined together, but we never finished that one. We got into something else.

—*Brian*

The duo focused on farm life; the Old West; the natural environment; ethnicity; American roots; "Child Is Father to the Man" was inspired by the concept of the phrase itself. "Cabin-Essense" would deal with a quiet little cabin in the woods—the atmosphere of a log cabin—subtitled "Home on the Range."

On "Cabin-Essense," there's a line in there—"truck-driving man" which I sang. I got off so much doing that. It's mixed way down in the track and it's syncopated all the way through. Right there is my biggest turn-on.

—*Dennis*

With humor and affection, Brian and Van Dyke were approaching subjects that had not been expressed in rock and roll. The music of *Smile* was so different, so exciting in the way it employed sound as a means to express emotions and visual ideas that it defied characterization. It had the vitality of pop and the sophistication of classical music. It wasn't really rock and roll, it was just "new music."

Brian was constantly speaking about "new plateaus" for the group. Despite the commercial reception for *Pet Sounds,* Brian was fully confident of his new musical direction. "Good Vibrations" would be a hit. The next album would top the Beatles. He had a tremendous drive to keep the Beach Boys "on top," and at the same time he was anxious to free rock and roll of its thematic restraints by relating his new experiences and feelings through music. He wanted to make music that was a joy to hear. Most of all, he wanted to make people laugh. To Brian, a state of laughter was a sublime release—a beautiful moment when a person could be happy, open, and fully expressive. Making an album that would put people into a state of laughter would be almost religious in its significance. Making people happy was one of the highest things he could do. At the same time, this "cosmic humor" could remove the stigma of "serious music" from the experimentation he had planned. Brian was worried that "the kids" would look at his new music and say it was pretentious. After all, *Pet Sounds* with its symphonies had tested the commercial limitations of rock and roll. By making the listener laugh, however, Brian hoped the new album would say, "Hey! This arty music's not heavy! It's real, it's fun!"

By July 1966, he began extensive work on the sound. As Capitol's first *Best of the Beach Boys* collection shot up the charts, it was clear that Van Dyke Parks would play a major role in the new music. With Brian, he'd provide lyrics and dozens of new musical concepts.

I was there for "Good Vibrations" and then "Heroes and Villains," which was as big if not bigger than "Good Vibrations" in its original form.

I thought it was a fantastic song, a great, rich full sound. It was just a full-sounding record and the voices blended right in...like an extra part of an instrument.

We had our basic unit—an organ, drums, basses, and guitars. Mostly everything we did had the same amount of basic instrumentation.

I think there was a harpsichord in the back of the room and a harp played by Mike's sister, Maureen.

——*Chuck Britz*

Brian and Van Dyke worked on a song called "Heroes and Villains," a vibrant, melodic collage of musical harmonies and highly visual lyrics. Although "Good Vibrations" had not been finished yet, they were sure this new song would top it. The music was exuberant with counterpoint and harmony that was both innovative and—characteristically—"fun."

The version we did originally was just voice holds and no gimmicks...like where they just drop out the orchestra and did an organ thing for a solo....It moved from beginning to end.

——*Chuck Britz*

We wanted to do something spiritual with no verbal connotations to it so that people could be influenced by the feeling of it.

——*Mike*

"Our Prayer" was an a cappella song that swept by like a gossamer cloth. Its soaring harmony was a stunning example of Brian's use of the voice as a musical instrument.

"Do You Like Worms" had little to do with its title. The song was a magnificent example of Brian's production style for *Smile*. Each element of the song was recorded live, then overdubbed with the Beach Boys' use of words-as-music—monosyllabic lyrics coupled with a spare narrative chorus that followed the opening of the song.

The first sound in "Do You Like Worms" is a pounding combination of steel guitar and kettle drum, which quickly fades to the second element, an unadorned string with a sweet "Rock, rock, roll, Plymouth rock roll over, roll overrrrrr" chorus dubbed over it. The harmony for the word "over" is stretched up and out, lightly blending with a third element—a beautiful music-box rendition of the main theme from "Heroes and Villains" on harpsichord.

From here Brian recorded two alternate elements, both Hawaiian chants. The first was a deep, comical *"Umacah buh ummagah,"* backed by steel guitar. The second, sweeter and more harmonic, was *"Wahhla loo lay, wahhlaloola, kee nee wakapoola."* Mike Love sang lead on the latter. The *"wahhla"* version was repeated six times, each linked to the addition of another instrument or sound on the instrumental track. (First chorus, Mike and drum; second chorus, Mike, drum, and surfing guitar; third chorus, Mike, drum, surfing guitar, and soft background group "lalalalala" chorus; fourth chorus, Mike, drum, surfing guitar, and harder chorus—like a sea breeze; fifth chorus, repetition of the fourth.) On Mike's *"wahhla"* of the sixth chorus, the song takes a one-beat pause and returns to a cello with a single-note series

backed by harpsichord. A reprise of the "music box"/"Heroes and Villains" theme follows, eventually meandering to a close, as if the music box itself were winding out.

A final mix on "Do You Like Worms" was never completed.

In his musical experiments, Brian would go to extraordinary lengths to find new—and in his mind, more expressive—sounds. By early September, he was playing with a fragment called "Bicycle Rider" ("Bicycle rider, now see what you've done done"). Here Brian's obsession was with the sound of "light" wheels—the gentle clicking of a coasting bicycle. He toyed with bells and a cello. Then he turned to nonmusical objects for musical sounds—glass, paper; they generated more experiments and pushed Brian ahead on two cuts about the Old West, "The Iron Horse" and "(Have You Seen) The Grand Coulee Dam?"

The song was about railroads...and I wondered what the perspective was of the spike. Those Chinese laborers working on the railroads, like they'd be hitting the thing...but looking away too, and noticing, say, a crow flying overhead...the Oriental mind going off on a different track.

——*Brian*

A panorama of American history filled the room as the music shifted from theme to theme. The tinkling harpsichord sounds of the bicycle rider pushed sad Indian sounds across the continent; the Iron Horse pounded across the plains in a wide-open rolling rhythm that summoned up visions of the Old West; civilized chickens bobbed up and down in a tiny ballet of comic barnyard melody; the inexorable bicycle music, cold and charming as an infinitely talented music box, reappeared and faded away....

——*from "Goodbye Surfing!"*

Work on one cut began and then was abandoned. Mike remembers, "A lot of tracks were titled a couple of different things." Like toys, Brian would play with musical concepts and then set them aside. Between Brian and Van Dyke there was no shortage of ideas, and the eldest Wilson was spurred on in a self-invoked competition with Lennon-McCartney and Jagger.

Mike Love, Carl Wilson, and Al Jardine huddle around one of the big playback speakers at Columbia Records, Studio A...Twelve takes on one small section of background voices for "Heroes and Villains" have just been completed. Mike is not quite satisfied with his singing on a few bars. They go back into the studio. Over and over they rerecord the difficult and complex harmony pattern until it is perfect. Then Brian takes them to the piano and teaches them more background to be overdubbed. The creative process here is as spontaneous as in the earlier track sessions. Carl has an idea and goes to the microphone alone, laying in a lovely and funny little riff behind the chorale effect.
The Beach Boys and their producer work together well. The communication is not limited to words, there is a profound spiritual rapport. They are turned to one another and it shows up in the music.

——*Teen Set, Volume 4,*
a semi-accurate/semi-put-on by Brian and Mike Vossi for
a fan magazine published by Capitol Records

Brian's enthusiasm was extraordinary. There was talk in Brian's sauna about how the album would be pieced together. "Bicycle Rider" could be part of "Heroes and Villains." Or would "Bicycle Rider" fit better as part of a "Barnyard Suite"? Or would "Barnyard" be part of "Heroes and Villains"? "Surf's Up" could close the album. "Heroes and Villains" could open it.

The master for "Good Vibrations" was at Capitol. The other Beach Boys were about to embark on another tour. Work on *Smile* would continue in their absence.

The fall concert schedule for the Beach Boys began at the University of Ann Arbor in Michigan. Brian flew out to rehearse the group for the first date. His head was full of new plans for the group. Among them was the idea of their own label, separate from Capitol Records.

Preparation for the Michigan date was strained. Mike, Al, Carl, Bruce, and Dennis would be touring Europe in the wake of "Good Vibrations." Performing the complex number "live" was a challenge they had never faced.

The college concert went surprisingly well. The group got Brian out on stage for the closing number—a feat they hadn't accomplished since his "retirement" in Texas. Sans Brian, the Beach Boys then left for what would be the most impressive and critically successful tour in their history.

Brian returned to California and the studio. Working on the tapes, he'd sometimes mix down Carl and Dennis's voices and push up his own—no lack of self-confidence when it came to music. Even in live sessions with the group, Brian's recording decisions were rarely challenged. There was immense respect for his work. If there were any problems with the direction of *Smile*, the Beach Boys voiced them outside the studio.

ously simple and sophisticated music and arrangements with Van Dyke's complex poetry and puns produced a deep, joyful, personal sound that really did make you want to smile.

Perhaps the most beautiful thing about this fascinating work was what it represented to the evolution of popular music. Brian's *Smile,* for all its humor, was a serious work. It had a theme, a consistent method of construction, and a series of emotional and aesthetic goals. The Beach Boys—a rock-and-roll group from the suburbs whose youngest member had just recently turned twenty—were continually moving beyond their earlier achievements into the realm of modern art. If the hits of the early sixties had their roots in Southern California, then *Smile* stretched them across the American West.

Had things remained as exciting and positive as they had been that fine October of 1966, *Smile* could possibly have been the biggest musical event in rock and roll since the sounds of Chuck Berry's guitar and Elvis's voice.

Bruce, Carl, Dennis, Alan, Mike

I never objected to musical progressions...the only thing I ever objected to was lyrics—I think lyrics should be used to communicate. Music or sound which will communicate a feeling. Meaning and feeling together make a musical whole....Although I thought they were far-out, I didn't relate to them. When I heard a lyric that made no sense to me, I could appreciate it on an aesthetic level, but it didn't sit right with me. I had a difference of opinion from those who did.

————*Mike*

Van Dyke Parks's lyrics and Brian's music transcended other innovative rock because it operated on so many levels. Brian's simple concept of a modern musical "humor" album had never been fully explored. Nor had rock and roll focused on the evocative mixture of music and sounds as extensively as both Brian and Van Dyke had planned. The songs themselves were sensational. Van Dyke's lyrics were obscure but not oblique. The effect of coupling Brian's simultane-

They're all vignettes. You see, that's Brian Wilson's greatest work—not the sustained riffs of a blues band, but the little musical vignettes—ten or twenty seconds of verse, a chorus, a shot here or there and then out. And that's what the whole Smile *era was—vocal trips, musical trips, little trips, experiments, they'd go down this alley and maybe it would be a dead end. It didn't mean it wasn't good, it just didn't fit with something, and sometimes things were dropped. Sometimes things fit together and sometimes they were dropped. There's no way it could be made sensible and logical. It doesn't follow any patterns you could trace.*

————*Mike*

Had Brian concentrated on completing *Smile* and nothing else, the album might have been ready for December release. Acetates of instrumental tracks for the LP littered Brian's house. Yet his concentration was split among a dozen interests. He was getting involved deeply in the business decisions of the group. This frustrated him. The financial problems could not be controlled as quickly or as directly as a hit record. By the end of October, rock prodigy David Anderle was on the payroll to explore the possibility of establishing "Brother Records" as a Beach Boys-owned entertainment company. In addition to releasing Beach Boys' records, "Brother" would be a channel for the group's work in music, publishing, television, film, and other media. Progressive in structure, "Brother" would be responsive to the needs of the entire group. As a record label, it would give Brian the opportunity to handle other musicians such as the Honeys and Danny Hutton and the Redwoods. Carl could also produce other artists. David Anderle began discussions with Capitol Records and other companies on the Coast to find "Brother" a home.

Meanwhile, while the group was in Europe, Brian continued intellectual sidetrips with his friends. Astronomy, a preoccupation of his youth, resurfaced. Health foods, meditation, numerology, scheduled vitamin intake, and the natural environment all fascinated him. He spent a few days in Big Sur to experience its beauty. He'd sit in his swimming pool at three in the morning and hold meetings.

It was crazy, it was fun, it was even too intense. Yet it was Brian and he did it.

In the living room of his house, Brian erected a huge red-and-gold print meditation tent. Sewn from his own design, it lacked proper ventilation. Brian rarely set foot inside. Downstairs, in the vestibule, there was a portable sauna. Another room was converted into a gym.

The night the tent went up Brian didn't like it. I think Brian was in it twice.
———*Mike Vossi*

Back in the studio, Brian worked on instrumental tracks and overdubs. His preoccupation with the environment blossomed into the *Elemental Suite,* a beautiful four-part polychromatic collection of songs that would express the feeling of the elements.

Yeah. There was a cut—a piano piece, an instrumental, no vocals—we never finished that.
———*Brian*

"Air" would be a lovely, wordless piano tune. "My Vega-Tables," Brian and Van Dyke's funny love song to carrots, beets, and assorted greens, would be the "Earth" section. "Fire" was "Mrs. O'Leary's Cow," a cacophony of strings—a mad, impressionistic piece that crept up on you with the emotional chill of a real fire. For the sessions Brian had toy fire hats purchased for the musicians. As they played, a bucket of burning wood was kept in the studio for effect.

Brian did more than a dozen takes of the song, using an actual sound-effects record of a fire on some of the versions. He was decked out in tight white pants, striped t-shirt, lime bowling shoes, and firehat for the occasion. As with the use of swimming-pool meetings for business, Brian used the absurdity of the red firehats to loosen up the studio musicians. By getting *them* to smile and relax, Brian could get a more natural and possibly more evocative performance.

Two takes of "Fire" reveal just how fast Brian could change a track and build on an extemporaneous musical experiment. "Fire" opens with an oscillating duet of violins and cellos. They whine up and down in a repetitive wave, punctuated first by the sound of a triangle to gently simulate a fire bell and then by a sharp series of drum beats with cymbal shading. The use of violin and cello continues through the short piece, playing perpendicular to each other, like sirens to a flame at a street corner blaze. The song's finale is a quick series of snare-drum beats. The effect disappears with the track.

When a rash of fires broke out in Los Angeles after the tapings, Brian grew upset. When another flared up in a building across the street from the studio, he abandoned the song entirely. Bad vibrations.

It is another night at Goldstar. A group of older musicians whom Brian has never met are there to perform on French horns. Five minutes after producer meets players, the men are creating laughing effects and having conversations with their horns.

It was just an idea I had and I'm glad to see it works.

"How does he do it?" somebody in the hallway asks.
———*Brian with Mike Vossi in* Teen Set

There was one part of the *Elemental Suite* that fascinated Brian as far back as the spring of '66. It sprang from his interest in using sound effects such as those he had sent Mike Vossi out to record in June. "I Love to Say Dada" was planned as an ode to water, reflecting not only the element but the pleasure people experienced with it. Light, full of cute vocal tricks and real water sounds, "Dada" and another cut, "Surf's Up," were briefly considered as part of a grand "Water Suite" within the *Elemental Suite* itself.

"Old Master Painter"–that was an old, obscure...black gospel sort of thing, sung by an old fellow that came by Brian's house one night.
———*Mike*

In addition to the *Barnyard Suite,* "Surf's Up," the *Elemental Suite,* and the "western" cuts— "Iron Horse," "Cabin-Essense," "Heroes and Villains," and "(Have You Seen) The Grand Coulee Dam?" Brian and Van Dyke toyed with other pieces, often generated by a passing suggestion or visitor to the Wilson house. The soulful, black-spiritual "Old Master Painter" was an example—quickly recorded, then ignored.

By November the group had returned to California. Brian was still dynamic and creative. His "Heroes and Villains" had as much chart potential as "Good Vibrations," but Brian refused to commit himself to any version. In the old days things were ostensibly simple—work hard, have fun, make a hit. Now the picture was complex. Three problems took the fun out of much of the work—problems that in many ways were instituted from without as well as from within Brian Wilson. They were the commerciality of the work in light of its artistic nature; the quality of the music in relationship to the other innovative rock and roll being made; and the viability of Van Dyke's lyrics in the context of the Beach Boys' music. Personally Brian had no crippling doubts about any of these things. He may have been insecure as a person, but as an artist he had confidence in his work.

The rock community also had little reason to doubt Brian's direction. Anybody who heard the *Smile* tapes walked away impressed. The Beatles are reported to have written "Here There and Everywhere" after hearing *Pet Sounds.* Yet these people did not play a large role in Brian's personal life. There was pressure from Brian's father to keep within the successful boundaries of the group's early music. There was unspoken pressure from Capitol Records to be consistent with the Beach Boys' name.

Brian continued to play with musical fragments. With harmonica, rhythm guitar, plunking violin, and snare drum he developed another light instrumental section to be overdubbed for "Heroes and Villains." The music was beautiful but the distractions continued.

The Smile *thing was not a real comfortable time.*
———*Diane Rovell*

Abe Solmer, an attorney, sat down with Mike, Brian, Carl, Dennis, Al, and David Anderle to explain what would be involved in the formation of Brother Records. Relations with Capitol had not improved. There was still tension over their corporate attitude toward the Beach Boys' new music. Capitol's anxiety for a follow-up single did not help.

Shortly after the Solmer meeting, matters grew still more complicated. The Beach Boys filed suit against Capitol Records on the

grounds that they had not been paid sufficient royalties for their work. An estimate of alleged damages, tied to an archaic "breakage" clause, ran as high as $250,000. Relations with Capitol worsened.

All right, Brian, he was told one day, at this point in order for us to get what we have to get for Brother Records, we've got to have a single out. That old, lousy thing that still exists in our business: You've got to have a single out. So Brian is told that he's got to have a single. He was getting very uptight, he was getting disappointed, he was getting disappointed in me because I was being business...I wasn't hanging out any more.

——*David Anderle*

Brian wanted a deluxe color booklet for the forthcoming *Smile* album. In an age when jackets had been less an art and more a necessity, deluxe color books were the exception rather than the rule. That *Smile* might be on the level of "serious" music did not persuade Capitol at all. The shadow of a lawsuit, however, gained Brian an extra bargaining point. Capitol agreed to the plan. Pop art was commissioned from Frank Holmes for a special sixteen-page photo-and-picture section. A cheery childlike illustration was prepared for the front cover. Guy Webster shot Al, Bruce, Dennis, Carl, and Mike while on tour in Boston. A double portrait of Brian would be used in the center.

We were touring a lot. I wasn't involved in working in the conception a lot at that time.

——*Mike*

I wasn't there. I heard about it just like anybody else...I was home.

——*Al*

By mid-November there were enough distractions to keep Brian from working on *Smile* whenever he wasn't in the mood. A promotional film based on the music to "Good Vibrations" was prepared for use on British television. In the vein of *A Hard Days' Night*, it would later function as a promotional device for Capitol in the States.

There are so many screwed-up people in the music industry. The good guys and the bad guys....That's one thing Brian had in mind when they did "Heroes and Villains." There was a part Brian didn't use. It went, "In the cantina..." I only heard it twice.

——*Marilyn*

As he worked on sweetening some of the *Smile* tracks, Brian was relayed a $50,000 offer by the head of merchandising at Capitol on behalf of a car manufacturer who wanted a jingle for a new model.

Brian was not amused. Another session was canceled. Another day's work on the *Elemental Suite* was gone. Friend Lauren Schwartz came by with an idea for a clothes store to specialize in robes. Brian loved the idea. He rode down Sunset Boulevard to check out available stores. Another afternoon lost.

Jasper—Jasper Daly, he was a photographer—he came up with an idea for a song that I thought was clever. "Teeter-Totter Love"—"When I am up, my baby goes flying down." Simple but poignant. I mean, how many times have you been on a teeter-totter love affair?

——*Mike*

People would drop in with new ideas and Brian would pick up on them. The problems with Capitol continued. Pressure came down for a single. Brian's reaction to the pressure was compounded by another problem. Drugs.

I didn't know how affected he was by the drugs in terms of paranoia and stuff....Otherwise I would have freaked out more.

——*Mike*

Brian's problems with drugs have never been fully documented. The effect of drugs on his personality was tied closely to his other emotional problems at the time. He had trouble dealing with the sudden burden of "artistic" success. He was compelled to turn out music that satisfied him intellectually and he was *sure* (as "Good Vibrations" had shown) that this personal success would mean financial success in the stores. It was a conviction, however, that was challenged by Murry Wilson, who still exercised a measure of control over Brian. Brian felt trapped, depressed—for the sake of the group, he didn't want to jeopardize their financial standing; and on the other hand, he refused to compromise his creativity. Drugs, specifically amphetamines, aggravated the problem. It is clear that Brian was abusing them and the resulting symptom was casebook: paranoia. In addition to amphetamines, Brian was naively susceptible to whatever drugs friends would bring into the house. This resulted in even more "retreats" to his room—or into moods in which nobody could talk to him. Carl remembers a period when Brian took a lot of LSD over a short span of time, then stopped taking it completely. Brian credits acid and speed as the prime reasons for his "breakdowns." In his words, "Acid shattered my mind." Brian was the focal point of an entire mini-industry. He loved making music but could not handle all the hustles being laid down on the group. The business problems made it more difficult to concentrate on getting *anything* done. Drugs made the problem circular. He'd retreat to avoid problems. Then he'd take drugs that intensified his feelings of paranoia. The intensified paranoia made him want to work even less. He was afraid that people would steal his ideas; afraid of "conspiracies."

Overworked and scared, he'd retreat again.

Into this scene walked David Oppenheim, an articulate director for CBS Television. For eight months he had been planning a news special on rock music and the youth culture, to be hosted by Leonard Bernstein. "Inside Pop: The Rock Revolution" would begin with an introductory "rap" by the famed conductor on new musical styles. Music from rock stars, from the Beatles to Janis Ian, would be played and then analyzed for the viewer by Bernstein. For the second half of the show, Oppenheim's camera would reveal the emerging counterculture in L.A. and its philosophy in the context of rock and roll.

Oppenheim flew out and spoke with Frank Zappa, Tandyn Almar, and members of Canned Heat, Gentle Soul, and UFO. As one of the highlights of the program, Beach Boys' leader Brian Wilson would be recorded at work.

The director was quickly caught up in the L.A. scene. By late November, the friction between police and young people hanging out on Sunset Strip and Crescent Heights developed into violence. A clash outside Pandora's Box, where Brian had met Marilyn a few years earlier, spurred Stephen Stills to go over to Terry Sachen's house and write the song, "For What It's Worth."

A march against an eleven P.M. curfew was organized and support from rock personalities was solicited. Brian sent Mike Vossi and David Anderle down to represent the group.

David Oppenheim and his cameras showed up to film the event. It was a peaceful march until the end, when two groups of police came in and blocked off the protesters. Van Dyke's friend Paul Robbins was hit on the head. Coverage by the CBS crew helped prevent a full-scale disaster and managed to slow down the clash and eventually cool things off.

The level of tension was a preview of things to come. The Beach Boys became involved with a benefit for the protesters. Once again, attention was diverted from *Smile*. When Brian *did* work, it was in his own idiosyncratic pattern of recording fragments. A session for the CBS cameras was so musically inaccessible to the "average" viewer that Oppenheim was unable to include it in the film. He decided to try and get Brian on film at home.

Brian had a big dinner for Oppenheim. He wanted to shoot Brian singing. Brian said he wanted to do some sort of underwater ballet thing. So the crew arrived equipped to shoot underwater. I think Murry dived in and they shot that too.

———— Mike Vossi

Finally, one night in Brian's house, Oppenheim was able to set things up. At first, he attempted to get Brian to sit and talk about his work and the pop culture. Brian wouldn't, so Oppenheim focused on his music. A group of Brian's friends were over at the time and they coaxed him to the piano. It wasn't easy. Unshaven, with reddish-brown sideburns and a tired look, Brian Wilson was reluctant to play in front of the cameras.

Muted lighting bounced off the walls of the room. A candelabrum sat on top of the piano. At last, after many false starts, Brian began to play. From memory he performed the song he had written in one night with Van Dyke Parks—"Surf's Up."

…poetic, beautiful in its obscurity, "Surf's Up" is one aspect of the new things happening in pop music today.

———— Leonard Bernstein, on "Inside Pop"

If the rock community had been eager for *Smile*, Brian's television performance sent them through the roof. "Surf's Up" was the highpoint of the Parks/Wilson collaboration. Subtle, shifting, enigmatic, a kaleidoscope of music, poetry, and elliptical humor, "Surf's Up" was equal to if not better than "Good Vibrations." Played in its most simple musical form for Bernstein's spring special, it poignantly displayed Brian's musical vision.

SURF'S UP *by Brian Wilson and Van Dyke Parks*

A diamond necklace played the pawn,
Hand in hand some drummed along,
To a handsome man and baton,
A blind class aristocracy,
Back through the op'ra glass you see
The pit and the pendulum drawn.
Columnated ruins domino.
Canvass the town and brush the backdrop
Are you sleeping?
Hung velvet overtaking me.
Dim chandelier awaken me
To a song dissolved in the dawn.
The music hall a costly bow.
The music all is lost for now.
To a muted trumpeter's swan.
Columnated ruins domino
Canvass the town and brush the backdrop
Are you sleeping, Brother John?
Dove-nested towers the hour was.
Strike the street quicksilver moon.

Carriage across the fog,
Two-step, to lamp lights cellar tune.
The laughs come hard in Auld Lang Syne.
The glass was raised, the fired rose.
The fullness of the wine, the dim last toasting,
While at port adieu or die.
A choke of grief heart hardened I beyond belief.
A broken man too tough to cry.
Surf's up mm, mm, mm mm, mm mm,
Aboard a tidal wave.
Come about hard and join the young.
And often Spring you gave
I heard the word, wonderful thing,
A children's song.
The child, the child, the child is the father of the man
The children's song and the message that they play.
The song is love, and the children know the way.

Copyright 1971, 1972 by Brother Publishing Co.

At home, as the black acetate dub turned on his bedroom hi-fi set, Wilson tried to explain the words.

"It's a man at a concert," he said. "All around him there's the audience, playing their roles, dressed up in fancy clothes, looking through opera glasses, but so far away from the drama, from life—'Back through the opera glass you see the pit and the pendulum drawn.'"

The music begins to take over. "Columnated ruins domino." Empires, ideas, lives, institutions—everything has to fall, tumbling like dominoes.

He begins to awaken to the music; sees the pretentiousness of everything. "The music hall a costly bow." Then even the music is gone, turned into a trumpeter swan, into what the music really is.

"Canvas the town and brush the backdrop." He's off in his vision, on a trip. Reality is gone; he's creating it like a dream. "Dove-nested towers." Europe, a long time ago. "The laughs come hard in Auld Lang Syne." The poor people in the cellar taverns, trying to make themselves happy by singing.

Then there's the parties, the drinking, trying to forget the wars, the battles at sea. "While at port a do or die." Ships in the harbor, battling it out. A kind of Roman Empire thing.

"A choke of grief." At his own sorrow and the emptiness of his life, because he can't even cry for the suffering in the world, for his own suffering.

And then, hope. "Surf's Up!…Come about hard and join the once and often spring you gave." Go back to the kids, to the beach, to childhood.

"I heard the word"—of God; "Wonderful thing"—the joy of enlightenment …and what is it? "A children's song!" And then there's the song itself; the song of children; the song of the universe rising and falling in wave after wave, the song of God, hiding the love from us, but always letting us find it again, like a mother singing to her children.

———— from "Goodbye Surfing"

Even Bernstein admitted it was "too complex to get all of it the first time around."

I think the group felt that the visit of CBS—the "musical genius" stuff—was ruining Brian…making him too worried that people wouldn't like him.

———— Mike Vossi

I think he got caught in a trap with "Good Vibrations." He became a prisoner instead of a poet. He had the plaudits, the accolades, and touched the masses. I know music is a very important thing to him, besides a vocation. It became cluttered in the last few years. Your attitude is in the grooves and it's a very personal thing. But Brian thrived on competition.

———— Phil Spector

After Oppenheim's visit, Brian's behavior grew worse. Increasingly paranoid, he suspected that his house was being bugged. Meetings in the pool, originally held to loosen up the formality and pretentiousness of business, became a way to avoid detection. There was the word of "theft" of concepts from *Smile*. The Capitol relationship further deteriorated.

Brian worked on "Heroes and Villains" again, in the hope of having a single out before the end of the year. To please Capitol, the Beach Boys provided a list of projected side-one and side-two cuts for the *Smile* album. Frank Holmes prepared cover art, which went out as part of a winter promotion for *Smile* in the music trade. To the outside, *Smile* seemed weeks away. Billboard ran a full-page ad, complete with the news of the appearance of "Good Vibrations" on the album. A back cover, in black and white, was prepared with a picture of the group sans Brian. A suggested order for the cuts may have gone something like this—*Side 1* "Do You Like Worms," "Barnyard," "Cabin-Essence," "You Are My Sunshine," "Who Rode the Iron Horse," "Grand Coulee Dam," "Bicycle Rider," "Heroes and Villains;" *Side 2* "Good Vibrations," *The Elemental Suite*, "My Vega-Tables," "Surf's Up," "Child Is Father to the Man."

ILLUSTRATED BY
JAMES McMULLAN • RALPH REESE

I'm waiting for the Day
Brian Wilson-Tony Asher

I came along when he broke your heart
That's when you needed someone
To help forget about him
I gave you love
With a brand new start
That's what you needed the most
To set your broken heart free.
I know you cried and you felt blue,
But when I could I came straight to you.
I'm waiting for the day when you can
   love again.
I kissed your lips when your face looked sad.
It made me think about you
And that you still loved him so
But pretty soon,
I made you feel glad that you belonged to me

Your love began to show.
He hurt you then but that's all gone.
I guess I'm saying you're the only one.
I'm waiting for the day when you can love again.
You didn't think that I could sit around and let you go.
You didn't think that I could sit around and let you go.

Here Today
Brian Wilson-Tony Asher

It starts with just a little glance now,
Right away you're thinking 'bout romance now.
You know you ought to take it slower,
But you just can't wait to get to know her.
A brand new love affair is such a beautiful thing,
But if you're not careful, think about the pain it can bring.
It makes you feel so bad.
It makes your heart feel sad.
It makes your days go wrong.

It makes your nights so long.
You've got to keep in mind, love is here today
And it's gone tomorrow;
It's here and gone so fast.
Right now you think that she's perfection.
This time is really an exception.
Well, you know I hate to be a downer, but I'm the guy
   she left
Before you found her.
Well, I'm not saying you won't have a good lovin' girl,
But I keep on remembering things in a whirl.
She made me feel so bad, she made my heart feel sad,
She made my days go wrong,
And made my nights so long.
You've got to keep in mind, love is here today
And it's gone tomorrow.
It's here and gone so fast.

  Love is here today

And it's gone tomorrow.
It's here and gone so fast.
Love is here today and it's gone tomorrow.
It's here and gone so fast.

Wouldn't It Be Nice
Brian Wilson-Tony Asher

Wouldn't it be nice if we were older
Then we wouldn't have to wait so long,
And wouldn't it be nice to live together
In the kind of world where we'd belong.
Though it's gonna make it that much better
When we can say goodnight and stay together.
Wouldn't it be nice if we could wake up in the morning
When the day is new;
And after that to spend the day together
Hold each other close the whole night through.

The happy times together we'd been spending
I wish that ev'ry kiss was never ending.
Oh wouldn't it be nice?
Well maybe if we think and wish and hope and pray it might come true.
Baby then there wouldn't be a single thing we couldn't do.
We could be married
And then we'd be happy.
Oh wouldn't it be nice?
You know it seems the more we talk about it.
It only makes it worse to live without it.
But let's talk about it.
Oh wouldn't it be nice.

God Only Knows
Brian Wilson-Tony Asher

I may not always love you,
But as long as there are stars above you

You'll never need to doubt it;
I'll make you so sure about it.
God only knows what I'd be without you.
If you should ever leave me
Life would still go on, believe me.
The world could show nothing to me,
So what good would living do me.
God only knows what I'd be without you.
God only knows what I'd be without you.

Don't Talk, Put Your Head On My Shoulder
Brian Wilson-Tony Asher

I can hear so much in your sigh
And I can see so much in your eye.
These are words we both could say,

But don't talk,
Put your head on my shoulder.
Come close, close your eyes and be still.
Don't talk.
Take my hand and let me hear your
  heartbeat— Listen, listen, listen—
Being here with you feels so right.
We could live forever tonight.
Let's not think about tomorrow
And don't talk,
Put your head on my shoulder.
Come close, close your eyes and be still.
Don't talk,

Take my hand and listen to my heartbeat—
Listen, listen, listen.

You Still Believe in Me
Brian Wilson-Tony Asher

I know perfectly well I'm not where I should be.
I've been very aware you've been patient with me.
Every time we break up you bring back your love to me,
  And after all I've done to you, how can it be
    you still believe in me.
I wanna cry; I try hard to be more what you want me to be.
  But I can't help how I act when you're not here with me.

I try hard to be strong but sometimes I
Blame myself
And after all I promised you so faithfully
You still believe in me.
I wanna cry.

I Know There's an Answer
Brian Wilson-Terry Sachen

I know so many people who think they can do it alone.
They isolate there heads and stay in their safety zones.
Now what can I tell them
And what can you say that won't make them defensive?

I know there's an answer. I know now, but I had to find out for myself.
They come on like they're bashful, but inside they're sewed up tight.
They drift through the day and waste all their thoughts at night.
Now, how can I come on and tell them the way that their days could be better?
I know there's an answer, I know now but I had to find out for myself.

Caroline, No
Brian Wilson-Tony Asher
Where did your long hair go?
Where is the girl I used to know?
How could you lose that happy glow?
Oh, Caroline, no.
Could I ever find in you again

Things that made me love you so much then.
Could we ever bring 'em back
Once they have gone?
Oh, Caroline, no.
Who took that look away?
I remember how you used to say
You could never change
But that's not true.
Oh, Caroline
You break my heart.
I wanna cry.
It's so sad to watch a sweet thing die.
Oh, Caroline, no.

I keep looking for a place to be where I can speak my
   mind
I've been trying hard to find the people that I won't
   leave behind now
They say I got brains but they ain't doing me no good
I wish they could
Each time things start to happen again
I think I got something good going for myself but what
   goes wrong?
Sometimes I feel very sad. Sometimes I feel very sad.
I guess I just wasn't made for these times
Every time I get the inspiration to go change things
   around
No one wants to help me look for places where new
   things might be found now
Where can I turn when my fair weather friends drop
   out? What's it all about?
I guess I just wasn't made for these times.

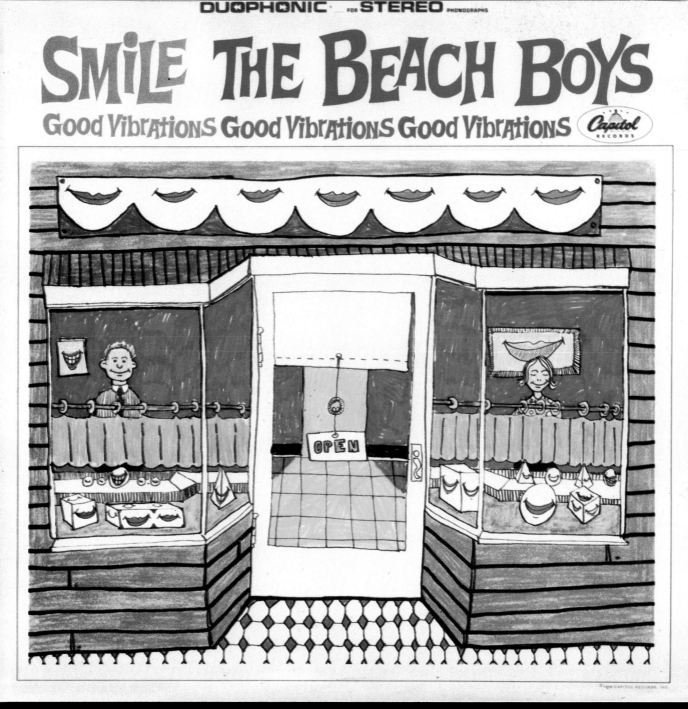

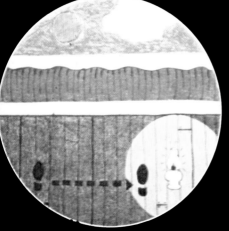

GOOD VIBRATIONS

I, I love the colorful clothes she
   wears
And the way the sunlight plays
   upon her hair
I hear the sound of a gentle word
On the wind that lifts her perfume
   through the air
I'm picking up good vibrations,
   she's giving me excitations
I'm picking up good vibrations,
   she's giving me excitations
Good, good, good, good vibrations
Close my eyes she's somehow closer
   now
Softly smile, I know she must be
   kind.
Then I look in her eyes, she goes
   with me to a blossom world
I'm picking up good vibrations,
   she's giving me excitations
I don't know where but she sends
   me there
Oh my, my, what a sensation
Gotta keep those good lovin' good
   vibrations
A-happening with her.

        —Brian Wilson and Mike Love

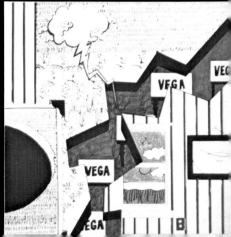

Above is a color interpretation for the music of the Beach Boys' classic "Good Vibrations." Each note is represented by a different hue: C = Magenta, D = Red, E = Orange, F = Yellow, G = Green, A = Blue, B = Violet. The music ranges over four octaves, and the correct octave is indicated by the exact shade of each color, from the darkest values for the lowest notes to the lightest shades for the highest notes. (For example, a high C is light magenta; a low A is dark blue.) Sharps and flats are denoted by blends of two basic colors. A single note in the treble staff is shown by a solid block of color; a chord is represented by a stack of smaller color blocks. Bass notes appear as either two or four blocks of color per measure beneath the corresponding treble notes. Measures are divided by thick black bars, and within each measure, thin black bars separate the notes. The song is composed primarily of single notes and three-note chords in 4/4 time.

GOOD VIBRATIONS *paintings by John Pound*
SMILE *booklet photographs by Guy Webster*
SMILE *booklet illustrations by Frank Holmes*

I been in this town so long
that back in the city
I been taken for lost and gone
and unknown for a long, long time

Fell in love years ago
with an innocent girl
from the Spanish and Indian home
of the Heroes and Villains

Once at night,
Catillion squared the fight,
and she was right in the rain
of bullets that eventually
brought her down

But she's still dancing
in the night unafraid of
what a dude'll do in a town
full of Heroes and Villains

PAINTINGS BY DAN GREEN

Heroes and Villains, just see what you've done done
La la la la la la la la la la la la la la
Stand or fall I know there shall be peace in the valley
and it's all an affair of my life with the Heroes and Villains.

My children were raised, you know they suddenly rise,
They started slow long ago, head to toe, healthy, wealthy and wise.

I been in this town so long, so long to the city,
I'm fit with the stuff, to ride in the rough,
and sunny down snuff, I'm all right by the Heroes and Villains.

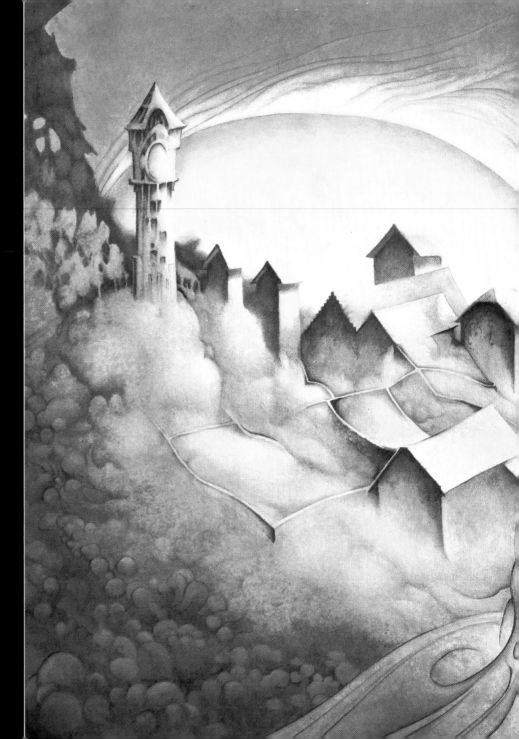

Kenneth Smith

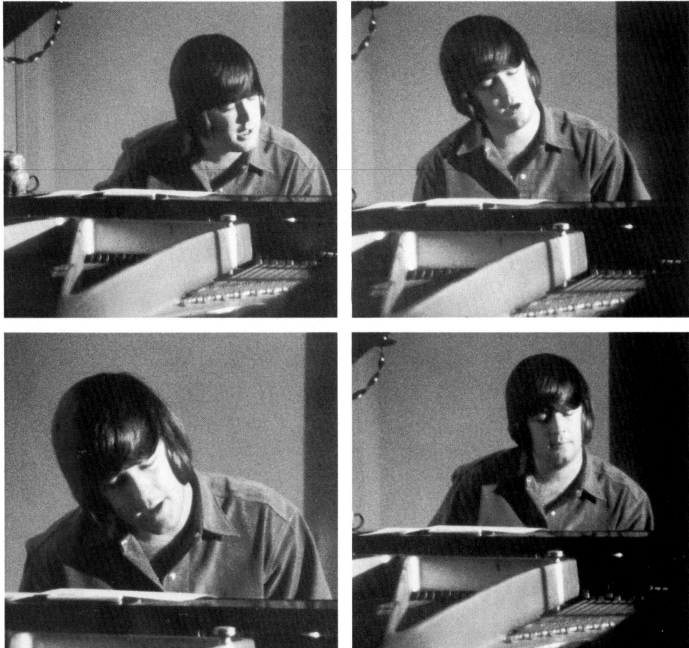

Brian performs Surf's Up, 1966

There was also talk of a physical fitness cut, "I'm in Great Shape," a logical extension of Brian's preoccupation with health and natural foods.

Smile, however, was not delivered to Capitol. Brian was still working.

At the same time, Van Dyke's enigmatic lyrics were under attack. There had been resistance to them from the group and Brian, whose music had always been accessible and emotionally direct, was also starting to feel somewhat frustrated by his partner's work.

Plans for Brother Records were not moving smoothly, either. There was no agreement with Capitol, Warner, or any of the other labels who were interested in the Beach Boys' operation.

Decisions were not being made. Numerous TV and film offers, including a ninety-minute animated special, went unanswered.

Smile was an intense, complex, and ground-breaking effort. Brian still had his professional confidence. When he worked the results were sensational, but his work became more and more infrequent. Recording sessions were canceled and there were emotional scenes among Brian, his family, and friends. Brian's rapport with Murry was especially strained at this time; beyond the drugs and whatever conflicts Brian had had with his father in the past, the normal metamorphosis of a father-son relationship had also been affected by the Beach Boys' success, something that Murry Wilson had worked for from the start. Both Brian and Murry were stubborn. Both wanted to dominate the group's affairs.

We had an argument…a basic argument.
——Brian

Their parting was kind of tragic, in the fact that they were two separate people who absolutely did not want to separate, but knew that they had to separate, that they could not work together, 'cause they were too strong in their own areas.
——David Anderle

In February, *Smile* suffered a fatal blow. After repeated conflicts, Van Dyke left Brian. The frustrations involved with the songwriting and production had pushed them apart and an offer for a solo album from Warner Brothers was too important to Van Dyke's career for him to turn down—at least in the context of the idiosyncratic indecisiveness that now surrounded *Smile*. Versions of "Heroes and Villains" were complete and *Smile* itself had been overdue for two months, yet nothing was being released.

If completion of the album had seemed an elusive goal with Van Dyke present, it became a crisis after his departure. Who else could work with material like "Columnated ruins domino"? Brian's own emotionally direct lyrics rarely went beyond a three-syllable word.

Still, there was enough material to get an album out. The problem was Brian's perfectionist nature. No material was ready for release until he said so.

For the Beach Boys, a group whose last single had been the most commercial and critically respectable innovation of the past year, things were a mess.

With the Beatles, both of us being on the same label, made it even more competitive. Both our names started with "BEA" and both on the same label. I thought that was very amusing.
——Brian

February saw the release of "Penny Lane," "Strawberry Fields," and Stevie Winwood's "I'm a Man." Brian loved them all. He'd ride around and listen to them on AM. Musically, he was as far ahead as before, but emotionally …

It seemed as if people were conspiring to make things difficult for the Beach Boys. Brian just wanted to make music, have fun, and expand the focus of the group, but there were these *problems*.

He couldn't get [studio] time when he wanted time, which would be like three in the morning. Brian could work those knobs better than anyone I've ever seen, including any engineer. He would mix a lot of his things right there as they were recording. He wouldn't have to wait, he'd be adding his echo, mixing and blending right while they were recording.
——David Anderle

The other Beach Boys had their own personal concerns. Dennis was going through the trauma of an unsuccessful marriage. Mike Love spent time with his young children and toyed with a collection of expensive cars. Carl was growing—after Brian, he was considered the most promising composer in the group. Al Jardine avoided the hassles. He enjoyed touring. His wife Lynda accompanied him from time to time, photographing the group. Commenting on the Beach Boys, Brian, and their music in a December 1966 *Melody Maker* interview, Al said:

"California Girls" is my concept of what most people feel the Beach Boys are or should be. That is, a nice compromise between the sophisticated and the simple heads. Everybody loves it because it's completely passe—and out-dated by Brian Wilson's standards. Easy to sing and to identify with. Everything was there…The retaliation of the Beatles and English pop music came just when we were beginning to get very big in America. The mystique of the English groups distracted everybody's attention…Man, when we heard, "I Want to Hold Your Hand" we thought somebody was putting us on! The thing is, the coming of the English invasion gave us a chance to look at ourselves and reflect.

I now feel our success is completely legitimate. If we'd got in there three years before the Beatles hit America or waited until years after—our true position as far as popularity was concerned may have been false…Brian realized the position and had time to develop musically…when the disc we did during the English invasion flopped midst all the English records, we sat down, analyzed the situation, and took off in another direction.
——Al Jardine

We moved into the Bel-Air house about April 1967. We were in the first house about eighteen months. I think the move may have had something to do with what happened to Smile. *You know, new house, new things. We had a studio in the house.*
——Marilyn

Smile was a collection of vocal and instrumental experiments. When Brian and Marilyn moved to their new Spanish-style mansion in the spring of 1967, Brian had the idea of putting a studio right in the home. By having the equipment nearby at all times, the off-hour and sudden impulses to experiment would present no problem. All Brian would have to do is walk into the next room to record.

When we started at the house we had remote equipment. It was rented and brought into his house. They have one large room which had been a music room for the former owner and there was a hallway and an office and all the console and tape machines were set up in the office. The cables ran across the hall into the music room and there was a closed circuit television so you could see what was going on…We started working in that method.
——Jim Lockhart

Excited by the new surroundings and assisted at home by ex-Western engineer Jim Lockhart—who had worked briefly on *Pet Sounds*—Brian reinvolved himself with *Smile*. The personal problems he had faced during the winter continued, but he also enjoyed having people at the new house. Late at night, with a closed circuit camera in front of him, Brian would play "Johnny Carson" to whoever was hanging out.

Every day there was recording…Brian was really working…We worked every day—some. We might work one hour or six hours. The guys were very understanding. We supposedly would start every day at two o'clock. A lot of times some of the guys wouldn't get there until four or five o'clock for their parts. When everybody got there we'd work. If somebody got tired then they'd say, "Let's quit." I'd work until midnight if they wanted to go that long. I'd say, "Hey guys, I'm tired, let's go home" and they'd say, "One more take" or "One more time." They were cooperative. They would know if somebody really didn't like working they did not get the best of what they wanted.

——Jim Lockhart

Even as he developed a new version of "Heroes and Villains," Brian experimented with other tracks. Van Dyke was gone; the lyrics for new songs were less complex.

Just a very winsome…melancholy…almost rubato type of rendition, sung by Dennis.

——Mike

Brian developed his idea for a new version of the classic, "You Are My Sunshine," a warm, wistful production that opened with a stately cello sound. The intro was followed by a single, lighthearted violin string, then a stomping bass drum. The main theme of the song was structured around a melancholy cello and violin with a woodblock sound syncopated behind it. A lovely clarinet provided the bridge between the last verse and the finale, a slow cello that echoed the first chorus.

I think we did that one night about midnight. We put the cello on about twelve-thirty … We'd done the track we'd been working on and at about eleven o'clock he picked up the phone and called a man that did some of his contracting with musicians and told him he needed so many cellos. Two o'clock in the morning he'd get them. People enjoyed working with Brian because they learned. Brian was ahead of his time. I guess it was because the life his father put on the group when they started out….

Brian had the knack of transmitting to other people what somebody wanted. He had the knack of transmitting, of communicating….He would take over the sessions and run them. The other guys had ideas, but it would solidify with Brian because he had the feeling for the situation, he knew what the end was gonna be.

——Jim Lockhart

With the new surroundings, Brian's mind also moved *away* from the *Smile* LP. There was no clear-cut plan to finish the "album." The "album" was many, many pieces. Brian worked on the tracks but did so without any set schedule for completion. Other new ideas and musical experiments held his interest. Whatever fragment, old or new, that appealed to him would be put into momentary production.

"Can't Wait Too Long," an uptempo love song with phenomenal Beach Boys' harmonies, was one example. Carl sang lead, and Brian pulled the group, piano, falsetto, tambourine, vibrato, cello, snare drum, distorted rhythm guitar, and thudding drum together for one of the most vibrant performances of the *Smile* era. The piece fea-

---

CAN'T WAIT TOO LONG *by Brian Wilson*

"OOH—MMM	Can't wait too long baby
AHHHHHHHH	Wait too long
Been too long	Can't wait too long baby
OOH—MMM	*chorus*
AHHHHH	I've been away too long
I miss you darlin'	Been way too long baby
I miss you so hard	Baby you know that I can't wait forever
Di-di-dip-di-dip-di-dip	Woke in the night again we were together
Miss you darlin'	Been way too long
Miss you so hard	Been way too long baby
Been too long	Windows of darkness are all I can see through
Been way too long baby	Searching the shadows
Way too long	Hoping to see you
Been way too long baby	Way too long
Wait too long	I can't wait too long baby
Can't wait too long baby	Baby you know that I
Wait too long	OOOOOOOOO"

---

tured the full range of Brian Wilson techniques—luscious four-part harmony, wordless bridges, spiraling *"woo"* falsetto, dazzling tempo and chord changes, and a simply beautiful, beautifully simple, melody.

The tapes for "Can't Wait Too Long" were a wonderful insight to the incomplete work on *Smile*. The music is so clear and yet so instrumentally complex—there's a guitar distortion that wavers like a neon wisp on the edge of your senses. Brian couples piano and bongos, syncopates cello string against cello chords and background chorus behind Carl's vocal. There's a single moment of falsetto by Carl that must be considered among the most beautiful sounds the group has ever recorded. Just when you think the vocal strength and beat of the song have reached their peak, everything moves into 3/4 time, a stunning shift that keeps repeating until the song gently fades.

"Can't Wait Too Long" remained in fragments. The tapes were evidence of Brian's working method on *Smile*.

1. Record "live" instrumental sections in the studio. Each section would be a possible fragment for the final editing of the song.
   or
   Record the entire instrumental track "live" in one take, the same method used for *Pet Sounds*.

2. Separately record Beach Boy vocals "live" for each instrumental section; then overdub the voices on each musical fragment or complete track.

3. Combine the fragments into one complete cohesive song—the final mix, at times "sweetened" by additional instrumental highlights.

It was most frequently the final step that was not completed. "Can't Wait Too Long" stayed in the can; the overdubbed sections were substantial enough to form an entire song, but they may not have been sufficient enough to meet Brian's expectations. Or perhaps he had just become distracted. Another song. Another experiment. Another problem. Although he was producing a considerable volume of music, Brian was still in a difficult emotional period.

We went shopping one day and we brought home some wind chimes. We hung them outside the house and then one day, while Brian was sitting around he sort of watched them out the window and then he wrote the song. I think that's how it happened. Simple. He does a lot of things that way.

——Marilyn

"Wind Chimes" would reflect the beautiful sounds Brian heard outside his window. With some unusual harmonies, the group produced an airy, soft, drifting sound. Interlocking vocals were planned for an elaborate chorale, but work on this aspect was not expanded.

By the end of June, Brian's *Smile* album became more dream than soon-to-be reality. On the second of the month, the Beatles had released *Sgt. Pepper,* and the level of excitement Brian had expected for *Smile* was bestowed on the Lennon-McCartney-Martin sound instead. All across the Western world, the airwaves were filled with "All You Need Is Love" and "A Day in the Life." It could have been "Surf's Up" or "Cabin-Essense." Brian had been so close, yet it all seemed so far away. He was changing and the people around him were changing, and the music—there were so many pieces—needed his concentration.

There was enough for a whole album. More than enough. There was an awful lot of music. "Wind Chimes," "Cabin-Essense," "Vega-Tables," "The Iron Horse"—that one was magnificent: the first trains going across the country…the buffalo…the Indians…there was a selection about Kansas. Sitting in the studio, the kettle drums booming, you could see big black crows sweeping across cornfields.

——Tom Nolan, "A California Saga," 1971

David Anderle departed and Beach Boys' attorney Nick Grillo finished negotiations for "Brother" with Capitol.

hit the top twenty was a measure of the group's continued popularity. Eccentric high-pitched vocals, unusual tempo changes, a short playful chorus of babylike sounds blending into a bubbling harmony, inventive instrumentals and characteristically oblique phrasing made the radical harmony of "Heroes and Villains" a challenging puzzle every time it played AM.

I was very happy with that.

——*Brian*

"Heroes and Villains" was released in July.

Brian took a benign, passive interest, instead of a dominating interest. At that time something had happened to his whole ego drive. It had been very powerful until the time of "Heroes and Villains" release—he was about ready to come out with the Smile *album and he was feeling very dynamic and creative and then something happened...* chemically *that completely shattered that—that made him the complete opposite...that made him want to withdraw....But he was always shy; he was too sensitive. There was a fine line and he went over that line....He was still creative though. Instead of* Smile *he did* Smiley Smile. *It was light, mellifluous, laid-back. It was dynamic in a passive sort of way, it was a revelation of where his psychology had gone to. It dropped out. He dropped out of that production race—the next big thing after* Sgt. Pepper.

Brian had lost interest in being aggressive and he went in the other direction—still creative, and different, but it wasn't competitive.

——*Mike*

I think it was the drugs.

——*Dennis*

The tapes from *Smile* still exist. The album became a legend. Songs and beautiful musical fragments would emerge over the years, but *Smile* was to have been a whole musical direction, and the individual songs, taken from their natural surroundings, were deprived of what could have been a stunning collective emotional effect. The work had started with "Good Vibrations" and it had expanded with the help of a friend Brian had met on Cielo Drive. Now, a year later, *Smile* was still a dream. Too much pressure. Too many drugs. Too much anticipation. Too little support. It was the end of an era.

I'm not a genius. I'm just a hard-working guy.

——*Brian*

Brian had become a member of the board of directors for an open-air rock extravaganza scheduled for the weekend of June 15, 1967, in Monterrey, California. The Beach Boys would top the bill for a huge, hip, predominantly Northern California audience on Saturday evening. Shortly before the event, Brian withdrew the group. Carl's draft problem, the pressure for "Heroes and Villains," final negotiations with Capitol for Brother Records, and, significantly, a lack of communication about the economic status of the event billed as "The Monterrey International Pop Music Festival" were cited as reasons. Whatever the cause, the Beach Boys missed a crucial chance for acceptance by the growing "counterculture" rock audience.

Brian kept his focus on "Heroes and Villains," editing and re-editing different sections of the song. A shorter, more flowing mix was discarded. Brian overdubbed group vocals on earlier instrumental tracks, putting a *"hum-hum de doobie doo"* chorus on his harmonica-snare drum interpretation of the main theme. He finally decided on a 3:36 version after playing with tracks up to eight minutes long.

We had the complete song, but they just wanted to use part of it. Brian wanted to change what had been done on the rest of it. I think he wanted instrumentally and vocally to make it more complex. I think he wanted to finish the song, it was a challenge to him ... We went and rerecorded from where we started off the old tape, the rest of the song at the studio in the house. We did the parts and the music tracks and most of the guys played their own instruments ... It was done in pieces and the vocals were done to complete the song.

——*Jim Lockhart*

As a fitting send-off, Brian personally planned a trip to L.A's number-one pop station with a dub of the single in hand. A full parade of Beach Boys limousines drove up to KHJ-AM for the event. They had to argue before they could even get through the gates. By the time they reached the DJ it was almost midnight. Brian presented the tape to the resident jock and was told that it couldn't go on the air because it wasn't on his playlist. Brian freaked out.

After checking with the station manager, the DJ was told to put the song on *immediately*. For Brian the concession was a little late. He had been hurt again.

"Heroes and Villains" was a hit, but not of the size of "Good Vibrations." The song had more of the shifting stop-and-start patterns foreshadowed by "The Little Girl I Once Knew" and "Good Vibrations." Van Dyke's words took it off on a yearning, playfully innocent fantasy.

The fact that a piece of such musical and lyrical subtlety could

The summer of '67 was the summer of love, a transition period for rock and roll. Surrealistic lyrics, which had come into play during much of *Smile*, surfaced in the Procol Harum hit, "A Whiter Shade of Pale." A laid-back love song to Sunday afternoons went top ten in "Groovin'." *Sgt. Pepper* dominated the radio. Otis Redding died. Sam and Dave triumphed. *Rolling Stone* appeared. Dylan crashed. Memphis, Muscle Shoals, and San Francisco were the centers of musical action. The Jefferson Airplane played the Fillmore. Ex-Beach Boy Glen Campbell had his first major hit, "By the Time I Get to Phoenix." Jim Morrison and Linda Rondstat imbued rock and roll with its original meaning. Psychedelic, introspective, and soulful music was "in." The media read: *love*, *trip*, and *hippie*.

For the Beach Boys there was a sense of departure from the intense period of recording that had begun with *Pet Sounds* and had dissipated in the final days of *Smile*. The group and the family were back together again. Brian's circle of friends from the *Smile* days had moved on. "Heroes and Villains" was a bona-fide hit, and Capitol wanted it on a new album along with "Good Vibrations." In the meantime, a second *Best of* collection traveled up the charts less successfully than its 1966 counterpart.

Smiley Smile *was a very simple album to make. It took a couple of weeks at Brian's house. Tops, two weeks. We had a remote come into Brian's library*

and we set up a console on his desk with two speakers, ran wires up to the gym, down to the sauna, and out to the pool—anywhere....

———*Carl*

We found a room adjacent to the large music room and built a control room in there and installed a remote console and speakers where we could do it. We were in the office before that....We physically changed the music room into a recording studio with isolation and baffles and sound treatment so we could do some recording in there without problems.

———*Jim Lockhart*

Brian had gotten into doing vocals again and some tracks—experiments, really—called for little more than Brian, the group, and an engineer.

Brian's swimming pool had a leak in it and was empty, so we put a microphone in the bottom of this damn near Olympic-size swimming pool and the guys laid down inside the pool and sang so the sound would go down the wall of the concrete pool into the microphone—and that was part of the vocals on one of those songs....We had to watch out for the planes coming in over L.A. airport. We did it late at night so hopefully we wouldn't have that kind of noise bothering us.

We did some other vocals—all the guys got into the shower and we put the shower on. We had the microphone above the shower head so it wouldn't get wet. We recorded them singing in the shower. I learned a lot from those guys.

———*Jim Lockhart*

Still fascinated with the effects of noninstrumental sound in a musical context, Brian continued to pair aural humor with advanced melodic themes. The most obvious example was his later production work on the "Earth" section of the *Elemental Suite*, "My Vega-Tables."

Paul McCartney and the Beatles were friends of theirs....He was a guest of Brian's and normally I was up in the control room. There was much experimentation.... [On "Vega-Tables"] we had celery coming out of our ears—and carrots!—you'd never believe the stuff the guys were chewing in front of the microphone. I don't remember what all the vegetables were. They had a basket of them and they were tryin' to see how they sounded and to make up their minds which to use.

———*Jim Lockhart*

By midsummer, it was over one year since the Beach Boys' last LP. Even for Brian, the lapse had become intolerable. To remedy the situation, the group sprang a wildly determined plan to combine uncompleted *Smile* cuts and post-*Smile* Bel-Air studio experiments into a whole album.

Beach Boys 1967-1971

FRIENDS 1967–1973

Smiley Smile, the first Brother Records album, was framed by a Rousseauesque jungle scene with a smiling house in the middle. Side one of the record led off with "Heroes and Villains," side two, "Good Vibrations." As far as commercial openings were concerned, Capitol got their wish.

The balance of the album was the Beach Boys' most eclectic offering. The "Earth" part of the *Elemental Suite,* "Vega-Tables," proved the best evocation of the album's spirit. It was clever, silly, funny, and superbly produced. Real vegetable-crunching sounds were mixed with jug-blowing, water pouring, and the group's incredibly happy vocals for a celebration of fresh greens and carrots. The chromatic range for the closing chorus ("I know you'll feel better/when you

---

VEGETABLE ("My Vega-Tables") *by Brian Wilson and Van Dyke Parks*

I'm gonna be a-round my vega-tables
I'm gonna chow down my vega-tables
I love you most of all
My favorite vega-table
I'm gonna keep well my vega-tables
Cart off and sell my vega-tables
I love you most of all, my favorite vega-tables
I love you most of all, my favorite vega-tables
I know that you'll feel better when you send us in
    your letter
And tell us the name of your favorite

vega-table
If you brought a big brown bag of them home
I'd jump up and down and hope you toss me a
    carrot
I've tried to kick the ball but my tennie flew right
    off
I'm red as a beet 'cause I'm so embarrassed
I know that you'll feel better when you send us in
    your letter
And tell us the name of your favorite vega-table.

Copyright 1967 by Irving Music Co., BMI

The Smiley Smile *album was done on eight track in segments that were never put together in one tape. The intro was on one reel of tape, the first verse was on one reel of tape.... When you take a song you have an intro, first verse, a chorus, second verse, a chorus, and then you have an ending. Each segment of that thing was on a different tape for each cut of the album.*

We had all the component parts with all the first verses on tape. We went into Wally Heider's Studio Three one night at five o'clock, we mixed the intro of each song as we went to a two track, then we mixed the first verse, then we went back and wiped off the verse that was on that tape and we put on the second verse or the third verse or whatever was on that song.

We overdubbed the same tape, wiped out the vocals that were there. We didn't have another take of it. They didn't want to make copies of it to put it together. So we'd do the first verse and mix it down and then we'd wipe off the vocals on it and then go in and sing all the harmony parts and lead parts for the second verse and record it onto the tape. Then we'd go in and mix it down.

They were overdubbing the instrumental track. We'd overdub on the same instrumental track. You'd wipe out the first voice and put the second verse voices on it. We had one piece of tape for the verse. We'd mix it to a two track, we'd erase the vocals on the verse, and we'd rerecord the second set of vocals on it. We mixed each piece of this down as we went along.... We'd cut the piece together so that the song was almost together by the time we were through. Almost every cut was this way. "Vega-Tables," "Little Pad," "She's Goin' Bald."

When we came out the next morning at six o'clock, the album was mixed down, cut together, and was complete. One of the guys from Wally Heider was my second engineer and he said, "Well, I never believed in miracles but I saw one tonight."

That's the way they did it. It wasn't my idea. They mixed it chorus and verse, chorus and verse and intro, and all the levels had to match.

——*Jim Lockhart*

What Capitol received in the summer of '67 was an avant-garde production of vocal humor, druggy digressions, bizarre time signatures, extemporaneous rock, and tracks from *Smile.*

Smiley Smile *was a bunt instead of a grand slam.*

——*Carl*

Very spacy, weird album but it's so subtle and so damn innovative.

——*Bruce*

---

send us in your letter/and tell us the name of your/favorite vega-table") was a stunning showcase for variations on a single melodic theme. Brian would later cut another memorable version with Dean Torrence.

"Gettin' Hungry," at 2:27, was an odd combination of energetic chorus, electric bass, and bluesy meandering.

As the second 45 on the "Brother" label ("Heroes and Villains" was the first), "Gettin' Hungry" was credited to only Mike and Brian who "just thought it would be a good single." It had the stop-and-start drive of "Heroes" but lacked its eccentric cohesiveness.

Smiley Smile... *when we put that one out we almost double-dared anyone else to try and record anything like that. Take "Wind Chimes." People just don't sing like that.*

——*Dennis*

We'd play the track and they'd work out their parts until they got them and we'd put it on—and they'd listen to it and if it was what they wanted they'd go in immediately and double it or overdub it with another part. Then the last thing they used to do is go to the high parts. Brian would put his part on last most of the time. The high part.

——*Jim Lockhart*

More impressive were "Wind Chimes" and "Wonderful," abbreviated efforts from the *Smile* era. "Chimes," with real chime sounds in the background, had innovative fragments of soaring vocal beauty. "Wonderful," with Carl's intimate lead and a good-time "chorus" was less focused but also affecting. The "Woody Woodpecker Symphony" ("Fall Breaks to Winter") had Brian stretching his instrumental capabilities with a strange blend of triangle, woodblock, vibes, harmonica, and monosyllabic sounds.

WIND CHIMES *by Brian Wilson*

Hanging down from my window
Those are my Wind Chimes, Wind Chimes
In the late afternoon
You're hung up on Wind Chimes, Wind Chimes
Though it's hard I try not to
Look at my Wind Chimes
Now and then a tear rolls off my cheek
On a warm breeze the little bells

Tinklin' Wind Chimes, Wind Chimes,
Close your eyes and lean back,
Listen to Wind Chimes, Wind Chimes
It's so peaceful, close to lull-a-bye.
Oh, Wind Chimes ting-a-ling.
Whisp'rin' winds send my Wind Chimes
    a tink-l-in.

Copyright 1967 by Irving Music Inc.

Brian liked to experiment. If he came up with an idea we'd try it. I remember one of the songs we had the echo chamber on while we were mixing it and we were rewinding a tape and Brian said, "How'd you do that?"

I said, "Simple. Just rewind it." So he said, "Let's do it again" and so we did. "She's Goin' Bald"—that has the sound of a tape being rewound in an echo chamber at full speed backward.

It was a weird, eerie sound, like somebody screaming. We just accidentally hit that and we recorded part of it.

——Jim Lockhart

"She's Goin' Bald" was the weirdest cut of all, merging surreal word play ("She flipped her wig"), Mel and Tim humor ("She drew a comb across her scalp and brushed what she had left" à la "Along Came Jones"), sexual innuendo ("real blown"), inflated fifties chorus ("Sha-na-na-na"), and funk ("you're too late, Mama...") in what could be called a fully flipped-out alternative to "Good Vibrations."

"Little Pad" copped a touch of the old surf, a lot of the simple Brian Wilson, and a classy fade. Carl sang lead on it and on "Whistle In," the short (1:02) closing cut that featured a beautiful rolling fragment ("Remember the day, remember the night, all day long"). To top the album off, the credit "Produced by the Beach Boys" appeared for the first time. *Pet Sound's* blend of forties soundtrack, sixties romanticism, and Spectorian instrumentals had been all but forgotten. Listeners were baffled as to what would come next.

Between takes he held up this can of honey. He says, "How about that—wild honey." I said, "That's a great name for a song, Brian. I'm going to make up a set of lyrics about a girl, a wild little thing ... that the boy's mother doesn't really care too much about—because she knows a little too much and she's a little too wild, but the guy's really hung up on her...."

——Mike Love

October saw the fast (but temporary) fade of Brother Records and a new single on the Capitol label. Piano and theremin rose with a beelike sound, bongos joined in, and a "sweet-sweet" high-pitched chorus and soulful vocal by Carl took off. The sound was raw and unpretentious. The album was *Wild Honey.*

When we did Wild Honey, *Brian asked me to get more involved in the recording end. He wanted a break. He was tired. He had been doing it all too long.*

——Carl

Something to clear my head out.

——Brian

Working in Brian's home studio, Mike Love and Brian collaborated closely on a set of nine songs for the new album. Carl came into prominence singing leads and working on production. The focus was something thoroughly unexpected: *a Beach Boys' soul album.* The group had turned around, getting closer to their R&B roots. *Wild Honey* was an exuberant and genuinely happy record.

Basically it was a fragment thing. The songs were done in pieces and parts by experimentation and each one of them had his own idea of the song and each one of them...had a song in mind when they started the album. They were on a health-food kick at the time. "Wild Honey" would make a good song—and titles like that....The vocals were not always done in one take. They were done in pieces. Instrumental tracks were pieced together also....It was laid-

BEACH BOYS

back....I think there was a break between **Smiley Smile** *and* **Wild Honey**. *They wanted to change but not too much.*

———*Jim Lockhart*

Wild Honey was a musical exercise in the tradition of *Beach Boys' Party*. The group had an "ambience" they wanted and a feeling that the ambience would express. The sound for *Wild Honey* was an open-air, vibrant spontaneity. It was a splendid example of their importance to rock and roll. They were embarking, casually, on a new direction—a sound nobody else with their background was doing. They were developing new music that was outside of their usual body of work, and they were doing it in a way that would violate neither their approach nor the roots of their style.

They worked toward spontaneity. They felt if it was worth doing they wanted to do it with feeling. So they kept that feeling going all the time. If they didn't have that feeling, then it didn't work.

———*Jim Lockhart*

I really didn't get into the **Wild Honey** *album until* **John Wesley Harding** *came out and everybody started saying, "Dylan told 'em what to do....He told everyone to go back to simplicity and forget wild production albums, and just put it right where it's at." And all of a sudden I realized that once again Brian had been first. That's exactly what* **Wild Honey** *is—it's getting right back to simplicity and right back to music....In terms of his music... everything with Brian is direct and forceful and the quickest way it can get said—and, again, this is* **Wild Honey**.

———*David Anderle*

The album debuted in December and rose to twenty-four on the charts, a significant improvement over *Smiley Smile*. *Wild Honey*

birthed two vital singles ("Darlin'" went top twenty), eleven cuts, and no piece of music over 2:42.

We all really dug Motown, right?...So Brian reckoned we should get more into a white R and B bag. I also recall around that time the band, and Brian in particular, getting criticized very heavily for sounding like choirboys....

———*Carl*

DARLIN'   *by Brian Wilson*

You know if words could say
That darlin' I'd find a way
To let you know what you meant to me
Guess it was meant to be
I hold you in my heart
As life's most precious part

Oh darlin', I dream about you often
My pretty girl you're so fine
I love the way you soften my life
With your love, your precious love un-huh

I was living like half a man
Then I couldn't love but now I can
You pick me up when I was feeling sad
More soul than I ever had
Gonna love you every single night
Yes, I will
'Cause I think you're too doggone
out of sight

(Repeat chorus)   *Copyright 1967 by Irving Music Inc.*

On the *Wild Honey* album, the group sang their hearts out. Both "Wild Honey" and "Darlin'" showcased the most uninhibited rock vocals the Beach Boys had cut in a long time. On "Darlin'" the simple and contagious at-home studio sound of the Beach Boys, snare drum and constant tambourine, sped spectacularly from start to finish.

On the soft side, there was "Let the Wind Blow," one of Mike's most beautiful compositions. Written while in his car, Mike took it to Brian, who changed the melody line, gave it a different beat, and went into the studio to record. The "Don't take her out of my life" refrain tugged at the heartstrings and took *Wild Honey* closer to the romanticism of *Pet Sounds* than anything else on the album.

"Aren't You Glad" was a sensational upbeat love song rounded out by horns and Carl's mellow lead. Backed by vibes and a homespun chorus, it epitomized the simple energy of the album.

AREN'T YOU GLAD?   *by Brian Wilson and Mike Love*

Today could be a lot of fun and precious one
I feel good just to walk with you
Tonight will be a special treat
You're so sweet, and I feel good just to talk with you
You know that I've been a long time needin' you
You say you've been a long time needin' me
And don't you know there's so much more to come
I've got a heart that just won't stop beatin' for you
I've got a love that just can't stop feelin' for you

Today is another day

Another way to get this feeling across to you
Tonight will be another night
That's out of sight
'Cause I know the way to get close to you
You know I've been a long time lovin' you
You say you've been a long time lovin' me
And don't you know there's so much more to come

Aren't you glad now darlin' there's me and you
Aren't you glad each day there comes something new?
Oh, oh, oh, aren't you glad
So glad.

Copyright 1967 by Irving Music Co., BMI

The Beach Boys' long-standing respect for Stevie Wonder's music was crystallized in a frenetic cover version of his "I Was Made to Love Her." Carl's lovely vocal on "Country Air" followed.

Sometimes the last thing I hear at night before falling asleep is from "Country Air," Carl holding that note ("Mother Nature she fills my eye ye ye ye ye y") and rhyming it to the rooster's crow that begins the cut.
———*Arthur Schmidt*, **Rolling Stone**

COUNTRY AIR *by Brian Wilson and Mike Love*

Get a breath of that COUNTRY AIR,
Breathe the beauty of it ev'rywhere,
Get a look at that clear-blue sky,

Come on.
Mother Nature she fills my eyes, Come on
Rise up early, the day won't let you sleep.
Copyright 1967 by Irving Music Inc.

For an old California surfin' band, the Beach Boys shifted easily into a "down-home" feeling.

"A Thing or Two," "Here Comes the Night," and "How She Boogalooed It" followed suit, simple rockers with tight vocal arrangements. "I'd Love Just Once to See You" characterized the album's casual beauty. It went from rough mix to master recording in a single day. The group played all the instruments on the track.

Wild Honey closed with an a cappella rendition of Brian and Mike's "Mama Says." The harmony is as good as ever and as the cut goes into a freaky fade, the album leaves you with an upbeat feeling.

The Friends *album...a really easy project. Brian enjoyed it....My dad sang on that album.*
———*Carl*

"Friends," the single, followed *Wild Honey* in the spring of '68. It was a cheerful and euphoric tune with a textured production that returned the group to the standards of the *Smile* era. Drum, harmonica, vibes, and cello backed a four-part harmony that soared right out of the record. It aptly previewed the album of the same title that followed in May—the first total Beach Boys' studio effort to be produced in stereo.

We met the Maharishi Mahesh Yogi in December 1967 when we did a United Nations' show in Paris. We heard about the Beatles meditating.... Maharishi was talking about being able to increase the use of your conscious mind, so it sounded pretty good to those of us who were in a profession that demanded creativity.... He said you don't have to give up the pursuit of material pleasures...and that sounded real good to me.
———*Mike*

Nineteen sixty-eight was the start of a heavy involvement for the group, especially Mike, Carl, and Alan, with the work of Maharishi Mahesh Yogi. Once again, the group was attracted to new ideas and preoccupations. Unlike other rock groups, however, the Beach Boys were quite serious about popularizing the practice of transcendental meditation. Mike Love was the most affected; he spent considerable time in the East with the Maharishi and other students. Fellow TM enthusiasts the Beatles sent Love a combination "Happy Birthday/TM song" from India.

As usual, the Beach Boys, experience with TM soon found its way into song.

Transcendental meditation can
emancipate the man
and get you feeling grand.
It's cool, it's cool.

Fusion of the never changing
with the everchanging
with the never-changing world.
It's cool, it's cool, it's cool.
——— "*Transcendental Meditation,*"
from Friends

The Beach Boys' contentment with their personal lives was evident in the musical atmosphere of *Friends*. If the group was feeling

STEREO
FRIENDS/THE BEACH BOYS

better individually, it was good timing. *Friends* and the TM Tour were two of the least commercially successful ventures in the Beach Boys' career.

The nonacceptance of both may be attributed in part to the times. The upbeat single "Friends" was released shortly after the death of Martin Luther King.

The tour with the Maharishi was aborted because the Reverend Martin Luther King was shot on the same night as we were playing Memphis. The National Guard came in....
———*Dennis*

The TM tour had been planned by Mike Love and the group for college campuses. Instead, the Beach Boys found themselves booked into cavernous rock arenas like the Philadelpia Spectrum. Half-Beach Boy, half-Maharishi, the concerts suffered walk-outs, cries for oldies, empty halls, and finally, suspension.

The climate in America was somber and pessimistic. The Beach Boys' California dream seemed years away. With the assassination of Robert Kennedy in Los Angeles in June and the subsequent brutality at the 1968 Democratic National Convention in Chicago, America faced a nightmare unlike anything since the Second World War. Depression was not at the country's doorstep. It was inside. Massive protests against the Vietnam War intensified the mood.

Good-time California music by clean-cut Beach Boys was unacceptable even as a panacea, let alone as a cultural force. On a stereo in a college dorm, the group's music seemed strangely out of place. You were not *supposed* to be listening to anything as "irrelevant" as "Mama Says," no matter how good it made you feel. The personal revolution in values and ideas had been suddenly supplanted with overwhelmingly political concerns. Stop Johnson. Stop Nixon. End the war.

The Beach Boys, however, were experiencing the pleasures of California family life. Fully aware and concerned about the war, they refused to give up the integrity of their work. For the first time, the Beach Boys' music was fully out of sync with the American mood. The songs ironically reflected a feeling everybody wanted to have but which nobody could accept. There was too much going down to be mellow.

The title was Brian's idea.... It was just a collection of cuts. He'd get the ideas and we'd sit down and write the words together. It was done in Brian's house. 'Most everybody teamed up together.
———*Al*

Friends was the closest thing to a "group album" that the

take a simple thing—doing "nothin'"—and make it so musically beautiful that in retrospect the importance it is given seems natural from the start. And when you thought about it, why not? It was a style consistent with what Brian had been doing since the early days of the group—cars, beach girls, surfboards, drive-ins, and vegetables had received the same affection.

BUSY DOIN' NOTHIN' *by Brian Wilson*

I had to fix a lotta things this morning.
'Cause they were so scrambled;
But now it's okay.
I tell you I've got enough to do.
The afternoon was filled up with phone calls.
What a hot sticky day.
E ya, e ya; the air is coolin' down.
Take all the time you need, it's a lovely night.
If you decide to come,
You're gonna do it right.
Drive for a couple miles,
You'll see a sign and turn left for a couple
  blocks;
Next is mine.
You'll turn left on a little road,
It's a bumpy one.
You'll see a white fence;
Move the gate and drive through on the left side,
Come right in and you'll find me in my house
somewhere keeping busy while I wait.

I get a lotta thoughts in the morning,
I write 'em all down;
If it wasn't for that I'd forget 'em in a while.
And lately I've been thinkin' 'bout a good friend,
I'd like to see more of.
Yea, yea, yea, I think I'll make a call.
I wrote her number down, but I lost it,
So I searched through my pocketbook
I couldn't find it.
So I sat and concentrated on the number and
  suddenly it came to me:
So I dialed it and I let it ring a few times,
There was no answer,
So I let it ring a little more;
Still no answer, so I hung up the telephone,
Got some paper and sharpened up a pencil
And wrote a letter to my friend.

Copyright 1968 by Sea of Tunes Publishing Co.

Beach Boys had done to date. Each member had a hand in the songwriting. There is casual ambience to the title cut that helps explain why Brian considered *Friends* his favorite Beach Boys' LP. The record is affectionate, spontaneous, and unpretentious, much like Brian himself.

Brian and Mike's "Meant For You" functioned as a thirty-eight-second prologue. Its mellow sound gave way to the exuberant "Friends." An irrepressible "Wake the World" followed with delectable four-part harmonies and an understated mix of tuba, drum, and vibes. It epitomized the album's focus: a celebration of life without stress. Once again, *Friends* mirrored *Wild Honey*'s concerns. "Wake the World" expressed homespun themes and everyday feelings. The album was stronger harmonically, substituting sweet vocals for *Wild Honey*'s ragged enthusiasm.

"Be Still" and "Little Bird" showcased Dennis's budding songwriting talents. "Bird" featured a precious vocal style uncommon to Dennis's hard-drumming, rugged stage presence.

"Transcendental Meditation" was the first of many songs about TM. It was a low-key example of the Beach Boys' individuality. TM was the "in" consciousness of the 1967–1968 period and the sound of a sitar could be heard on everything from *Magical Mystery Tour* to AM radio. The Beach Boys approached the same theme without a major concession in style. Whereas the Beatles' TM sound displayed a prominent Far Eastern influence, the Beach Boys' song maintained its Southern California roots. The shrill, good-humored "Transcendental Meditation" exploited driving horns, drums, and another wordless chorus.

Brian's whole thing all along has been the juxtaposition of the dumb and the brilliant.

——*Carl*

The lyrics of "Busy Doing Nothin'"...I thought they said something.

——*Brian*

With a bossa nova beat and tranquil singing, "Busy Doin' Nothin'" took us inside Brian Wilson's head. The song was little more than a recitation of a morning in the life of a composer, but it was done with such clarity and self-effacing strength that the melody kept playing over and over in your mind. In singing about phone numbers, the path to his Bel-Air house, and early-morning work habits, Brian pulled off a conversational classic of whimsy, innocence, and endearing simplicity. His voice was as charming as ever and the portrait it painted of a sensitive man-child fit comfortably with the album's affectionate nature. Once again, the music reflected Brian's peculiar genius: the ability to

---

Stack-O-Tracks was Capitol's idea....They picked the cuts.

——*Brian*

If *Friends* did not garner the public attention it deserved, *Stack-O-Tracks* had to be the most obscure album in the group's history. Capitol #2893 did not even show up in most stores.

You sing the words and play with the instrumental background to fifteen of their biggest hits. Includes booklet with printed lyrics, chord symbols, lead and bass lines...and many photos of the Beach Boys.

——*from the cover of*
Stack-O-Tracks

Stack's jacket featured all six active members of the group, with Brian in horn-rimmed glasses and psychedelic flowered shirt. Stacked high between them is a pile of recording tapes, original tracks from their albums.

Stack was a gem. It offered the best of the Beach Boys, instrumental tracks without words.

You'd probably be surprised at what was under the vocals. It was what was

really behind them too. Just the music tracks. —I like that.

——*Carl*

The cuts from *Pet Sounds*—"Wouldn't It Be Nice," "God Only Knows," "Here Today," and "You're So Good to Me"—were exactly what Brian had called them—lush "pocket symphonies." "Let Him Run Wild" was a complex track of comparable sophistication. The rest were simply a pleasure—giving new meaning and understanding to Brian's music. The album was released in early summer.

Touring was fun. It's amazing, isn't it? I just do the music and enjoy it. I knew we were great and I didn't think about it....This group is heavier than anybody can imagine.

——*Al*

The Beach Boys' sunny California heritage was coming head-on with the politicized attitudes of the late sixties. The prevailing hard-rock esthetic conviction was that if you weren't heavy, black, or pessimistic, you weren't worth hearing. The Beach Boys' innovations, from four-part California harmonies to "summer" singles, remained popular, but for the Beach Boys as a touring group, these were hard times.

They came on stage decked out in matching ice-cream colored suits...and since generally Fillmore habitues like their groups grungy, raw and au courant, the Good Humor hallucination on the stage couldn't help but bring out the sadistic side of the audience.
——*from a* **Rock** *article covering the Beach Boys at the Fillmore East*

Even on tour with Buffalo Springfield, American rock audiences couldn't accept the Beach Boys for being the Beach Boys. People who came in contact with them personally found the Beach Boys to be refreshing, unpretentious, and friendly. Mike and Alan acquired a reputation for getting together with college students after concerts to medi-

tate. On stage, however, it was still a matter of their old rep being "unacceptable" to the kids. The group itself was still having trouble—both artistically and commercially—with Capitol Records. Mike Love talked things over with Paul McCartney, who suggested upgrading the physical "album" image. Rock was becoming more of a product. The Beach Boys still focused entirely on their music.

Back in California, Mike took a ride out to an old surfing haunt with his friend Bill Jackson. As they drove back up the coast from Camp Pendleton, Mike thought about the surfing, the girls, the beach, and the original Beach Boys' mystique. The nostalgia motivated a new song and he rushed back to talk it over with Brian.

I remember when Mike came over....They worked on it in the studio at the house. I remember I didn't like it at first, then it grew on me.
——*Marilyn*

"Do It Again" was the first top-twenty single for the group since "Darlin'." Capitol rushed it out for summer, accompanied by the tag "A Summer Single." The familiar Love voice mixed with a funky, razzy opening that sounded terrific on AM radio. A driving *Ditdit/ba ba* chorus bridged the song's evocative soft and fast sections and the lyrics, filled with hooks like "the lonely sea," "suntanned bodies," and "California girls," pulled you back to easier times. It was an instant hit, tapping an undercut of nostalgia and romanticism in the late sixties and capping it with the *Smile* era.

DO IT AGAIN   *by Brian Wilson and Mike Love*

It's automatic when I talk with old friends and
Conversation turns to girls we knew, when their
Hair was soft and long, and the beach was
The place to go
The suntanned bodies and waves of sunshine,
The California girls and a beautiful coastline
With warmed up weather, let's get together and
Do it again.

With a girl the lonely sea looks good with
   moonlight,
Makes your night times warm and out of sight,
Well, I've been thinking 'bout all the places
We've surfed and danced, and all the faces we've
   missed,
So let's get back together and do it again.
Copyright 1968 by Irving Music Inc.

Mike, Alan, Dennis, Carl

It all started in 1967. I got arrested in New York City for refusing to submit to induction. Which was a hype, see. They called me a few days before and said, "OK, listen, there's a warrant out for your arrest. You just come into the office in New York and we'll arrest you. Then we'll release you on personal recognizance bond and you'll go back to L.A. and take care of it." So I did that, but they really wanted to do a news thing. They got a photographer, actually arrested me and did a hoked-up trick, held me in jail for a few hours....When I had to file I asked for 1-O Classification. It's cost me thirty thousand dollars to fight this thing so far. Imagine what'd be like for somebody who didn't have the money.

———Carl, October 1971

It's not a matter of us changing our name. People have to be reeducated.

———Al

It's just a record company—Capitol, making money—and that's all there was. What control did we have?

———Dennis

The Beach Boys have never broken the faith with their fans by selling out to faddism or by jumping from musical gimmick to gimmick. The Beach Boys have always been trend-setters and never fad-followers....their music never loses the flavor of their zest for living and love of life....In concert or on record they have the rare ability to reach out and touch their audiences.

———From Capitol Records concert book, 1968

    August 1968. Carl was hassling over his draft status and with Annie taking care of their first son, Jonah. Brian retreated to his estate in Bel-Air with Marilyn and first daughter, Carnie. Dennis was the divorced father of Scott and Jennifer. Mike drove a 1938 Rolls Cabriolet, spent time with his kids Hayleigh and Christian, and meditated in Manhattan Beach. Bachelor Bruce surfed, scubaed, rode a Yamaha cycle, and did the L.A. scene. Al Jardine was happily married with one son, Matthew, one Jaguar, one Mustang, and a home in Brentwood with his wife, painter Lynda.

    In seven years the Beach Boys had won international fame, but 1968 was more frustrating than any year in the group's history. In Europe, their popularity remained high, but in the States the Beach Boys were saddled with the problems of their name and public profile. There was no immediate follow-up to "Do It Again." The lawsuit against Capitol Records continued and one of the most important bands in the history of rock was virtually ignored by their label. A redundant *Volume 3* in the *Best of* series was released and did not make the top one

hundred. Yet the strength of the Beach Boys' music could not be denied. Even with the identity problems, the group continued to tour heavily through the rest of 1968. Without the Maharishi, a twenty-one-city sweep, including Alaska, was set for July. In August they came East, did three days at the Steel Pier in Atlantic City, and continued on for twenty other concerts. Through it all, the Beach Boys maintained one of the most sophisticated sound systems in the history of rock.

    In November they covered the Midwest, then returned East for two Thanksgiving Eve concerts in Boston. December saw them return to Europe. On the first of the month they played the Palladium in London, accompanied by a full symphonic orchestra. Germany, France, Denmark, and Holland followed in early 1969.

    Against this background, the group began their last contractual new album for Capitol, *20/20*. Three remakes capped the effort, which was released in January '69.

I expected "Cottonfields" to become a hit. I know what the formula is. It's like anything else. You follow the rules and the axioms and it'll work. Brian liked the song and cut the first version his way. Then I went in and cut the second version my way. It was awkward—I really wasn't a producer but I knew how it should sound. So I went in and said, "Look." Brian was steadfast. So we wound up leaving it the way it was. I thought there was potential for a single, but again, there was a state of flux going on in America—but I was in the roots department. If I had waited I might not have done it at all. It was a number-one record in foreign countries.

———Al

    "Cottonfields," the old Huddle-Leadbelly folk standard, was revitalized by Al's lead and a down-home approach. Horns and piano sweeten the track, which is backed by a tight mix of bass, snare drums, and tambourine. A year later another version, with steel pedal section added, became a major hit in Europe.

    The second oldie was "Bluebirds Over the Mountain," co-produced and arranged by Bruce Johnston. It was a funky remake of Ersel Hickey's composition with an angular chorus backing Mike's lead. The single was punctuated with some vintage psychedelic licks by Beach Boys' guitarist Ed Carter.

    The trio was completed with Carl's cover of the old Ronettes' song, "I Can Hear Music." True to the other Beach Boys'-Phil Spector interpretations, "I Can Hear Music" featured a sweet, full-bodied wall of sound and ultra-smooth lead vocal. Carl did Brian proud as a student of the "Phillies" style. The production was spectacular. An airy chorus, bell-tree, driving bass, and a cappella bridge highlighted the cut. As the new Beach Boys' single it fared better than "Bluebirds" (it went top thirty) and provided *20/20*, their last new Capitol album, with a solid start.

    Dennis Wilson made his appearance with three songs on *20/20*—"Be With Me," "All I Want to Do," and "Never Learn Not to Love." The first was a yearning, circular piece backed by horns that played eccentrically off the word "free" for its chorus. "All I Want to Do" was a hard-driving rocker, concise in both music and lyrics.

Bruce Johnston's "The Nearest Faraway Place" was the exact opposite. Much like something out of a fairy tale, its piano and strings swept innocently through a gentle melody.

Brian contributed two new songs to the album. "I Went to Sleep" embraced the tranquil sound of "Busy Doin' Nothin'." Casual lyrics and soft vocals gave it the feel of an adult lullaby. It was backed by a dreamy combination of clarinet, flute, conga, and strings.

I WENT TO SLEEP *by Brian Wilson*

I took a walk and sat down in a park,
The gard'ner walked out and the sprinklers went on.
They watered the lawn and I WENT TO SLEEP.

At ten thirty I turned my radio on,
Some group was playing a musical song.

It wasn't too long and I WENT TO SLEEP.

Again at the park on a nice summer day,
High up above me the trees gently sway.
A bird flew away and I WENT TO SLEEP.
Copyright 1968 by Sea of Tunes Publishing Co.

"Our Prayer" was the classic a cappella fragment from *Smile*. Evoking memories of the Dick Taylor days, it opened with a deep sigh, and then soared for little over a minute. The Beach Boys' harmony had rarely sounded better,

---

"Cabin-Essense" ...there's an example of a piece of material that should wait for its time. It didn't belong on that album.

——*Al*

We had to find stuff that Brian started and put it together.

——*Dennis*

To cap *20/20* (named after the eye chart on the inside jacket), Carl and Dennis turned to tracks recorded during the days of *Smile*. There were whole instrumental tracks for some songs, fragments for others. They began to work on a collage that would feature pieces of

Alan, Carl, Bruce, Mike, Brian, Dennis (seated)

"The Iron Horse," "The Grand Coulee Dam," and "Cabinessense" for which Dennis was to have recorded the lead vocal.

The result, simply titled, "Cabinessense" intensified the loss of *Smile*. The track was a tantalizing blend of harmony, musical inventiveness, and sounds of the Old West. Once again it showed how close Brian had come to the good-natured, metaphysical atmosphere he had wanted for the entire album.

"Cabinessense" is labyrinthian. There are basically five sections to it: the opening, the bridge, the repetition of the opening, a repetition and variation on the bridge, and the closing.

The opening is backed by banjo, harmonica, piano, and a subtle *"boing-boing"* vocal. Van Dyke's words are delivered softly, and the track maintains the famed Brian Wilson immediacy without losing a sense of the Old West. This part is from the original "Cabinessense," as Brian described it, "about a funky little cabin in the woods." It fades on the phrase "home on the range."

The bridge, a driving clockwork of tambourine, a cello, and soaring vocals, consists solely of the line "Who ran the iron horse?" (from the *Smile* cut of the same name). It conjures up a locomotive engine ramming its way across the Great Plains. This section slows down to a single cello and then gives way to the repetition of the opening theme.

The "Cabinessense" opening plays again, then fades on "range" to a more complex version of the "Iron Horse" bridge, with vocal overdubs by Dennis. A cello signals another fade.

The final part of "Cabinessense" opens with chimes, three-part harmony, piano, and the words, "Have you seen the Grand Coulee working on the railroad?" It is as soft as the first section, but the music is more expansive. The fragment, "Over and over the crow flies uncovers the cornfield" takes you right up into the air. It is an astonishing mix of wordless vocals, the main theme, and an elaborate instrumental track. It fades slowly as the voices swirl around, leaving you mystified and delighted at the same time.

CABINESSENSE *by Brian Wilson and Van Dyke Parks*

Light the camp and fire mellow,
CABINESSENSE timely hello, welcomes the time for a change.
Lost and found you still remain there,
And find a meadow filled with grain there,
I'll give you a home on the Range.
Who ran the iron horse? Who ran the iron horse?
Who ran the iron horse? Who ran the iron horse?
Who ran the iron horse? Who ran the iron horse?
I want to watch you wind-blowing facing,
Waves of wheat for your embracing,
Folks sing a song of the Grange.
Nestle in a kiss below there,

The constellations "evan" flow there,
And witness our home on the Range.
Who ran the iron horse? Who ran the iron horse?
Who ran the iron horse? Who ran the iron horse?
Who ran the iron horse? Who ran the iron horse?
Have you seen the Grand Coolie working on the railroad?
Have you seen the Grand Coolie working on the railroad?
Over and over the crow flies uncover the corn field.
Copyright 1968 by Sea of Tunes Publishing Co.

20/20 enjoyed a modest success in America, with "Cabinessense" once again enhancing the group's status as *artists*. From January to the summer of 1969, there was little in the way of new recording. For the Honeys, Brian went into the studio and produced "Tonight I'll Be Loving You" backed by "Goodnight, My Love." Appealing girl-group rock, it came out on Capitol (#2454) and disappeared. Then Murry Wilson and his eldest son collaborated on a wonderful new tune called "Breakaway."

We wrote a song one day. He helped produce it with me....It wasn't included on an album.

——*Brian*

Released in June (Murry used the name "Reggie Dunbar"), "Breakaway" was an exuberant and eclectic single. An early sixties-style rock chorus was overlaid with a mellow surfing harmony and transcendental motif. The melodic range was stunning and Brian's production, with everything from castanets to Carl's guitar, managed to be fragile and dynamic at the same time.

Although "Breakaway" was an ideal summer single, Capitol

gave it the half-hearted support record companies reserve for departing artists. Still it rose midway on the charts.

People look at the Beach Boys and think we're surfing Doris Days.
———*Bruce*

The thrust of the Beach Boys' popularity remained in Europe. At Royal Albert Hall, Capitol/EMI recorded a live performance for U.K. release the following year.

Rumbo is the father of Dumbo the elephant and that's Captain Keyboard—Daryl Dragon.... I just thought it would be fun to put out as a single in Europe.
———*Dennis*

"Sounds of Free" (backed by "Lady"), with echoes of "Be With Me" chorus, was Dennis's first solo offering, from Capitol/EMI under the name Dennis and Rumbo. The single was more loose rock and roll, highlighted by Dennis's lead and an interesting mix of harpsichord and bass.

For the balance of 1969, the Beach Boys toured the U.K. and played smaller concerts at home. The band was going through a period of anxiety and depression; it was eager to move away from Capitol in order to forge a strong direction for the seventies.

We met each other in sixty-nine at the Corral in Topanga. After that we were up at the Monterrey Folk Festival.... Talked about meditation. Ever since that time we just hung out.
———*Mike*

Charles Lloyd, an accomplished flutist and fellow TM enthusiast, was slowly brought into the fold by Mike Love. A keyboard wizard, Daryl Dragon, his brother, and pianist Toni Tenille also became involved with the Beach Boys as members of the touring band.

While on tour in England, the Beach Boys saw the Flame, a South African rock group containing (surprise) three brothers as members.

I saw them in London.... I insisted everyone else come and see them. When they did, Carl flipped out and totally fell off his chair. He says, "Well, they've got to come and record."
———*Al*

They're very eclectic—some acoustic things, some very hard rock stuff. Mostly their own, a very far-out synthesis. They're East Indian and African, so their music reflects a little of the different cultures.
———*Mike*

Carl Wilson befriended the group and grew anxious to record them under a Beach Boys' label. Through the work of their attorneys, that possibility became more and more likely as 1969 drew to an end.

In the summer of 1969, the group played to an enthusiastic crowd at New York's Central Park, but missed an important chance to display their new music to a spectacular audience in a meadow one hundred miles north. Woodstock was the concert sensation of the year. The Beach Boys' music was missing, but their spirit wasn't. The whole event, a celebration of peace, love, and music, was an extrapolation of the California dream. From the harmonies of Crosby, Stills, and Nash to the laid-back atmosphere of the crowd itself, Woodstock echoed the down-home, natural atmosphere of *Wild Honey* and *Friends*. The event, of course, went beyond that, with the debut of music from *Tommy* and the presence of such artists as Jimi Hendrix and Sly Stone. Yet Woodstock was an important sign that the Beach Boys had chosen a correct path even in their obscurity. By remaining faithful to their original vision, by extrapolating their new music from their California

dream, the Beach Boys' music was actually in sync with the spirit of the times. It was just that the times were speeding by in a frenzy of political and social change. Their early music had both influenced and reflected the times. Although disregarded, it retained a cultural integrity.

The Beach Boys' music had grown just as America's youth had grown. But while America's youth had changed from clean-cut mop-headed innocents to members of a sociopolitical movement clad in jeans and old sneakers, the Beach Boys' profile had generally remained the same. Much of the problem could be traced to their name. As one rock critic noted, "If only they'd called themselves *The Band*...." Yet the Beach Boy identity was still too much a part of the group for it to be totally discarded. The name "Beach" was tossed around but rejected. Instead, they forged ahead on a characteristically sweet new single. "Add Some Music to Your Day" was similar in its simplicity and warmth to "Friends." The song would become their next release.

We have now got two albums ready for release, **The Fading Rock Group Revival,** *which will be our last for Capitol, should be out around the end of July. It will contain ten tracks, including "Loop de Loop," "Deirdre," which I co-wrote with Michel Colombier, our previous hit "Breakaway," possibly an unaccompanied version of the "Lord's Prayer," and a song called "Forever," which we are also considering as our next single. After that album, we shall be bringing out* **Sunflowers,** *which will be on our own reactivated "Brother" label.*
———*Bruce, 1970*

The end of the sixties was the end of the working relationship between Capitol Records and the Beach Boys. The group, its old "Brother" imprint, and all post *Party* albums would be licensed to Warner/Reprise. The label's reputation for distribution and promotion, plus a substantial advance and the personal commitment of executive Mo Ostin, attracted them to the company. A Nashville distributor, Starday/King, would release all non-Beach Boy "Brother" works, such as the Flame. In Europe, Capitol/EMI would distribute their records for two more years. There was some confusion about what would be the first release.

The Fading Rock Group Revival was never released. "Loop de Loop, Flip Flyin' in an Aeroplane," a tour de force by Al Jardine and Brian, was the outgrowth of a simple piano session. Brian played a tune, Al wrote lyrics. Then Al became so enamored with the piece that he decided to go wild with it. Taxing Capitol to its limits, he brought in equipment from adjoining studios to develop a gigantic production number. "Loop de Loop" kept growing more and more complex.

...the most fun I ever had and the most frustration. Brian would help with it. I am going to finish it. After sitting on it for seven years I think I can!
———*Al*

They went on the air at progressive N.Y. rock station WNEW FM and previewed tapes for four new songs, including "Good Time," a lighthearted, percolating track with lovely background vocals; "I Just Got My Pay" ("Five long days and I'm tired of working, I'm going to see my boss today/In fifteen minutes I'll be on the train 'cause I just got my pay"), another upbeat song by Brian and Al, with a new *"Deh deh dih deh dih duh duh deh dih dih"* choral invention; "Burlesque," also upbeat; and "San Miguel," Dennis's rollicking *"I wanna be in Mexico"* song filled with castanets, tambourines, and cheery Beach Boy vocals.

Instead of fading in early '70, the Beach Boys blossomed. The first album for Warner Brothers would be named after the single they had planned for Capitol. "Add Some Music" became the first test of Warner's commitment.

Mo really believed that Brian and the Beach Boys represented a crucial, highly appealing slice of Americana, which was simply unique to them and which should not be dismissed or ignored.
———*Van Dyke Parks*

The "Add Some Music" single made its debut in March 1970, amid fanfare and a high-visibility campaign in *Billboard*. The distribution force went all out, insuring airplay and shipping an unusually large quantity of records. Initial response to the single was strong, but it soon leveled off and left the group with a hit of "Breakaway" proportions. It was a major disappointment.

"Add Some Music" did not provide Warner with the sendoff they had wanted for the group. The forthcoming album underwent a name change to *Sunflower*, but retained the same concept and design.

The entire group was active at this time. "Susie Cincinnati," the flip side of the single, was an Al Jardine song. As a camp rocker, it came closer to Dennis's material than anything else the group was doing. It was a memoir/fantasy about a woman cab driver Al had met in Cincinnati.

"Susie Cincinnati" was a put-on. It was really a put-on with regard to a group called the Flame....I said, "If they can do it, we can do it." Kind of interesting....Daryl Dragon played drums on it.

——Al

It became a local favorite.

The prospect of real record company support energized the Beach Boys and brought Brian out of semi-retirement from the studio. Carl pursued an individual production role with the Flame. "See the Light" and an album, *The Flame*, were planned as the first Brother/Starday release. Dennis began writing his own album.

Stephen Desper was hired by the group to serve as engineer on both *The Flame* and *Sunflower*. He shared the group's enthusiasm for electronic advances that would enhance the sound of rock. Together with the Beach Boys, he advanced the commercial prospect for quadraphonic sound. The Beach Boys'—and teenage America's—love affair with technology had been transferred from cars to musical equipment.

"Brother's" studio has recently been modified so that records may be mixed-down utilizing the Dynaco-derived center channel system of quadraphonic sound....The beauty is in the fact that our system takes into account the true goal of quadraphonic sound—that is to engulf the listener in the ambience of sound.

——Stephen Desper, 1970

The ambience of *Sunflower* would be lovely and innocent—more sweet, lush Beach Boys' harmony. Production values would rival *Pet Sounds* for innovation and complexity. It was clear from Brian's new work that he was excited about recording again. The period from *Friends* through *20/20* had found Brian in the role of observer more than producer. The traumas of the *Smile* era, the ongoing drug abuse and a feeling, according to Marilyn, of having taken the Beach Boys, spotlight too long, contributed to his inactivity. Now, with renewed enthusiasm, Brian wrote one of the most beautiful songs of his career, "This Whole World." In his "spare" time, Brian also produced a country-western album for friend and sometime Brother Records publicist Fred Vail. As with many of Brian's pursuits, the record wasn't completed, but over a period of a few weeks, Brian, Fred, Marilyn, and Diane Rovell worked on about fifteen instrumental tracks. The whole effort was more out of friendship than business. Vail had no recording contract. He and Brian just picked up on tunes of the "Black Man in Georgia"/"Fool Such as I"/Sonny James schools and developed them with Jim Burton, Red Rhoades, Freddie Weller, and others. As work began on the vocal tracks, Brian decided to shelve the whole effort. The tapes were not completed.

Carl, Bruce, Mike, Brian, Alan, Dennis

Al, Mike, Carl, Bruce, and Dennis continued to tour. They did six weeks in Australia and New Zealand. They followed Tony Bennett into the Chevron Hotel and made their cabaret debut. They shot a TV special. In June they did a huge outdoor concert in Milwaukee with the Supremes and B. J. Thomas. A three-day festival in Alaska and a starring performance in the TV Show "Good Vibrations from Central Park" followed in July.

See the Light—Strongest group yet to emerge from South Africa, the Flame ignites itself in a Beatle-modeled performance that carries the impact of searing harmony and instrumental electricity…the team is also garnering live receptions on the West Coast to star this side up the charts.
———*Cashbox*

Carl's protégés, the brothers Fataar and Blondie Chaplin (Flame), made their recording debut in June. Things were looking up for the Beach Boys. In August they would play a peace festival in Japan. Their touring schedule would take them to Seattle, Vancouver, and the Northwest. These concerts were highlighted by cuts from the new album. *Sunflower* appeared at the end of August.

We made records, singles for the kids, but they didn't buy them. For a couple of years in a row, '67 and '70, singles just didn't make it. We thought that they were great, we figured that they were super.…I think the kids left us.…
———*Brian*

To kick off *Sunflower*, Warner issued a new single, Dennis's undulating "Slip on Through," backed with Brian's beautiful "This Whole World." To Warner's chagrin, it didn't dent the top one hundred. A November release, "Tears in the Morning"/"It's About Time," met the same fate.

Many of the commercial problems the Beach Boys encountered with *Sunflower* had to do with the attitude and preoccupations of the music. Their experiences—family life, domestic tranquility, California's natural beauty—were removed from the concerns of the primary rock market—kids. As much as there was talk about ecology and world peace, most teenagers still thrived on the simple me-and-you romance rock currently popularized by solo singers such as James Taylor and Carole King, and the dance-rock of groups like the Jackson Five.

For the college market, *Sunflower* was still too sweet, too close to m.o.r.

As a work of music, however, *Sunflower* was extraordinary. It was the best received, most beautiful, cohesive, harmonic album since *Pet Sounds*. It had the unpretentiousness of *Wild Honey* and a more sophisticated ambience. Even the jacket looked happy.

But *Sunflower* was not a commercial success. It was an aural confection in a grimly political time.

I felt blue. I felt upset that they didn't make it.…I just thought that they could have, should have.…They were beautiful but they didn't go as well as we thought.
———*Brian*

Sunflower, I'd say, is the truest group effort we've ever had. Each of us was deeply involved in the creation of almost all the cuts. Say, someone would come to the studio early and put down a basic track, and then someone else would arrive and think of a good line to overdub…
———*Carl*

Dennis composed four cuts with assistance from Al, producer Gregg Jakobson, and Bob Burchman. "Slip on Through," which opened the album, was a sensual, wailing 2:15. Its "baby believe" chorus was a full and intricate interpretation of the Beach Boys' sound. "Got to Know the Woman" was a mixture of straight and put-on sexuality. Dennis parodies the macho vocal style of the late fifties as a camp

"oo mow mow" chorus rumbles out behind him. Even Dennis breaks up after shouting, "Come, come on and do the *chicken!*" Shades of *Beach Boys' Party.*

"It's About Time" channeled the same rocking energy in a more serious and autobiographical direction.

"Forever," Dennis's fourth contribution, was unabashed tenderness. "If ev'ry word I said could make you laugh,/I'd talk forever;/I asked the sky just what we had,/it shone forever." The lead vocal was heartbreaking, a loving, slightly sad, and very beautiful rendition.

Romanticism blossomed fully in Bruce Johnston's two songs, "Deidre" and "Tears in the Morning." The former was incredibly sweet, from its "Dear-dear-Deidre" chorus to the refrain, "Baby, one, two, three and you're back with me." Yet in the context of *Sunflower* the production worked. Placed after the raucous pulsation of "Got to Know the Woman," "Deidre" sounded as if the Beach Boys had walked out on the set of a Roger Corman sixties exploitation film and started singing the score to *Oklahoma!* "The trouble you had,/it wasn't so bad,/it's only life/and watcha livin' for?" White shoes, Main Street, and sunshine, all wrapped up in the Beach Boys' harmony.

"Tears" was lyrically morose and musically lactose, with concertinas, mandolins, and Michel Colombier's arrangement enhancing the tale of a broken love affair.

"All I Wanna Do" was tinted by the use of delayed echo and a repetitive arrangement for drum and guitar. The song took a simple, lovely melody off in an expansive direction—a cosmic resonance not unlike that of Brian's classic, "This Whole World."

THIS WHOLE WORLD by Brian Wilson

I'm thinkin' 'bout-a this whole world
Late at night I think about the love of this whole world
Lots of different people everywhere
And when I go anywhere I see love, I see love, I see love
When girls get mad at boys and go
Many times they're just puttin' on a show

But when they leave you wait alone.
You are there like everywhere like everyone you see
Happy cause you're livin' and you're free
Now here comes another day for your love, for your love.

Copyright 1970 by Brother Publishing Co.

He doesn't want to get locked into a particular mode. He gets bored very easily…and that probably is why his music has retained through the years a feeling of freshness and spontaneity…because you never find Brian doing an eight-minute riff on anything.
———*Mike*

Brian's solo composition was a dazzling tapestry of textured sound and harmonic changes. The overlapping vocal tracks—Carl's lead, the funky transcendental *"aum-bop-diddit"* chorus, the *"woo-woo,"* Diane and Marilyn's thrilling "This whole world" tag—showed Brian at his best. What was almost as incredible was the song's length—a mere minute and fifty-five seconds for a score of musical experiments.

It was taken from a French tune…from the Kingston Trio days. A song called "Raspberries, Strawberries"—a French country tune about wine and lovers. I wanted Brian to sound like a French schoolboy. He sounded more like a Chicano.…Brian's daughter Carnie is in there—her first vocal performance.
———*Al*

"At My Window," Al's contribution, a homespun, fluffy celebration of a little bird. Once again the sublime harmony of the group elevated an everyday occurrence to a moment of unexpected beauty.

We actually went out and bought a Moog synthesizer. All of the albums from now on will have more Moog. We used it on "Cool Water" on Sunflower. *We're also working with quadraphonic sound. "Cool Water" is recorded quadraphonically.*
———*Brian, 1970*

Capping *Sunflower* much in the way "Cabinessense" had done for *20/20* was another "lost" piece from *Smile*.

WIND CHIMES
Mike Skaret/The Workshop

VEGETABLES

Joey Epstein/Tom Hachtman   Photograph by Ben Asen

DARLIN'
John Collier

Busy Doing Nothing

Edward Gorey

I Went to Sleep

Walter Simonson (after Gorey)

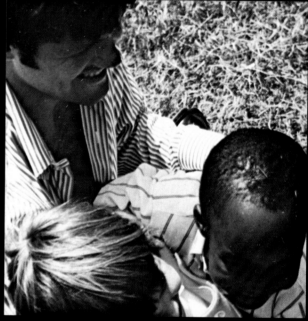

CABINESSENSE *Wayne McLoughlin*

THIS WHOLE WORLD *Dennis Pohl*

COOL, COOL, WATER

Bobby London

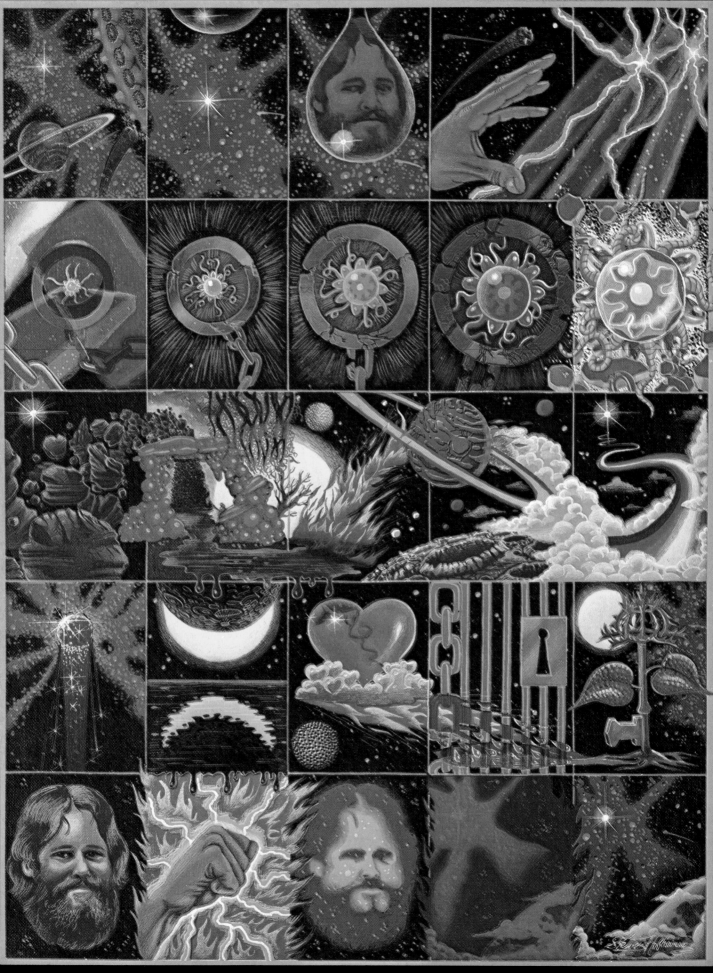

LONG PROMISED ROAD
Steven Holbrook

ALL THIS IS THAT
Gabriel Csakany

CUDDLE UP
JoEllen Trilling
Photograph by Ben Asen

"Cool Water" —Carl, Mike, and Bruce Johnston and I spent forty-eight hours straight dubbing down "Cool Water." It was like being on another planet. It was really something.... We didn't realize the time was going by, it was so enjoyable.

——Al

COOL, COOL WATER by Brian Wilson and Mike Love

Cool, so cool, coolin' me, cool, so cool, coolin'
  me
Have yourself some coolin' water
Have some coolin' water *(Repeat 5 times)*
Have yourself some water

Cool, so cool, coolin' me
Cool, so cool, coolin' me
Have some coolin' water *(Repeat 4 times)*
Have yourself some water

Water, water, water
Water, water, water, water

Now *(Repeat 22 times)*

Oo
Ah
So cool, coolin' me
Cool, so cool, coolin' me

Cool
It's so
Cool, coolin' me

When the heat's got you down here's what you
  oughta
Cool, coolin', coolin' me
Get yourself in that cool, cool water

Get yourself in some cool, cool water.
When the heat's got you down
Here's what you oughta

Get yourself in that cool, cool water

Cool, cool, coolin' me

Get yourself in some cool, cool, water

In an ocean or in a glass,
Cool water is such a gas
It's so coolin', coolin' me
Oo
From the mountains on down to the sea
Cool water keeps on coolin' me
When the night is too hot to keep cool
I keep on dreamin' 'bout a swimmin' pool
When I'm just too hot to move,
Cool water is such a groove
In a shady spot I'm laying down
The only thing moving are the
  ants on the ground
When I'm thirsty and I reach for a glass,
Cool water tastes like such a gas

From the mountains on down to the sea
Cool water keep on coolin' me.

Copyright 1972 by Brother Publishing Co.

Happy, precious, crystal clear, "Cool, Cool Water" was a 5:33 expansion of "I Love to Say Dada" from *Elemental Suite* of *Smile*. Named for its original "dada" background chorus (which remains in the *Sunflower* version), "Cool, Cool Water" was meant to reflect the liquid in a cleverly shifting series of lighthearted fragments. Real sounds of pouring water blend with the Beach Boys' unassuming chorus for a bubbling effect. The song gurgled along through airy vocals and Moog droplets, funny rhymes, and a distorted a cappella bridge, of which Brian later said, "It fits all right but there's something I don't think is right in it." At what could be called an extreme length for a Beach Boys' tune, "Cool, Cool Water" still retained their characteristic spontaneity and warmth.

In order to spread their "good time" profile and counter the nonacceptance of *Sunflower* on a commercial level, the Beach Boys embarked on a strategic touring schedule for the remainder of 1970.

It went fine.... I only wish that we had a little more time. There were a lot of acts so even with two sets we didn't get a chance to play as much as we'd have liked to. I like playing there, though.

——Carl

Sans Dennis (who was off acting in a film called *Two-Lane Blacktop* with James Taylor) and Brian (who stayed at home), the Beach Boys made amends for their 1967 withdrawal and performed enthusiastically at the 1970 Big Sur Folk Festival in Monterrey. They did carefully planned sets of oldies and new songs, salting "Vega-Tables," "Darlin'," "Aren't You Glad," and cuts from *Sunflower* with late sixties and classic "surfin'" tunes. A full horn section and back-up band provided instrumental support. Mike and Carl, sporting beards, sizzled. To add more rock to the act, the entourage jammed on a version of the old Robins' song, "Riot in Cell Block Number Nine."

That film scared me. It was the hardest work I've ever done; up at five in the morning...James is good. A true friendship developed there. We'd never met before and all of a sudden we were there in front of a camera. "What are we doing here?" It was that sort of thing. We got on well, and argued a bit.

——Dennis

Around the time of "Good Vibrations" the audience, which had been quite

cheerless as the set began, picked up and went into some semi-dutiful joy of rock and rolling of its own. It was nice, good old rock and roll.

——Robert Christau, **Any Old Way You Choose It**

The Monterrey date was a major success. On its heels were plans to play the other end of the rock spectrum—a relatively intimate gig at the Whiskey à Go Go in Los Angeles.

At 28, Brian Wilson was the proud owner of The Radiant Radish, a soon-to-be-defunct health-food store in West Hollywood. He could also claim a title reserved for the upper echelon of rock and roll—reclusive genius. Having retired from the road and having shown only recent interest in an active role in the group, Brian found himself at the center of a hyped-up legend which pictured him as something of an "Orson Welles of rock." In reality, however, he was rarely far from the music.

I forget sometimes that he's straight above the recording studios. He can hear everything that's going on. In fact, every once in a while he'll call down a part from the house phone to the studio phone.

——Carl

I don't think a studio in the home is a good idea because it cuts into your privacy. Don't ever have a studio in the home. People are always walking around.... You get an idea and people are in the studio—you can't go in there. Brian wanted a studio so bad and all of a sudden, when he got one he grew out of it real fast. It started to drive me crazy because it was like a circus. A lot of people would be hanging out and Brian would see them working and he would not feel that motivated to work. It was a real drain having people around all the time. A lot of them were a bad influence on Brian because he's a really giving person—really open person. He could never say no to these people, and some of them took advantage of him.

——Marilyn

To counter the problems of the '67–'69 period, the Beach Boys had hired Pacifica DJ and sometime-journalist Jack Rieley to act as their new director of public relations. Rieley had interviewed the group for a broadcast in early summer, and they had come away favorably impressed. Rieley was a fan of the Beach Boys' music, and his plans for improving their profile in the rock community included a contemporization of the act and exposure to an audience filled with celebrities from the record industry. A series of shows at L.A.'s Whiskey à Go-Go would give the Beach Boys a direct opportunity to show the business just what the group could do. As an enticing bonus, these dates would be touted for the reappearance of Brian as an active member of the on-stage band.

It was good to get up there again. When I first got up on stage I felt a little self-conscious....So I thought, "Okay, I'm going to have some fun." But on the second night I started to feel dizzy from the amps.

——Brian

Brian's debut lasted one night, but Mike, Carl, Bruce, Dennis, and Al went on to overwhelm the audience with an exuberant mixture of early hits and songs from *Wild Honey, Sunflower,* and *Pet Sounds.* There were even a few solos, such as Bruce's rendition of Elton John's "Your Song." The group was backed by a nine-person team including horns, bass guitar, and Daryl Dragon on electric keyboards and drums. They packed the house.

In late November, the Beach Boys left for a tour of England. The group was riding a new wave. With the momentum from America they played the new Sheffield Fiesta.

The Beach Boys had never lost their audience in England, but as they headed back to the States after another successful European tour, they felt a renewed public interest was blossoming in both their music and their careers. Back on the Coast with Flame, they played the Santa Monica Civic Center and were greeted like old friends.

Then, just as Monterrey had been the turning point in the West, a special sold-out concert in Carnegie Hall elicited a crucial response in the East. Their performance of February 24, 1971, became one of the most written-about rock events of the year.

Mike Love, Bruce Johnston, Carl Wilson, and Alan Jardine singly and in perfect harmony were in good vocal form, while Dennis Wilson, a steady drummer, came front for a couple of good vocal leads, including "Forever." The enthusiastic audience drew out several encores, including such oldies as "California Girls," "Surfer Girl," and "I Get Around."

From their opening "Heroes and Villains" to the closing of "Good Vibrations," the Beach Boys combined the best of their many standards with different material and treatment, producing a contemporary feel. The second half opened with solos by Carl Wilson, accompanying himself on acoustic guitar, and Johnston, backing himself only on grand piano.

Among the good numbers not usually associated with the Beach Boys were a rockin' "Cottonfields," a tongue-in-cheek "Okie from Muskogee," and "Riot in Cell Block Number Nine." Throughout the bill (they were the only act) the Beach Boys exuded fun, which was contagious.

Other numbers associated with the unit, which were highlights, included "Wouldn't It Be Nice," "Darlin'," "Vega-Tables," and "Sloop John B." Most numbers were aided by eight back-up musicians, including a five-man brass section.

*——Fred Kirby, **Billboard***

The "new" Beach Boys, a group that had grown within itself rather than changing to suit the times, was suddenly "in." Their musical integrity and timeless sound was finally getting through to a wider audience.

I think our stuff has been guilty of being simplistic. Avant-garde, but simplistic. I think that eventually through interpretations like this being read by people who know or care or listen or feel the interpretation of what the artist felt at the time and what his surroundings were like, pretty soon it will be understood as some kind of folk art form that a group of guys from California who liked to sing all their lives got together and did.

——Mike

Crawdaddy smiled:

They were brilliant…their excellence that night equaled any rock performance I have ever seen….They strolled on into the spotlights smiling and waving, Mike Love with his long red beard and white hat;…Carl in black-and-yellow spangled cowboy shirt; Al elfin and unchanging; Bruce Johnston, the dapper, manicured playboy who oozes gleeful energy; and Dennis, chewing gum as an athlete's body sprawled out behind the headset. Also on stage were two permanent back-up musicians, Daryl Dragon on piano and Ed Carter taking turns with Bruce and Al on organ, bass, and guitar, and five New York horn and woodwind players. They did two sets of beautiful music, with their pristine harmonies….They were totally without the pretentiousness and egocentric melodrama that has absorbed so much of rock's vitality in recent years.

Their vocals are so good and if you listen to the instruments you say, Hey, they're not taking any solos. But if you listen, the blend of their instruments sounds like one instrument, all of it is rhythm … but it's so full, it's incredible.

——Ed Carter

The revival they had strived for since *Wild Honey* had arrived. Now all the Beach Boys needed was a hit album to complete the renaissance. "Cool, Cool Water" in a shortened single version was released in March, but did not get the airplay it needed to take off. The concerts continued.

Yeah, it really happened…at around one o'clock in the morning…the two greatest California groups played together for the first time. They opened with "Searchin'," the great Coasters' classic. They did "Riot in Cell Block

Number Nine," "Sweet Little Sixteen," "Help Me Rhonda," "Good Vibrations," "Okie from Muskcogee"…The interplay between Garcia's guitar and Mike Love's theremin…I loved it…the bands loved it.

*——Toby Mamis, **Action World**, June 1971*

On April 27, the group added to their new-found acceptance by jamming with the Grateful Dead at the Fillmore East. The white suits were gone but the music was the same.

To add to the excitement, completion of *Smile* was rumored, supported by comments from members of the group.

*We just listened to **Smile** week before last. We'll get it out now that we have a fair deal with Warner Brothers.*

——Carl

Dennis pushed ahead with his solo album.

A lot of the solo is Moog….What I want to do is, instead of renting a bell for ten dollars, try to get my bell sound with the Moog, or a snail crawling or what sound would a liver make for an alcoholic? But it takes time. I've only been at it a year.…I have a whole new way of overdubbing; I've overdubbed my voice like ninety-nine times. Parts of it for choir, parts for voice. Like within five seconds, it'll go from one voice to two-hundred.

——Dennis

The group spoke of expanding the influence of rock; using a percentage of every band's profits to affect national policy on ecology and social welfare. They had been one of the first bands to go behind the Iron Curtain.

We had a lawsuit with Capitol and decided to go—go outside, like to Europe

Top: Carl, Mike, Dennis　　　Middle: Mike, Carl　　　Bottom: Bruce, Ed Carter, Alan, Carl

and Czechoslovakia....It's real bleak back there; not very much freedom but one of the most tumultuous audiences we've ever had was in Prague.
———Bruce

The political awareness that permeated the early seventies was felt by the group. Al Jardine had become very active in the movement to save California's environment. Mike Love spoke of revolutionizing the economic system of rock, so that the artists could share more equitably in the profits from their music. Carl pressed the idea of free concerts—suggesting the Beach Boys play prisons such as Soledad and Isla Vista.

Uninhibited television dates, such as "Vega-Tables" for David Frost, spread the word to a national audience.

Observing the audience we're getting now is really freaky. I would expect a hip twenty-five-year-old audience, but we're getting a very aware seventeen to twenty-five-year-old group. Maybe they've rediscovered their American group.

———Bruce

With the legacy of their teenage music the kids had returned.

"Surf's Up"... he has a piano version with a voice on it and on another track, "Child Is Father to the Man," he's got several sections of that ... pieces and movements and stuff.
———Mike on Brian's Smile tapes

Amid the touring activity, Carl, Mike, Al, Bruce, Dennis, and even Brian were active in the studio. Carl planned to make good on the revival of *Smile,* but it was difficult to sort through Brian's miles of experimentation. The *Smile* tapes were now over four years old. Carl moved ahead on a composition of his own called "Long Promised Road."

Released as a single in May of '71, "Long Promised Road" showed Carl to be as exciting an interpreter of his own material as he had been of an old Spector gem like "I Can Hear Music." "Road" was

gentle and compelling, with a dense production that drifted easily from ballad to rock and roll. The lyrics for "Road" were composed by Jack Rieley. They were quixotic and visually grandiose—Van Dyke Parks-inspired poetry without the wit. Carl's delivery was so earnest that the song skirted pretentiousness and went for the heart.

LONG PROMISED ROAD　*by Carl Wilson and Jack Rieley*

So hard to answer future's riddle
When ahead is seemingly so far behind
So hard to laugh a childlike giggle
When the tears start to torture my mind
So hard to shed the life of before
To let my soul automatically soar

But I hit hard at the battle that's confronting me
Knock down all the roadblocks stumbling me
Throw off all the shackles that are binding me down

Sew up the wounds of evolution
And the now starts to get in my way
So what if life's a revelation
If the mind speaks of only today

So real, the pain of growing in soul
Of climbing up to reality's goal

Long promised road
Trail starts at dawn
Carries on to the season's ending
Long promised road
Flows to the source, gentle force, never ending

So hard to lift the jeweled sceptre
When the weight turns a smile to a frown
So hard to drink of passion nectar
When the taste of life is holding me down
So hard to plant the seed of reform
So set my sights on defeating the storm.

Copyright 1972 by Wilojarston Music Ltd.

Unfortunately it did not go straight up the charts. Backed by Bruce's "Deirdre," the "Road" single disappeared the same month it was released. An Ode Records "live" release of "Wouldn't It Be Nice," culled from their Monterrey Pop Festival performance went the same route.

To recapture the record-buying public, the group moved in a direction that had been seized by every other form of media at the time: "relevance."

Under the prodding of Jack Rieley, the group addressed themselves to student riots, ecology, and welfare, but more characteristically they composed a range of music on "natural" living, nostalgia, and isolation.

Fortunately, the Beach Boys approach "relevance" on their own terms. The lyrics were a bit forced but the music was consistent with the tranquil rock sound they had cultivated on *Sunflower.*

We all just love harmonies so much. Harmonies are our main purpose. Messages are cool, but we've never been big on messages, obviously. The quality of clean vocal sounds and little rhythmic trips against a very white track. We play very white music. We're probably the only group in America that does anymore....Our purpose is just to be us. We're not trying to lay out too many heavy messages.

——Al

The album had a working title to tie in with both an "ecological" theme and, ironically, the Beach Boys' frustration with their recent record sales. The second Warner/Reprise album would be called *Landlocked*.

If they call that album **Surf's Up,** *we can pre-sell 150,000 companies.*
——Van Dyke Parks, in the employ of Warner Brothers Records

Creatively the Beach Boys of the *Landlocked* era were a less cohesive band than they had been for *Sunflower*. The enthusiasm was still high, however, and they pushed forward with more independence than usual. Brian had retreated from his intermittent but pervasive role on *Sunflower* to become what Bruce Johnston described as a "visitor" for *Landlocked*. The work Brian did produce was notable for its characteristic beauty and a feeling of tragic isolation. More often he hung around the Bel-Air house, listening to the group producing the album.

Dennis, on the other hand, was as full of nervous energy and athletic passion as he had been in the sixties. He still surfed, sailed, and camped. His love of music had grown serious, but it was often challenged by a boyish anger that reached its peak one night when he accidentally smashed a hand through a glass door, thereby ending his work as the Beach Boys' drummer for over two and a half years.

Al Jardine and Mike Love were soft-spoken and deeply involved with meditation and the natural environment. Al had a tightly knit family life.

Bruce still drove a motorcycle and enjoyed the role of "Beach Boy" at home in L.A. He didn't respect Jack Rieley, however, and this resulted in a strain between him and the group. Bruce was much happier without the influence of a manager who wanted political messages in the Beach Boys' sound.

Rieley fared better with Carl. In the studio, the youngest Wilson was developing his songwriting talent more extensively than he had done in the past. In brother Brian's tradition and in an approach later popularized by such "Renaissance man" composers/producers of electronically synthesized sound as Todd Rundgren, Carl played almost every instrument on "Long Promised Road."

Musically, I'm most influenced by Brian. I mean, that's obvious....I've been writing a lot of songs lately. Dennis is writing a lot of beautiful songs. Everybody's writing. I don't know what's gonna happen yet. I just know there's gonna be a lot of music.

——Carl

Landlocked became *Surf's Up*, triggered by the inclusion of Brian's legendary *Smile* track as a part of the album's second side.

Carl did a major share of the production work on the album.

I really love doing it. I spend a lot of time in here. It's so perfect really, because we are completely free to record whenever we please. The sterile environments of most studios...make you feel so depressed, but this is ideal. When I get behind the board I can hardly communicate to other people as they come through. Everything I've got is going into the piece I'm working on.

——Carl

Carl mixes my stuff because I get too involved with every part. He's a good overall mixer...a great mixer. He can mix sixteen tracks because he has the feel for it. Brian lets him mix his stuff too. It's much more fun to hear what you're doing when somebody else is mixing it, because in the first place, I don't like all that sound coming down. It's not realistic.

——Al

By late August, the second Warner's LP was ready for release.

I played piano first and then I played organ. I played piano twice, overdubbed it, and used a variable speed oscillator to make the track different speeds so that the piano would be a little bit out of tune, sort of spread around.

——Carl

Surf's Up featured Carl's undulating and dreamlike "Feel Flows." The song revealed a light jazz influence and expert use of Moog technique to develop a blend of sequential sounds. Carl played bass, Charles Lloyd came in on a magical flute, and Woody Thews added percussion. The flute and sax rippled through the production, and Carl's piano hummed mysteriously behind his vocal. The song was a "good vibration," evoking mood and attitude more than any story or concept.

In England, I had this little tune and Mike said, "That's pretty nice." So when we got back to L.A. to do **Surf's Up** *it happened to be one of the tunes that came out. It was one of the first tunes I played banjo on....Mike inspired the lyrics.*

——Al

A quasi-commercial song titled "Take a Load Off Your Feet" was inspired by the instructions for a famous Earth-type shoe called the Birkenstock Sandal. Al Jardine's ode to podiatric health followed the same "formula" as "Don't Go Near The Water": simple lyrics, sweet vocals, and humor.

His final contribution, "Looking at Tomorrow (A Welfare Song)" was more sober. Phase distortion and impressive guitar work backed a folk-style lead and "Looking" echoed the Clapton/Winwood sound of "Can't Find My Way Home." It was the most successful "protest" piece on the album.

> "Hi Rick and Dave
> Hi Pop…Good Morning Mom
>
> Love get up, guess what
> I'm in love with a girl I found…"

"Disney Girls (1957)" was Bruce Johnston's sole contribution to *Surf's Up*, and it surpassed everything else he had written for the group. It was a classic, capturing in music and words the innocence of an earlier era—Johnston's own *Pet Sounds*.

> "Open cars and clearer stars
> That's what I've lacked
>
> But fantasy world and Disney Girls
> I'm coming back…"

Sentimental but not maudlin, with a lovely Beach Boys' chorus and understated use of guitar and Moog, "Disney Girls" painted a picture of gentler times—a world Bruce remembered from his adolescence.

I suspect the real reason they are being taken seriously again is their live performances: It is impossible to hear them…and not be knocked out.
——*Arthur Schmidt*, **Rolling Stone**, *October 1971.*

To close side one, their driving live version of "Riot in Cell Block Number Nine" was given new lyrics by Mike Love. An electrifying Fender performance from Carl and explosive use of horns updated the song and provided a fitting instrumental track for the Beach Boys' most political if incongruous, statement. ("The violence spread down south,/Where Jackson State brothers …" etc.) In a touch worthy of Brian, an actual siren was used as an instrument on the track.

Mike's vocal, picking up where the Coasters left off, was another reason for the Beach Boys' renaissance. It had not lost either its youthful or gritty edge.

Brian, I'm sorry, he is *a put-on.…He's really a very highly evolved person …and he's very sensitive at the same time, which can be confusing. Brian's Brian, y' know?*
——*Carl*

Three touching Brian Wilson songs were placed at the end of *Surf's Up*, and they provided the album with an exquisite finale. The first, "A Day in the Life of a Tree," complemented the album's ecological preoccupation and would have fit thematically on *Smile*. Delivered with childlike affection and urgency in a nonprofessional but suitably wavering voice by Jack Rieley, "Tree" walked a fine line between precious and pretentious.

Brian said, "Wait a minute, Jack! Come back! I want you to try the vocal!"…Brian went on and on about how much he loved it.…But you know, I still don't know if he was putting me on.
——*Jack Rieley*

The lyrics were written in the first person and Rieley's performance was backed by an understated and layered chorus, the *ba-ba* sound of "At My Window" and a simple organ line. Rieley's couplets were awkward, but set to Brian's music, they took on a sad, poetic feeling. Van Dyke Parks came into the studio and added his voice to the final track.

> I'm a cork on the ocean
> Floating over the raging sea
>
> How deep is the ocean
> I lost my way…

"Until I Die," written and produced (with a lead vocal) by Brian and a truly exciting chorus from the group, followed "A Day in the Life of a Tree." The song was performed in the sweeping, ecumenical style of "Our Prayer" and "Wind Chimes." The loneliness of the music and the soft, windy harmonies of the group echoed the emotions of the oldest Wilson brother.

Time *correspondent Tyler was invited out to the Wilson house for what promised to be Brian's first interview in four years. Brian never came downstairs.…Brian did manage to phone down to Tyler as he sat in the backyard with Carl. "I'm sorry I couldn't make it down but I just got to sleep." Brian explained. "Let me talk a while before I drift off again.…What'm I doing? Getting back into arranging, doing that more than writing right now.…I'm really excited about 'Surf's Up' right now. As a single it has a very virile sound.…Well…I'm drifting off again.…"*
——— Time, *September 6, 1971*

A reporter from **Time** *magazine once showed up at his house and Brian would only talk to him for just two minutes over the intercom, during which time he told the guy that he thought "Surf's Up" was a very virile sound, when in fact he was thinking just the opposite. He's always doing that. He's not very disciplined, but he's often very funny.*
——*Mike*

Mike Love was 30, Al, Dennis, and Bruce, 27, Carl, 25, and Brian, 29. Five years had elapsed since Brian and Van Dyke had sat down one summer night to write "Surf's Up." Rock radio was now dominated by Brill Building veteran Carole King, Motown singer-turned-composer Marvin Gaye, Cat Steven's "Peace Train," and the revived sound of the Bee Gees' "Lonely Nights." The Beatles were no longer the Beatles. George Harrison and Ringo Starr had emerged as solo artists with the production skills of Phil Spector on "All Things Must Pass" and "It Don't Come Easy." Janis Joplin, Jimi Hendrix, and Jim Morrison were gone, as was the Fillmore East. The Beach Boys had performed at the final concert on July 27, 1971. "Riders on the Storm" and "Me and Bobby McGee" were epitaphs for both the singers and their generation. Nixon was still in the White House and the Vietnam war continued. The noble dreams of the sixties were still dreams.

After five tumultuous years, "Surf's Up" proved equal to the legend that had surrounded it. The Beach Boys had added Brian and Van Dyke's "Child Is Father to the Man" to the end of the song and the eloquent, kaleidoscopic new version debuted live on September 24, 1971, during the group's successful return to Carnegie Hall. The concert was a happy occasion for Carl. After five years of hassles with the government regarding his draft status (he had been granted C.O. in '67 but refused the alternate duty of bed-pan changer, claiming it was a waste of his talent), a Federal District judge permitted him to begin playing with the Beach Boys at prisons, orphanages, and hospitals as a form of alternative service.

The return engagement opened with a set containing "409," "Disney Girls," and "Caroline, No," after which the group was joined on stage by a section of French horn players imported for the event. Carl took Brian's role as lead singer and "Surf's Up" stretched out across the cavernous hall with soft, shimmering beauty.

Although a single of "Surf's Up" and re-release of "Long Promised Road" were unsuccessful on the charts, the Beach Boys finished 1971 at the height of a new popularity. They had recaptured the artistic recognition they had gained with "Good Vibrations" and had restored their reputation in America as one of the most exciting touring bands in the world.

It was a scattered project.…It was not everybody pitching in. We were under an extreme pressure, we had grown out of touch.
——*Carl*

Dennis was a late bloomer. I think he's incredibly talented.…
——*Audree*

Blondie and Ricky are very close with Carl. Carl was more or less doing most of the work for **So Tough**.…
——*Diane Rovell*

Surf's Up was a cause for celebration at Warner Brothers. It received the crucial FM airplay and album sales Warner needed to commit its marketing forces to the group's future. Now they were eager for a follow-up and, hopefully, a winning single for early 1972.

Regrettably, the group's internal affairs were less stable than they had been only six months ago. Bruce Johnston, critical of Jack Rieley's plans to continually update and "revitalize" the Beach Boy profile, left the group.

Bruce's future... it's all based on individual musical taste and individual aspirations, which are fine, but not within the framework of a group....His lifestyle is changing like everyone else's....We're still friends.

———*Mike, 1972*

It was an amicable departure; but the timing was off. Brother Brian was as far from being active in the Beach Boys as he had ever been. Carl, Al, and Mike held the group together. Carl recruited two members of the Flame band to join the Beach Boys. Blondie Chaplin and drummer Ricky Fataar brought with them an admiration for the California sound and their own basic style of rock and roll.

We can play harder rock than we've ever been able to before with Blondie and Ricky in the group. At present we are doing something new, but we still have some elements of harmony. Brian is still writing for the group. This is being fused with the new element of creativity within the group from the other guys....Dennis is into strings and orchestrations, he wants to do classical things.

———*Mike*

Another heavy touring schedule, including England, filled the first half of 1972. In early spring, the "new" Beach Boys returned to Brian's home studio to produce tracks for an album. The sessions lasted ten days and were described by Mike as "very spontaneous."

The result was to be called *Carl and Passions—So Tough*. It suggested a throwback to the rougher mixes of the early sixties—"The Passions" had been a name from the "Pendleton" era. It wasn't a bad concept for an album, but the approach was fractured, individual, lacking cohesive musical direction. Ricky and Blondie brought more "rock and roll" to the Beach Boys, and Mike's "Student Demonstration Time" was well-received at their concerts. A rock album exploring aspects of their roots could have been valid. Later in the year, Eric Clapton would successfully use the approach with "Derek and the Dominoes" and "Layla."

Unfortunately, the Beach Boys were in the midst of change. Some cuts for *So Tough* were recorded before the album sessions. Dennis was into his own "serious" thing, and Ricky and Blondie's skill in composing for the group was an untested commodity at best.

I'm pleased with almost all the tracks. Brian was there with "Marcella," and "Mess of Help" has his harmonies with the vocal. "The Background Track" has almost a Stones kind of feel, with country guitars and violins and stuff. It's pretty funky.

———*Mike*

So Tough was more eclectic and "contemporary" than anything they had done since their departure from Capitol. At times you could not even be sure it was a Beach Boys' record. In changing the group and its musical goals, the Beach Boys misplaced the precious unity of sound they had achieved on *Sunflower*.

Their usual thematic concerns showed up intermittently. The problems with the record reflected the problems within the group. It was too diffuse.

The song that most successfully expressed what *So Tough* could have been was the infectious "Marcella." Written and produced by Brian (with synthesizer and chimes), it was a danceable turnaround from his brooding work on *Surf's Up*.

> Hey-yay Marcella!   Sandals dance at my feet
> Hey-yay Marcella!   Eyes that knock you right over
> One arm over my shoulders   Ooooo Marcella so sweet.

Runnerup was the eccentric, effervescent "You Need a Mess of Help to Stand Alone," which to the surprise of most B.B. fans, became their next single instead of "Marcella." "Mess" was another Wilson/Rieley combination, happy rock and roll with Brian's production less controlled than usual.

The other song is done in a gospel style, "He Come Down." On that one we're singing like a whole black church choir and it's a lot of fun.

———*Mike*

"He Come Down" was Al and Mike's TM-song-with-a-difference. It featured a strange rocking mixture of Beach Boys, gospel choir, and friendly exuberance—a one-toke-over-the line-sweet-Maharishi. Brian's arrangement was notable for a vibrant and euphonic six-part chorus and organ.

**Left:
Blondie,
Alan,
Mike,
Daryl Dragon,
Dennis,
Carl and
Ricky**

**Right:
Carl,
Alan,
Ricky,
Dennis,
Blondie
and Mike**

"Here She Comes," the initial Fataar-Chaplin composition, was funky, especially by mid-seventies standards, but it sounded more like Stevie Winwood than the Wilson band. Their vibrant "Hold On Dear Brother" was more like the group but less like a hit—a meandering chorus filled much of the song, punctuated by Carl's steel guitar.

Dennis's work *was* more elaborate. His two songs developed the vulnerable style of "Forever" with help from Daryl Dragon and Brian. The better half, "Cuddle Up," was swathed in heavy violins and Brian's sugary arrangement, but the aching romantic vocals, simple piano, and gentle melody were beautiful. "Make It Good," however, was lost in a wall of sound and a lugubrious arrangement.

CUDDLE UP   by Dennis Wilson and Daryl Dragon

The night has come, CUDDLE UP to me.
Keep warm, mm, close to me.

In dreams we'll dream,
Making love to wake
To find, mm, we're still one.

Your love, your love, your love, your love for me
is so warm and good to me.
Growing ev'ry day, honey, honey; I'm in love.
Oh, I know a man who's so in love, mm.
Copyright 1972 by Wilojarston Music Ltd.

I had another song based on a Robert Frost poem called "The Road Not Taken," which is really a pretty poem. I thought it would make a really nice song. I went into the studio and cut a track. Mike and Carl got involved and it became a whole 'nother thing. It just became another song. Mike wanted some meditation lyrics and Carl liked a certain type of production and so I stepped back and said, "Well, okay!" If somebody's really that inspired to do something then that's great. Then you work with it instead of fighting it and it comes out okay.

———*Al*

ALL THIS IS THAT   by Al Jardine, Carl Wilson, and Mike Love

Chorus
I am that, thou art that, and ALL THIS IS
    THAT.
I am that, thou art that, and ALL THIS IS THAT.
I am that, thou art that, and ALL THIS IS THAT.
This is that.

Daybreak and I take a climb,
Into the pool of peace inside;
Two waves and I, both traveled by life's
    supporting waves of bliss,
Mother divine precious kiss,
Brings with love the light of wisdom,

and the gift of eternal freedom.

Dusk time, the shadows fall,
Into the timeless time of all;
Two waves and I, both traveled by, golden aura's
    glow around you,
Omnipresent love surrounds you,
Wisdom morning as the sun,
You and I are truly one.

Two waves and I, both traveled by,
And that makes all the diff'rence to me.
Copyright 1972 by Wilojarston Music Ltd.

Between Dennis's two cuts was a cozy little gem called "All This Is That." The circular melody and airy vocals swirled out from the record. It was the most effective "meditative" sound to emerge from the group's TM experience. Carl's voice was as sweet as a newborn's father, and the harmony of Mike and Al finally floated the lyrics away. Carl's arrangement made the most of a warm, peaceful feeling.

If Brian's touch seemed missing from *So Tough*, it was not for lack of interest in recording.

In November 1971, the Honeys, reborn as Spring, released a new single on the United Artists label. "Now that Everything's Been Said"/"Awake" was produced by Brian Wilson and lanky young songwriter/producer David Sandler. Once again, it was Marilyn and Diane Rovell's "girl's group" sound, but this time the music transcended the inherently anachronistic qualities of their "Red Bird" style by adding a sense of loss to the vocals—the same edge that had characterized Brian's singing for the Beach Boys on *Pet Sounds*. In May, this approach became apparent on an entire album. Spring offered Brian an outlet for his talent with none of the serious business and commercial pressures of the Beach Boys. He even composed a new song, "When Girls Get Together."

—I think it came out because I had a lot of girl friends and we have a really good time when we get together and Brian used to get a kick out of it. They loved him. He was always into my girl friends. Brian doesn't have an easy time relating to people. I do. That's one of my qualities. We realize each other has them.

———*Marilyn*

Spring was a four-person production—Brian, Stephen Desper, David Sandler, and Diane Rovell shared studio credit.

The idea was to record all the songs that we have ever loved like "Tennessee Waltz"... Brian really helped out in all departments—he sang, arranged most of the background, wrote some of the songs, and picked out the material. Sometimes he would cry at the sessions because he liked a song so much he couldn't believe it. He's very emotional.

———*Marilyn*

There were twelve cuts, each very alive with three-part harmonies, sophisticated arrangements, and the dynamic combination of innocence and wistfulness of two sisters who had grown up together and shared so much.

"Good Time"—Brian and Al's ingenuous 1970 song about sex—was a highlight of the album. A coy (but *cute*) Annette-style lead sings "My boyfriend Eddie, he's always ready to help me in any way" and a loco-motion machine takes off on a good-natured tour de force, hollow percussion, and a funky harmonica.

Spring 1972, Diane Rovell (top) and Marilyn

"Mama Said," "Awake," and "Everybody" showcased the women's upbeat vocals—sweet and unpretentious singing framed by some of the most tasteful arrangements Brian had ever produced.

Another highlight was "This Whole World," the *Sunflower* spectacular, reinterpreted and expanded with a "Starlight, Starbright" bridge from Diane and a trippy fade by Desper. This piece soared with the Spring/Wilson harmony. The wall of sound for this and every other cut on the album was achieved in Brian's home, but the expansive sound belied its living-room—studio origins.

Two standards, "Superstar" and "Tennessee Waltz," derived their strength from Marilyn and Diane's "innocent" singing. Leon Russell's "Superstar" in particular became a genuine torch song, transcending the saccharin trappings of other contemporary versions.

Spring had the cohesiveness and emotional focus of the Beach Boys' late sixties work. It was well-received on both sides of the Atlantic. Marilyn and Diane embarked on a promotional tour in England where the group was billed as "American Spring" to avoid conflict with a British band.

Both *Spring* and *So Tough* made little impact on the charts, although *Tough* rose midway for a short time in late May. Despite the glaring contrasts, Warner's had coupled *So Tough* with *Pet Sounds* as a "double" release. There was strong resentment to this packaging. Few people liked the idea of having to buy a 1966 record to get one from 1972, especially if they owned the former already. The result was disastrous. Forced to make a comparison between the rushed *So Tough* and Brian's classic of teenage romance, rock reviewers jumped on the former with undue severity. If Warner Brothers was unhappy with *So Tough* as a piece of music, they were also upset with the harm their marketing was doing to the Beach Boys' hard-won acceptance in the FM market. When "Marcella" finally debuted as a single two months

later, it didn't even make the charts. On the tour, however, the Beach Boys' success story continued.

"Surf's Up" showed the ends they have gone to get the best possible sounds on stage. Three keyboards playing bass, guitar, a three-piece rhythm section with Ricky Fataar and Daryl Dragon playing cross rhythm on full kit, congas and kettle drum, and Eddie Carter—usually on bass or electric guitar—slowly playing a bellows to catch the swishing rhythm that fills out part of the record. The vocal parts are...quite amazing.
— **Melody Maker** *on the Beach Boys in Birmingham, spring 1972*

In the spring of '72 the group flew to the Netherlands to appear as featured musicians on "Grand Gala du Disc," a Dutch television show. The program was taped in Amsterdam, and following the sessions, the Beach Boys decided to make Holland their home for the balance of a European tour.

When the tour ended, the group's love affair with Holland continued. Enthusiastic about the concept of an album produced in an environment so different from California, they rented a barn in the town of Baanbrugge and sent for their families. At the same time, Jack Rieley made arrangements to ship four tons of studio equipment from Bel-Air to Holland. Even Brian would be making the move.

The Beach Boys had been touring in Europe and they really liked Holland. Carl thought it would be a different kind of atmosphere to be in—away from everything, even the telephones....We enjoyed the country.
— *Diane Rovell*

With Blondie and Ricky firmly established as part of the touring band, the group slowly began work on a new album. In contrast to the ten-day series of sessions for *So Tough*, the fourth album for Warner Brothers would be produced at a leisurely pace. The Beach Boys were well aware of the damage *So Tough* had done to their comeback. In England, the album was released without *Pet Sounds*. In America, Warner's was anxious to advance the creative and commercial progress initiated by *Surf's Up*.

Brian at this point was as shy and eccentric as ever. He missed his first two flights to Holland and showed up mysteriously asleep on an Amsterdam airport bench after the third. He could not be relied upon as a producer for the new work. Al and Mike were still deeply into the philosophy of TM, having spent over two months at the beginning of the year with the Maharishi on the East Coast. Dennis was actively composing with some help from keyboardist Daryl Dragon. His hand was slowly recovering from the injury that had forced him into semi-retirement. Carl continued in his role as producer/composer. His close relationship to Blondie and Ricky contributed to his expanded influence in the "new" Beach Boys band.

"California Saga" became a reality when we were in Holland and there was a dire need and necessity to do something creative...for me anyway. Mike and I were sitting on a car in this field, looking out at the cows in the Dutch evening, thinking about California. Two years earlier I had written a song and played it for Brian—about 1970. I had really enjoyed it then and thought, "It's great but what do I do with it?" Brian liked it—but unless you're a Brian Wilson you just have to wait for its time. Finally it did...it fit into that particular time when I was expected to come up with something. Mike had this tune "Big Sur" and I said, "Mike we'll just hook that up and then we'll run it all together." We had the Robinson Jeffers' verse—I had really gotten into him. He had this big house in Big Sur called Tor House. I started reading his work and books about him. So when Mike had his "Big Sur" song I said, "Why don't we melt them all together?" I thought it came out really nice....The thing I enjoyed most was the banjo. I really enjoyed playing banjo on that. Brian used to use banjo, even before "Cabin-Essence."
— *Al*

All the "Brother" recording equipment had arrived and was wired up for use by the band. In the barn a switch was thrown to make the initial test. Smoke poured out from the console. In thirty seconds a half-million dollars of the finest recording equipment in the world was damaged. Thus began the *Holland* recording experience.

You know, when the Beach Boys started, I wanted us to be a folk group. As it turns out, I feel that the Beach Boys became America's balladeers, recording in music the folk myths, the experience of this country.

——*Al*

It took a trip to the Netherlands for the Beach Boys to return a coastal consciousness (misplaced in *So Tough*) to their music. Al and Mike, with added elegance from words of Robinson Jeffers, composed and produced a three-part ode to California. The "California Saga" suite consisted of "Big Sur," "The Beaks of Eagles" (a Jeffers poem performed by Mike), and "California." It was a joyous aggregation of Memories, a celebration of the natural environment in airy Beach Boy vocals.

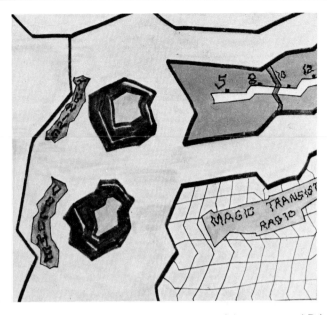

CALIFORNIA SAGA: BIG SUR   *by Mike Love*

Cashmere hills filled with evergreens
Flowin' from the clouds down to meet the sea
With the granite cliff as a referee
Crimson sunsets and golden dawns
Mother deer with their newborn fawns
Under Big Sur skies and that's where I belong.

Big Sur I've got plans for you
Me and mine are going to
Add ourselves to your lengthy list of lovers

And live in canyons covered with a springtime
   green
While birds and flowers to be heard and seen

And on my old guitar I'll make up songs to sing.

Sparklin' springs from the mountainside
Join the Big Sur river rushing to the tide
Where my kids can search for sea shells at low
   tide

Big Sur my astrology it says that I am meant to
   be
Where the rugged mountain meets the water

And so while stars shine brightly and up above
Fog rolls in through a redwood grove
And to my dying fire I think I'll add a log.

Copyright 1972 by Brother Pub. Co., BMI

CALIFORNIA SAGA: CALIFORNIA   *by Alan Jardine*

On my way to sunny California
On my way to spend another sunny day

Water, water, get yourself in the cool, clear
   water
The sun shines brightly down on Penny's place
The sun shines brightly down on the bay
The air's so clean that it just takes your mind
   away
Take your mind away
Take your mind away

Have you ever been south of Monterey?
Barrancas carve the coastline and the chaparral
   flows to the sea
'Neath waves of golden sun shine
And have you ever been north of Morro Bay?
The south coast plows the sea
And the people there are of the breed
They don't need electricity

Water, water, cool cascades of clear, clean water

The sun dance fiery scene sets the hills ablaze.
Horizon edges quick up the mountain's way.

Have you ever been down Salinas way?
Where Steinbeck found the valley
And he wrote about it the way it was in his
   travelin's with Charlie
And have you ever walked down through the
   sycamores
Where the farmhouse used to be?
There the monarch's autumn journey ends
On a windswept cypress tree

Have you ever been to a festival, the Big Sur
   congregation?
Where Country Joe would do his show
And we'd sing about liberty
And the people there in the open air, one big
   family,
The people there love to sing and share
Their new-found liberty.

Copyright 1972 by Wilojarston Pub., ASCAP

While listening to Randy Newman's *Sail Away* one night, Brian started writing a story. He was sitting in the barn, drinking apple cider, and thinking of the past—Mike's bedroom in the house on Mt. Vernon and Fairway, an AM radio under the pillow, the city lights of L.A. stretched out below them. He began to write a fairy tale, with Mike's house as a "mansion on a hill." As long as the *Sail Away* album played, Brian kept himself in the mood. He constructed a fantasy about kids and a *magic transistor radio*. Strange, beautiful music would come out of it—a magical experience for the children in the mansion.

That was in Holland. Written and done in Holland....There were no plans to do full musical pieces. We just wanted them as part of the "Fairy Tale."

——*Brian*

Some of the greatest music I've ever heard is buried. I have a tape I made of the studio sessions. I was so intrigued by what we were doing. I was listening to it the other day and it was beautiful...melody lines.

——*Al*

With Jack Rieley playing the part of the narrator and Brian himself as the strange visitor with a magic radio, the Beach Boys went into the barn to record "A Fairy Tale—Mt. Vernon and Fairway." To fill the musical requirements of the story, Brian composed fifteen-second musical fragments—tantalizingly complex and lovely melodies that appeared but briefly. Carl edited the entire tape, even adding a part in Brian's absence. After it was completed, the group decided to include "A Fairy Tale" as a separate seven-inch long-playing disc inside the album. Brian had wanted it as part of *Holland*, but the compromise spurred him to draw a special color sleeve for the ELP jacket.

Working with Jack Rieley's inflated lyrics, Carl composed, arranged, and produced "The Trader," an upbeat ballad with echoes of "Feel Flows." It overshadowed both "Leavin' This Town" (an undulating rock composition from Ricky and Blondie) and "We Got Love" (an undistinguished rocker intended for the end of side one).

Dennis, with Mike's lyrics, added another ballad to the *Holland* repertoire. The song, "Only With You," and his other cut, "Steamboat," were pleasant, well-produced rock-and-roll songs with a more casual approach than the string-laden outings on *So Tough*.

Mike and Brian (with more words from Rieley) wrote "Funky Pretty," a minor but infectious love song with few musical changes.

After sweetening and remixing a few of the tracks back in California, the group delivered the tapes for the *Holland* album to Warner Brothers in January 1973.

Warner's was not impressed. The beauty of "California Saga" did not insure a "hit" single. Warner's wanted a "comeback" song from Brian, a production that would get the group back on the charts and balance out the effects of *So Tough.* The Beach Boys were angry. The *Holland* outing had cost a small fortune and they were happy with the result.

It was Van Dyke Parks who finally emerged as an agent of compromise. Still under salary to Warner's and also on good terms with Brian, he headed up to Bel-Air to see what could be done.

"Hey no, Van Dyke, listen, listen, let me play you this other thing I just came up with. This other new song I'm working on, huh?"

"No, Brian, write a middle-eight."

A painfully prolonged session with his old partner finally yielded a tune. "Sail On Sailor," which Brian had been playing on piano at home, was given new Jack Rieley-Ray Kennedy lyrics, a Blondie Chaplin lead, added input from Van Dyke Parks and Tandyn Almer (of The Association), and a quick production. It was Blondie's most successful work as a Beach Boy, the best example of Flame's rocking style in sync with the Beach Boys' harmony.

Warner's was satisfied and the single went out in the dead of winter. *Holland* followed, with "Sail On Sailor" replacing "We Got Love."

The *Holland*/Warner's hassle had been an uncomfortable experience for the group, and there were no plans for new studio work on the Beach Boys' schedule.

From a business standpoint, the group had grown dissatisfied with Jack Rieley's management. He was fired in the spring of 1973. Mike's brother Steve Love was brought in to replace him.

Murry Wilson was a hard, oystershell of a man, aggressively masking a pushover softness which revealed itself at the sound of a beautiful chord or the thought of his wife and three sons. An unending source of high-powered

---

SAIL ON SAILOR Lyrics by Jack Rieley and Ray Kennedy
Music by Brian Wilson, Tandyn Almer and Van Dyke Parks

I sailed an ocean unsettled ocean
Through restful waters and deep commotion
Often frightened Unenlightened
Sail on Sail on Sailor

I wrest the waters fight Neptune's waters
Sail through the sorrows of life's marauders
Unrepenting often empty
Sail on Sail on Sailor

Caught like a sewer rat alone but I sail
Bought like a crust of bread oh do I wail
Seldom stumble never crumble try to tumble
   life's a rumble
Feel the stinging I've been given
Neverending unrelenting
Heartbreak searing Always fearing

Never caring persevering
Sail on Sail on Sailor

I work the seaways the gale-swept seaways
Past shipwrecked daughters of wicked waters
Uninspired drenched and tired
Sail on Wail on Sailor

Always needing even bleeding
Never feeding all my feelings
Damn the thunder, Must I blunder
There's no wonder all I'm under
Stop the crying and the lying, and the sighing and
   my dying
Sail on Sail on Sailor.

Copyright 1972 by Brother Publishing Co.

Holland surpassed *So Tough,* but fell slightly short of *Surf's Up* on the charts. "Sail On Sailor" was a critical success and as a single, scored in the lower half of the top one hundred.

With his home studio removed (Marilyn had finally had enough) Brian headed out to a friend's studio in Ft. Dodge, Iowa, to work on new material for Spring. With Diane and Marilyn, he recorded "Snowflakes" and "Shyin' Away," a pair of lovely songs coproduced with David Sandler. "Had to Phone Ya," written by Brian while Marilyn was in Europe, and "Falling in Love" were cut with an eye toward a Columbia contract for Spring. Diane and Marilyn were signed by Clive Davis shortly before his ouster and a single appeared on the Columbia label in June.

The Beach Boys resumed their touring schedule, adding "California," "Sail On Sailor," and occasionally, "Funky Pretty" to their repertoire.

Oldies were becoming more and more the backbone of each performance. The stigma of "surfin'" music had been lifted and songs from "I Get Around" to "Wouldn't It Be Nice" kept the young crowds on their feet. Even Bruce Johnston showed up for an occasional concert.

energy, he could wear down the strongest souls just by explaining his thoughts in a telephone call. A jealous guardian of the incredible career he helped build for his sons, he was the enthusiastic champion of any who sought to help them, and the scourge of those who used the Wilson name for personal gain.

His compassion for their good fortune was enthusiastic but critical when he saw them performing live about two months ago. After the concert Murry told someone: "Tell the boys to sing out more, especially Carl—he's not projecting enough. They're getting good but people pay to see them great. And tell Dennis to keep his hands out of his pockets. But don't let him know the old man said it."

——— Warner Brothers press release

On June 4, 1973, Murry died suddenly from complications following a heart attack. It was a traumatic time for the group—Brian could not bring himself to attend the funeral; Dennis and the whole Beach Boys' "family" retired to their Big Bear Lake retreat. Although he was no longer responsible for any of their professional affairs, Murry Wilson had continued to play an important role in his sons' lives. Dennis in particular had grown close to his father, and he suffered deeply after the funeral. It was a time of self-examination and contemplation for the entire group.

Alan

Carl

Dennis

Mike

Photos by Ed Roach

THE BEACH BOYS

THAT SAME SONG 1974-

Another moment in the history of the Beach Boys—another footprint. That's what's neat about the group; you have a history to look at. You can appreciate it for its periods; its focus changes, its moods. The same way you might look at an artist's work. You have his whole career as a perspective. It's different, though. Nobody ever looked at, say, "The Thinker" by Rodin and said, "It's nice, but it only made a number nine with a bullet."

———*Mike*

Nineteen seventy-three was a long way from the New Frontier idealism of 1961. Watergate seduced the country and a presidency became the biggest drama on network TV. Shuttle diplomacy promised world peace, and America's youth took their first steps away from the heated political activism of *"Hell no, we won't go."* Hair was shorter. Skirts were longer. Girls were women. Men watched the kids.

For a child of the sixties, the Beach Boys' sound was a symbol of romantic innocence. Their music evoked an aura of fun-loving youth, happily devoid of the pressure women's liberation, the Nixon era repression, the Pill, and the energy crunch had placed on America by 1973. In the world of the Beach Boys' music, you could ride away from it all in a little Deuce Coupe (and there was always enough gas).

The carefree nature of the Beach Boys' early music appealed to the seventies' teenagers as well—and a whole new generation of adolescents flocked to their concerts. The group's winter and summer tours were nostalgic love affairs, friendly, infectious concerts characterized by the shared experience of the Beach Boys' fun-loving songs.

Dennis, Mike, Carl, Alan, Brian

It now seemed as if the group had always been at the center of things. Their music had a unity and timelessness that much popular music lacked. With "In My Room," "I Get Around," and "Good Vibrations," the varied concert crowds entered a time machine. The Beach Boys' voices, seemingly unchanged in twelve years, offered an emotional security that "What's Going On," "You're So Vain," and "Ohio" did not. If the lyrics of their oldies seemed out of date ("Hey man, what's a woodie?"), the feelings of love were not. "Don't Worry, Baby" and "Surfer Girl" hit the same chord in teenagers as they had when the group played Santa Monica in '64.

The one thing that kept our family together was the music....The only thing that our family would share emotionally was to have our dad cry over something the kids did with music. It's hard to fathom that....The last couple of days of his life, he's lying in bed, dying of a heart attack going, "Son! You've got to play more rock and roll! Listen to this melody!" He'd get so excited.

————Dennis

You know, since my father died, it's been a lot different. I feel a lot more ambitious. It really does something to you when your father passes away. I got a new perspective on life. I'm gonna try a little harder now....It's makin' a man out of me. Makes me want to produce a little more.

————Brian

In June 1973, a new single by Spring, "Shyin' Away"/ "Falling in Love," took a shot at the charts. Joined by Terry Melcher's California, Dean Torrence's Legendary Masked Surfers, and Eric Carmen's Raspberries, Spring hinted at the new wave of white pop that blossomed in months to come. For the Beach Boys, the two-sided single "California Saga"/"Funky Pretty" didn't score in April/May, but plans for a "live" album (their first in America in nine years) proceeded under the supervision of Steve Moffitt, a noted L.A. engineer who had joined the group for *So Tough* on invitation from Dennis and Carl.

I didn't know it then, but my touring days were over. First I spent a week figuring out Brian's home studio, then we did the whole album. Then we packed up the whole studio and flew to do Holland, *where we set it back up and recorded the album* Holland. *When we got back, the equipment went into storage for about a year before Carl and Dennis asked me to help them put "Brother" together. Since then it's been a twenty-hour-a-day job for me.*

————Stephen Moffitt

The Beach Boys in Concert album, a double-record affair, was released in December. Capitalizing on Brian's repertoire and the recent enhancement of their instrumental act (Carter/Chaplin/Carly/Munoz/Fataar/Hinsche), *In Concert* mirrored the group's touring success in the stores.

The set charted twenty-five and mixed oldies ("Help Me Rhonda," "Surfer Girl," "California Girls," "Fun, Fun, Fun," "Don't Worry, Baby," "Good Vibrations," "Heroes and Villains"), four cuts from *Pet Sounds* ("Caroline, No," "Wouldn't It Be Nice," "You Still Believe in Me," and "Sloop John B."), a pair from *Wild Honey* ("Darlin'" and "Let the Wind Blow"), and six from their recent sessions ("Marcella," "Funky Pretty," "The Trader," "Leavin' This Town," "Sail On Sailor," and the previously unreleased rocker, "We Got Love"). *20/20, Sunflower, Surf's Up,* and *Friends* went untouched.

"Good Vibrations" and "Fun, Fun, Fun" were standouts, and the set as a whole was highlighted by exceptional bass lines from Carl and Ed Carter. The double album went gold, despite Brian's dislike for the effort as a whole.

In early 1974 finishing touches were put on Brother Studios, an elaborate yet comfortable recording facility designed for the group by engineers Stephen Moffitt and Gordon Rudd. Complete with a stained glass window and easy access to the beach, "Brother" boasted full twenty-four and sixteen track equipment, a Steinway piano, a Joe Pollard drum set, a Michael Pinder-designed Mellotron, a Roto-toms,

an echo chamber, and a classic Hammond B-3 organ. On Fifth Street in Santa Monica, it strove for the old Goldstar sound—a "live" open-mike atmosphere. Unlike many new studios, which reduced the impact of rock music by encasing it in a technically superb but emotionally antiseptic cavern, "Brother" was conducive to a warm, intimate yet "airy" sound—acoustically appropriate for the Beach Boys and such performers as Elton John and Eric Carmen, who would later use it for recording.

They are certainly the most important band America has ever produced. Melodically brilliant songwriting, complex arrangements, and the music interesting, inspiring, and yet always accessible.

Their vocal harmonies are unsurpassed....I think Brian was a French horn, Carl was a flute, Al Jardine a trumpet, Dennis a trombone, and Mike Love a baritone sax before their present incarnation as the Beach Boys.

————Eric Carmen

In the late spring of 1974, an inexpensive LP of their early hits (*High Water*) topped the national budget record charts.

The thirteen years during which the Beach Boys had produced music were the most turbulent in America's history. The music of Brian and the group evoked so much of these times that the Beach Boys had finally emerged as *the* American rock band. Anybody who had had one ear to AM radio in the sixties could not help but respond to the sentimentality of "Wouldn't It Be Nice?" The fragile melody of "Surf's Up" and soaring harmonies of "Fun, Fun, Fun" echoed the spirit of the post-war generation. Rock, and its accoutrements—the stereo, the concert, the car radio—had taken on unexpected cultural proportions. Identification with rock music was replacing the shared experience less mobile generations had found in hometown football and the corner store. The music was both a backdrop to and a language of adolescence. Everybody had special songs in his life, hits that triggered a memory of a certain person or experience. Tenth grade was Blood Sweat and Tears, your first love was Chicago...

No American band conjured up memories like the Beach Boys. A "Good Vibrations" or "In My Room," with Brian's well-crafted spontaneity, found its way into almost every teenager's past. As the band moved into the mid-seventies, this became all the more remarkable. A third wave of kids were still relating to their songs.

I was not only stunned but a little worried. I could have understood if she'd called out for a song of Holland, *but she was no more than ten years old and there she was asking us to play our very first national hit which we recorded at least two years before she was even born!*

————Mike

The continuing appeal was not lost on Capitol Records. In June 1974 they launched *Endless Summer,* a hastily assembled collection of the group's most popular early material. So quickly was the double set put together that Capitol did not even bother to find the 45 (hit) version of "Help Me Rhonda," or the tighter Honeys-backed "Be True to Your School."

I think you have to be constantly aware of the teenagers, because after all we are a young group of kids, so we should still be making music for the kids. I see no reason to desert them, you know what I mean?

——*Brian*

Backed by extensive television exposure, *Endless Summer* caught a wave to the top of the charts, and sent Warner executives into a re-issue frenzy.

The summer tour of 1974 hyped eight Beach Boys' records. In May, Warner's had separated *Pet Sounds* from *So Tough* and sent it out with the original San Diego Zoo photo. Capitol added a two-sided single, "Surfin' U.S.A."/"The Warmth of the Sun," to its schedule. *High Water* continued to float and Warner's rereleased *Wild Honey* and *20/20* as a discount set in July. The albums were accompanied by another single, Carl's classic remake of "I Can Hear Music."

As Ford moved in and Nixon went home, the Beach Boys' revival accelerated. Huge amphitheater concerts were packed with old and new fans. They played racetracks and stadiums with such seventies superstars as the Eagles.

For the first time since "Good Vibrations" the group was on the top of the charts. *Endless Summer* became the talk of the trade.

On the road, Chicago's producer, multi-talented James Guercio, joined the Beach Boys as a bass player. He didn't *look* at all like the group but his sizzling guitar riffs put him side by side with Carl. By the end of the tour, there was talk of the Beach Boys joining Guercio's group for a major series of concerts.

More than anything, I miss singing with the guys....I have that falsetto that I guess I could capitalize on. I love singing. I sing in the shower all the time. I sing alone and I think, "Wow! If only I had a microphone here!"

——*Brian*

I read an album proposal that Brian wanted to do on "helpful hints." I read the first two lines of the thing and fell on the floor laughing.... He was serious, he wanted to do it as an album project. How you put it into an album I'll never know. There were hints about how to get dressed faster. You find a top and practice shooting your arm in and out of the sleeve. He said that if you could practice this it will save you many valuable seconds when you're late for work. Also, there was a part on how to lunge for falling objects. You crouch down like this and then spring for it. He had some drink in the proposal too. How to stir it up and don't cheat and stuff. The whole thing was typed out one night. He stayed up all night, that's the kind of guy he is—completely maniacal, humorous, just deadpan.

——*Mike*

We're still there. If there was no media we'd still be doing it. We're still the same group, same people, same ideas, same everything. A little older. The Beach Boys just reported and sang about what was going on for them, what was so for us. I think we represent to people in other countries, and even in America something that they imagine that we do. Everyone has fantasies. People use the Beach Boys for their thoughts of America, or what America should be or the beach. The Beach Boys created a safe place for people. Even though I was in the band I could lie in bed at night and listen to the radio, the lights out, and "In My Room" would come on and I'd get into it. A place for people to let go and kind of drift, to enjoy themselves.

——*Dennis*

The business of rock had expanded exponentially in the years since Carl first took his Fender guitar into the top ten. The opportunities for an unknown band to do what the Beach Boys had done with "Surfin'" seemed more remote than ever. New and vital music could still make it big, but rock and roll was now a *business* that thought more in terms of moving "one million units" of a single album than one hundred thousand units of ten. Best-selling rock stars were accorded the attention and indulgence of Hollywood's most famous actors.

Alan, Brian, Mike, Dennis, Carl

Since I've been meditating, I've become calmer, at peace with myself, and I have energy to do what I want.

——*Mike*

We do solo projects for ourselves. There are hundreds of Carl Wilson tunes that he's recorded. There is a tremendous amount of solo things. We're in our studio every day, but we don't put it out. It's a hobby.

——*Dennis*

The Beach Boys avoided the prima donna trapping of rock stardom by getting more involved with nonprofessional concerns. Carl would experiment at "Brother" in Santa Monica, laying down tracks and expanding his expertise in the latest production techniques. Al and his wife Lynda focused on the ecology movement and began to raise Arabian horses on a ranch in Northern California, where they built a combination house/studio. Dennis worked intermittently on a solo album and spent his off-tour time in Hawaii and on the beach. Mike pursued a secondary career as a teacher of transcendental meditation, developing links with national organizations for the use of TM in prisons, drug programs, and institutions. Brian unfortunately retreated further into an eccentric and drug-related state of depression. The popularity of the group on the road averted the financial pressures that could have been created by the absence of a new album. With the experience of *Holland* not that far in the past, the Beach Boys were happy to concentrate on the concerts.

In October, Warner released another two-record set, *Friends/*

Smiley Smile, and watched it join the *Wild Honey/20-20* ensemble on the charts. Neither placed as high as *Endless Summer,* but given the sales record of the original release, the results were impressive. The group headed out to Jim Guercio's Colorado ranch and began to lay down tracks for a new album. Additional work was done at "Brother" in Santa Monica.

We've done about forty tracks. Brian is very involved with the LP. We did two tracks of his before we left to go on tour and he did three tracks while we were away. I've written about ten songs, Carl about five, and Al's done a couple. I have this one song, "Our Life, Our Love and Our Land," it's kind of an ethnic thing and has the feeling of "Trader" from Holland. *Al has this incredible thing about a landslide....There's a Carl song, "Don't Let Me Go," which I wrote the lyrics to....There's a Brian song that is reminiscent of "Surfer Girl," called "Good Timing." He also wrote another tune, which is very up and bouncy. The album's a combination of* Sunflower *and* Holland.*
——Mike*

Before the end of 1974, Blondie and Ricky left the group. Glen Campbell, another ex-B.B., had made his fortune in country western/pop tunes and had a weekly television show. The Captain (Daryl Dragon) and Toni Tennille were on the eve of their first major single, "Love Will Keep Us Together," and Bruce Johnston penned "I Write the Songs," a Grammy-award-winning tune that would propel Barry Manilow to the top of the charts. The entire Beach Boys' "family" was experiencing a successful year. Dennis Wilson rejoined the band as a working drummer.

I was frustrated. When the music was going and I was doing something, it was fine. But between the songs, I didn't know what the hell to do. I like to do things all the time....My drumming's starting slowly to come back. I'm not as quick as I used to be. When you stop playing for that long a time, you're bound to fall back. I was a little embarrassed, 'cause a lot of drummers have those fancy riffs down, so I kinda had to eat it a little, coming back to play.
——*Dennis*

In place of an LP, Warner Brothers received a new single in the final days of 1974. It was a melodic, funny, and somewhat obscure Spectorian melody with heavy use of bell-tree and Brian's "fairy tale" falsetto. The song, "Child of Winter," might have had some success as a holiday single but Brian delivered it too late for the seasonal promotion. Together with the flip side (another re-issue of Al's "Susie Cincinnati") "C.o.W." entered the ranks of rock and roll collector's item with uncommon speed.

Brian called me...he was down at the studio with Steve Kalinich. He says, "Honey, you got to come down and hear the song that we did!" So, I went and put on my stuff and ran off. He played me a song that just blew my mind...because it started real serious like a Bill Medley thing and then it had Bobby Hatfield—real high and vibratos...I think he did it as a put-on just to show himself that he could do it—do a piano solo with it. He just said after that, "Marilyn, I don't want to hear it again." The next day I called the engineer and said I want a copy of that—don't get rid of it. I just wanted it to play in my car.
——*Marilyn*

Throughout the year, Brian had returned intermittently to the studio to compose. "California Feeling" was a special example—a lovely extemporaneous experiment that worked. "Lucy Jones," a silly song about a six-foot-tall girl, was also penned with Steve Kalinich.

I don't consider Brian not going into the studio. He just wasn't there full force.
——*Marilyn*

Other tunes with Steve Kalinich were also recorded. These were usually up-tempo, simple melodies, such as "You're Riding High on the Music."

Right now there's talk about touring the world with Chicago. That should be dynamite ....We're getting together some orchestrations because many of the Beach Boys' songs lend themselves to symphonic arrangements. It will be great doing several of the Beach Boys' songs with an orchestra on stage.
——*Mike*

With *Endless Summer* going double-platinum, the group developed plans for two 1975 tours—a special American May–July schedule with Chicago and a solo circuit during August.

We were at [The Caribou Ranch] at the time recording "Wishing You Were Here" so Walter asked the Beach Boys to sing on it and they did.... We invited them to be on the New Year's Eve special we did on TV with Dick Clark and then we came to thinking it would be kinda nice to have the two groups on the same bill....So we worked it where we could have a finale with both groups playing together but something other than just a jam session.... I think we complement each other in a way. It's a good balance between the vocals and the instruments.
——*Pete Cetera, Chicago*

While the group extended its spectacular record on the road, Brian spent a lengthy but inconclusive session with Roy (*Wizzard*) Wood, cutting the classic "Honeycomb" and some basic material for a song called "It's OK."

Brian was seriously troubled at this time and suffered from a psychological weight problem. Emotional troubles, lethargy, and a near-addictive use of cocaine had made his presence in the studio foreboding—a frightening contrast to the extremely talented, energetic young man of seven years before.

Marilyn would always say, "Get him down there, get him working again..."

It was kind of a shock the first time I saw him—but I got right in there and we started working on a couple of things. With his wife, he sang, and then produced "Honeycomb." It was all done live—one take—he was so nervous, I decided just to go. We had four sax, three guitars, a bass, an organ. There were about fourteen or fifteen pieces.
——*Chuck Britz*

Sensing the strength of the band after its triumphant 1974 *Endless Summer,* Warner rereleased "Sail On Sailor." This time the single hit the middle sixties, on the charts.

Carl is R and B. He keeps the group in tune with rhythm and blues music. Dennis, I would consider him hitting the twenty-five to thirty-five bracket. Al Jardine is also like Mike Love—he sounds young. So Al and Mike are responsible for our youth, Carl and Dennis are recognizable for twenty-five to thirty-five and I think I'm responsible for the twenty-five to forty-five. So it's a careful blend of age groups we hit.
——*Brian*

In the spring of 1975, the joint Beach Boys/Chicago tour began its sweep of major American amphitheaters. It was an all-American event, with the late sixties/early seventies jazz-rock, socio-political overtones of Chicago complementing the exuberant, timeless harmony of the Beach Boys. Mike, Carl, Al, Dennis, bass player (and Chicago manager) James Guercio, Billy Hinsche, Ed Carter, and two additional keyboard artists opened every show.

From "Good Vibrations" to "Surfer Girl" every Beach Boys classic drew a standing ovation. Even the recent songs, such as "The Trader" and "Sail On Sailor" played well to hard-core fans that jammed racetracks, baseball fields, and college stadiums.

Chicago's set took a similar course, mixing standards such as "Make Me Smile," "Now More Than Ever," and "Ballad for a Girl From Buchanon" with cuts ("Harry Truman") from their latest record.

Carl and Dennis

A brief intermission followed, after which both bands appeared together on stage. Seventeen musicians blasted off with "Wishing You Were Here"—an overwhelming display of harmony and rock and roll karma.

A dazzling Beachago duet of "Darlin'" and "God Only Knows" followed, backed by horns. Then Carl and Mike boosted Chicago's "Saturday in the Park." The Beach Boys' climax came with "Fun, Fun, Fun" and "California Girls," an epic medley that kept the crowd two inches off the ground.

Then came James Guercio's dream version of "Feeling Stronger Every Day," with lead vocalists Jim Pankow and Mike Love sharing honors. The repertoire closed on an eccentric but rousing "Jumping Jack Flash" with a Jaggerish Mike Love leaping through his legendary stage act in time to the cheers of the crowd.

The Beach Boys overshadowed Chicago at every concert, if for no other reason than sheer accessibility of their music. Songs such as "I Get Around" were already ten-year-old classics and unlike Chicago's "25 or 6 to 4," the lyrics to the chorus were as easy to recite as your name.

On stage, the tour was a friendly affair. The bands did not compete, and the combined strength of the Beach Boys and Chicago's vocalists in the sunny weather was a memorable footnote to rock's history.

There's a mutual respect going on....It isn't like we're trying to blow them off the stage or vice-versa. We're just out to have a good time ourselves and give a good time.

——Pete Cetera, Chicago

I get tired of playing some of the old tunes, but many of them are timeless to me. As a musician you can let go with them instead of making them sound contrived. You can play with them in a new way each time and bring in little variations.

——Dennis

With a title that summed up the entire tour, Capitol released another two-album oldies set in April. *The Spirit of America* package climbed the charts at a pace worthy of Craig Breedlove. It stayed firmly in the top one hundred for the duration of the tour.

I guess that with the success of Elton ["Don't Let the Sun Go Down on Me"*], Chicago [*"Wishing You Were Here"*], those Wombles [*"Wombling Summer Party"*], and First Class [*"Beach Baby"*], you could say that the Beach Boys are never off the radio.*

——Mike

The summer of '75 found the Captain and Tennille in the top ten, 10cc harmonies ("I'm Not in Love") taking America by a storm,

and both of the Beach Boys' labels in a re-issue frenzy. As the group played Wembly with Elton John, "Little Honda" and "Barbara Ann" took a shot at the charts.

In July, still without new product, Warner's reluctantly distributed *Good Vibrations/The Best of the Beach Boys,* a solid anthology of songs from the group's post-*Party* albums. With a tasteful selection of hits ("Heroes and Villains") and nonhit classics ("Cool, Cool Water"), it settled into the top thirty.

In August *Shampoo,* a new movie about Los Angeles and the scramblings amid its '68 era counterculture/chic society, pulled "Wouldn't It Be Nice" out of its *Pet Sounds* berth for use in commercials, the film's soundtrack, and the accompanying album. Accordingly, Warner's released the song as a single, but constant airplay of "Wouldn't It Be Nice" over the years kept it from catching on as a "new" (or rediscovered) item.

Although rumors of new work from the group continued to circulate in the summer of '75, there was little actual recording. In preparation for the Bicentennial—Mike hoped the group would be declared the "official American 'band' "—the Beach Boys cut a modern version of the "Battle Hymn of the Republic."

I'm working with Terry Melcher. He had a group called California Music, and we're working on some projects for that and we hope to get them going soon.

——Brian

Brian, in a brief attempt to extricate himself from a reclusive and uncreative situation, accepted an offer from Bruce Johnston and Terry Melcher to work with their new RCA-backed Equinox label. Bruce had already formed a band consisting of singers Gloria Grinel, Kenny Hickle, and himself. A nonhit of "Don't Worry, Baby" was released by California Music in the fall.

Brian's contract with Equinox called for production services, but he also worked on arrangements and background vocals for California Music's version of "Why Do Fools Fall in Love," the Frankie Lymon hit that the Beach Boys had already recorded.

The experience whetted Brian's appetite for recording oldies, but, characteristically, his relationship with Equinox did not develop further. Instead, he sporadically sat in on sessions with family and friends. With Marilyn, he recorded background vocals for Johnny Rivers' cover of "Help Me Rhonda," and Jackie De Shannon's planned comeback album, *New Arrangements.*

It was really my fault because I was hiding in my bedroom from the world. Basically I had just gotten out of commission. I mean I was out of it. *I was unhealthy, overweight, I was totally a vegetable....In other words, my life got all screwed up....It happened through my starting to take drugs. I*

Mike, Dennis, Alan, Carl, Blondie, Ricky
Blondie, Dennis, Alan, Mike, Carl

SAIL ON SAILOR
Howard Chaykin

Dennis, Alan, Brian, Mike, Carl
Mike, Alan, Dennis, Carl

15 BIG ONES *Overton Loyd*

Guy Webster

CALIFORNIA SAGA *Photograph by Lynda Jardine*

Al, Mike, Carl, Dennis

THAT SAME SONG *Overton Loyd*

Carl, Dennis, Al, Mike, Brian
Carl, Al, Dennis, Brian, Mike, Charles Lloyd

WINDS OF CHANGE

Wayne McLoughlin

Carl Wilson

Michael Love

Dennis Wilson

Alan Jardine

Brian Wilson

Mike, Dennis, Alan, Brian, Carl
Al, Carl, Mike, Dennis

started taking a lot of cocaine and a lot of drugs and it threw me inward. I imploded. I withdrew from society through drugs and continued to do so for two, three, four years.... I made everybody angry at me because I wasn't able to get to work, to get off my butt. Goin' to parties....

———*Brian*

For the past three years Brian had been a shadow. He'd work in spurts, leaving things half finished. Then he'd return to his Bel-Air house, sometimes remaining inside for weeks. The behavior deeply disturbed his family, and Marilyn, in desperation, began talking to Dr. Eugene Landy, a high-priced psychologist, author of *The Underground Dictionary* and noted shrink-to-the-stars.

The Beach Boys are not a superstar group. The music is the superstar of the group. ———*Dennis*

The absence of brother Brian was largely responsible for the absence of a new album. In late 1974, the group had discussed a possible album with Warner Brothers, to include such cuts as "California Feeling" and "Good Time." Neither side was satisfied and the plan was dropped.

He'd go in like once in a while when he felt the need to....He was just more sporadic. ———*Marilyn*

The thing that made me go to Dr. Landy was I couldn't stand to see Brian, whom I just love and adore, unhappy with himself and not really creating....It was the worst, the absolute worst....a big drainer because of all the weirdos coming over, drug people. ———*Marilyn*

I do a thing that says you don't have to spend a lot of time... ———*Dr. Eugene Landy*

After a series of meetings, Marilyn decided to hire a doctor who worked the way her husband did—fast. Landy, his staff of bodyguards, and a nutritionist instituted a daily schedule for Brian. A combination of exercise, weight-loss diets, and strict supervision (to prevent him from taking drugs) was enforced around the clock.

It was a little scary because we weren't as close. There had been so many changes ... that getting back together was a bit scary and shaky, but we socked into that studio with the attitude that we had to get it done. A week or two of being in the studio and we started to get the niche again. ———*Brian*

The result of Landy's "treatment" was Brian's renewed interest in writing and producing. Landy's plans had called for writing sessions two or three mornings a week, followed on alternate days with recording sessions at "Brother." Brian gradually began turning out two and three songs per session.

Dr. Landy helped Brian a lot. Took all his money—made him want to work again! No, seriously, Brian just wasn't doing much. It was frustrating.... He wasn't into much and if he was, it was with the wrong people....He was just laying back and thinking again. ———*Marilyn*

I remember one night on "Back Home"—this was before **Fifteen Big Ones.** *Brian came in one night, and there were two or three Beach Boys around doing a track also. Two or three times Carl came into the booth and said, "Earle! This is the way it used to be! It's happening now!" Carl was so excited because it was really happening the way it always had been with Brian.* ———*Earle Mankey, Brother Records engineer*

The reunion had problems. The Brian Wilson of January 1976 was not the energetic twenty-three-year-old who had produced "Wouldn't It Be Nice" in less than a week. Brian still worked quickly and authoritatively, but his concentration and patience seemed limited.

Gradually, with support from the family, Brian's new music began to take on a personality and direction—simple, rocking, and unpretentious. Brian had developed a penchant for recording "oldies" and as it became apparent that his "comeback" was for real, the group made plans for two albums. The first would be composed entirely of cover versions of old songs. The second would be Brian Wilson originals.

The "oldies" album was to be a tribute to the Beach Boys' original influences and a collection of their favorite songs.

Phil Spector is just a hero. He gave rock just what it needed at the time and obviously influenced us a lot. We're doing three Spector songs on the album: "Just Once in My Life," which he co-authored with Carole King and Gerry Goffin, and "He's So Fine." I guess I chose most of the ballads on the album. Carl and Dennis are more into rock and roll and picked "Rock and Roll Music," "Money Money," and "Palisades Park." Al and Mike are the R and B fans and they suggested "Blueberry Hill," "A Casual Look," and "On Broadway." ———*Brian*

Working alone, Al produced "Come Go with Me," the Del Vikings *do-wop* classic.

It was my favorite record....I did it at Brian's house one night. We had rented a remote truck for fifteen hundred dollars a night and nobody showed up to use it...except me. So I said, "This is great. I'll do something I want to do."...I began putting one track on at a time. It was very difficult, Brian was upstairs listening to every track, because he was sleeping. I woke him and Marilyn up and they listened to me do this from ten P.M. to three in the morning, and Brian's up there saying to Marilyn, "He's going to do the whole thing!" When I heard it the next day it was so disjointed I started taking out what didn't fit....Now it's a whole different set of instruments and parts...and then I added the Beach Boys. It was beautiful...drums were still a little weird though....I had to add another set of drums. ———*Al*

The group rolled ahead on a dozen classics, from "Sea Cruise," "Tallahassee Lassie," and "In the Still of the Night" to the famous Spector/Hatfield/Medley "You've Lost That Lovin' Feeling."

What impressed me most was that Brian's voice is sort of foggy, and he does have trouble hitting notes more than he used to have, but when he did "You've Lost That Lovin' Feeling" he came in and went through and played every part without looking at the music or anything...then he went out and sang the vocal all the way right through, singing both of the Righteous Brothers parts, the highs and the lows, all at the same time...then he went back and doubled it, and he sang it exactly the way he sang it the first time. It was like the song was ingrained in his mind, he really had it down. ———*Earle Mankey*

The oldies were characterized by the group's use of keyboards. Coupled with Carl's bass, a piano, Baldwin organ, and Moog and Arp synthesizers provided a loosely textured wall of sound.

In a couple of cases, Carl is literally laying down the tracks, since the only position he can play in without considerable pain is flat on his back on the studio floor. Other guitarists featured on the album include studio guitarist Ben Benay and Ed Carter and Billy Hinsche, who are members of the Beach Boys back-up band on the road. ———*Modern Recording*

Cuts were often completed in one day. "Chapel of Love" with Brian's lead vocal was his first such performance in years.

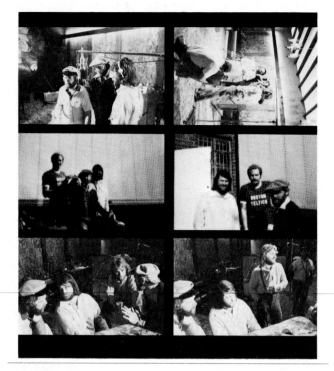

The Beach Boys have naturally unique vocals without even touching them. Their blend is usually accented further by having two or three of them sing background around the same mike, and by doubling the voices—sometimes with other instruments EQ and echo are added and the vocal tracks are usually limited a little then mixed up front.

——*Stephen Moffitt*

As the "oldies" were finished, talk surfaced of a double album instead of two separate efforts. The Beach Boys even discussed an album with one side of oldies and one side of Brian Wilson originals. New songs emerged from the Landy-instituted sessions—some genuinely exciting music. The group, especially Carl and Dennis, was anxious to fill the void that had arisen after the release of *Holland*. Brian was obviously happy to be working, and his brothers wanted the new compositions out before the public.

The truth is, Dennis and I were hoping that Brian would go back to the main plan. Dennis and I had a picture of doing an album of oldies just as a warm-up and then doing another album. But as it happens we started out to do the new stuff and then Brian said, "Well, I've recorded enough. I don't want to record any longer and the album's finished."

——*Carl*

Amid internal disagreements over the nature of the release, the Beach Boys sifted through the plethora of oldies and Brian's unevenly produced originals.

I'm very excited for Brian but I don't want him to lay back, the way he's been doing with oldies.

——*Dennis*

They finally selected Chuck Berry's "Rock and Roll Music," Trudy Williams' and the Teens' "A Casual Look," "Just Once in My Life," the Spector/Dixie Cup's "Chapel of Love," the Five Satin's classic "In the Still of the Night," Fats Domino's timeless "Blueberry Hill," Little Willie John's claim to fame, "Talk to Me," and Freddie Cannon's summer anthem, "Palisades Park," for which Brian returned to Western Recorders.

Even a Beach Boys oldie, the original *Sunflower*-era Wilson-Love-Jardine-Dragon-Johnston "Susie Cincinnati" was brought out of the can by Brian.

With summer on the way, the group turned to old friend Dean Torrence, who had moved from recording albums to designing them under his own firm, Kittyhawk Graphics.

*Let's see...one of the album titles I remember most is **Pick Ya Up** and **Pick Ya Up At Eight**. Dennis had a title he liked, **Group Therapy**. Then I came up with **Fifteen Big Ones**.*

——*Dean Torrence*

*This summer, the Beach Boys' fifteenth, Brian hearteningly is venturing out again....He also personally produced their first new material since 1972 for the album **Fifteen Big Ones**, one of the five by the Beach Boys now on the charts.*

——**People** *magazine, August 1976*

The Beach Boys' media blitz of 1976 rivaled that of New York's epic sailing armada. From *TV Guide* to *People* to *Rolling Stone*, lead features on the group showed up with the same motif—*Brother Brian was "back."* Mike and Al advocated TM. Carl was soft-spoken and supportive. Dennis with his new wife, strawberry-blonde model Karen Lamm, appeared to be the ideal surfer and surfer girl.

Warner Brothers pulled "Rock and Roll Music" off the album and sent it flying up the charts. It became the group's first top-ten single since "Good Vibrations" and helped position *Fifteen Big Ones* in a similar spot on the LP charts. With five best-selling albums and a TV special on the way, the Beach Boys experienced one of the most successful summers of their careers.

Halfway through the show a large sheet is unfurled in the center of the crowd, and a spotlight hits it, illuminating the message: "Welcome Back Brian!" The crowd cheers again. The Beach Boys smile and look over at their big brother. A smile flickers across his face. He extends his right arm and waves gently into the lights, like a little boy reaching up to pet a large dog he's not quite sure about....

——*Richard Cromelin*, **Sounds**

Brian's reemergence on stage came in July at the Oakland Stadium. His presence electrified the already ear-shattering crowds and his occasional vocals, delivered shyly from a piano to the side of the stage, were greeted with cheers. Brian's voice was terribly rough, out of shape, and coarsened by a bad cigarette habit, but he and the group shared a special sense of triumph. Things had not been this way since 1964.

Dennis, Alan, Brian, Mike, Carl

I feel more into it.... Rehearsals went real good. I got some of the old fire back and I feel more positive. I feel good about myself, and once you feel good about yourself you can touch other people. I lost weight and acquired self-discipline....I wanted to be a full band member again....In the early days I would also play bass....the period of adjustment wasn't as traumatic as some people think.

———Brian

Their pleasures as opposed to those claimed by such seventies inheritors as the Eagles and America have always radiated affection because those pleasures are rooted in friendship.　*———Greil Marcus*

I like to see a group or person entertain me....That's why I wear my gold lame jacket and turban. Even though Carl dresses pretty spiffy too, the rest of the group doesn't care so much. Of course, just because Al Jardine hasn't changed his underwear since the Japan tour in sixty-five—I mean, you can't ask for everything.

———Mike

The Beach Boys' sound once again permeated America's popular culture. The number-one single in the country, "Shannon," was a B.B.-style ballad about Carl Wilson's dog, sung in falsetto by Brooklyn-expatriate Henry Gross. Todd Rundgren released a single of "Good Vibrations," an audacious move that wound up on the charts and elicited Brian's sly comment: "Oh, he did a marvelous job! He did a great job. I was very proud of his version. Very close to the Beach Boys, incidentally." You can see Brian's smile. Eric Carmen's "Sunrise" and "Cruisin' Music" were nothing if not a homage to the Beach Boys. Flash Cadillac's "Sons of Beaches" was an entire album of B.B. surfstyle vocals. Television commercials for such "youth" products as Bonnie Bell (a "Warmth of the Sun" pastiche), Pepsi, and "Herbalessence" (an outright licensing of "California Girls") drove home the fact that the Beach Boys' music was *classic* teenage music—it possessed the same communicative properties a decade and a half after its debut. The children born when "Surfin'" was released were now responding to

Brian's compositions as if they had just been written. The entire phenomenon was summed up on August 5, 1976, with the airing of "The Beach Boys 15th Anniversary TV Special," an NBC program taped in June.

Produced by Lorne Michaels, the man behind the successful "Saturday Night Live" show, the Beach Boys' special reflected not only the Beach Boys' music, but their spirit of humor, unpretentiousness, and fun. The hour mixed footage of the Pacific Coast Highway, national air races, Big Sur, and a B.B. concert in Anaheim with behind-the-scenes interviews about the group. Van Dyke Parks showed up to laud their perseverence, Brian played "Bugged at My Old Man," and the entire group teamed up with the Double-Rock Baptist Church Choir for a spectacular, exhilarating, beautifully arranged rendition of "That Same Song."

In September Brian went on stage again, this time as presenter and nominee for Don Kirshner's "Rock Music Awards" program. As he walked out to announce the winner in the "Best Singles" category, Brian was greeted by a standing ovation, an overwhelming show of affection from the recording business. The Brian Wilson of September 18 was a far cry from the nervous man who had only nine months before begun a struggle against five years of depression and reclusiveness. His weight was down to 215, and in a stylish tuxedo, he handled himself with a renewed sense of self-pride. Landy's pressure and the happiness generated by his return to the group acted as a catalyst for Brian. Plans were made for a series of East Coast dates in New York and Boston around Thanksgiving.

---

*I thought the Beach Boys' special was fantastic...and the **Saturday Night Live** show—Dr. Landy thought would be a very therapeutic thing for Brian....It was very hard for him to do—go up there alone. Landy had a lot of good ideas. He'd get a little outrageous at times. We even had to hold the reins on the horse!*

———Marilyn

They just hired some musicians to play in the background and I did "Back Home" and "Love Is a Woman" from the new album. I did "Good Vibrations" too. My doctor at the time thought I should do it, so I did it. I enjoyed it. Yes, very much. The others, my brothers, that is, they liked it a lot too.

——Brian

As therapeutic as Brian's appearance on a November *Saturday Night Live* show might have been, it put off many viewers. Brian's coarse comeback vocals seemed jarring in comparison to the sweet Beach Boys harmonies of the past. In addition, Brian seemed terribly ill at ease. He *was* ill at ease; Landy's staff massaged him before and after the performance, but the simple act of going out and doing the show cleared another major obstacle.

I don't like to read about me as much as I used to, but I still do. I do like to read about the Beach Boys. Criticism doesn't offend me; I just take it....

——Brian

Between the end of their summer tour and a spectacular New Year's Eve show at the L.A. Forum—during which Brian played bass—the Beach Boy fever continued to grow. Despite his television performance, Brian's voice was getting better. More significantly, Brian had become highly motivated in musical composition. Back in L.A., he wrote two of the most beautiful songs of his career.

He felt very strongly about those songs....There was like this energy built up

inside him. He offered "Still I Dream of It" to Frank Sinatra, but we didn't hear from him.

——Marilyn

STILL I DREAM OF IT *by Brian Wilson*

Time for supper now
Day's been hard and I'm so tired
I feel like eating now
Smell the kitchen now
Hear the maid whistle a tune
My thoughts are fleeting now

Chorus
Still I dream of it
Of that happy day when I can say
I've fallen in love
And it haunts me so
Like a dream that's closely linked
To all the stars above

Young and beautiful

Like a tree that's just been planted
I found life today
Made mistakes today
Will I ever learn the lessons that
All come my way

(Repeat chorus)

I'm convinced of it
The hypnosis of our minds
Can take us far away
It's so easy now
You see someone's up there high in heavens
Here to stay

(Repeat chorus)

"Still I Dream of It" and "It's Over Now" were personal ballads, romantic, wistful songs with warm melodies and lyrics that defied the cute but banal phrasing of other, more extemporaneous work from this period. It was clear that these were *serious* songs, important songs for Brian, and the lyrics, ingenuous, with a gentle spirit of an adult who will not give up the emotions of his youth, were as moving as any work since *Pet Sounds.* A third song, "Life Is for the Living," an upbeat, forties swing piece complete with horns, went through the

whole arrangement trip. Brian called up Dick Reynolds (of the Christmas album) and had him do full charts for the song. Then, as if to restate his own roots even further, Brian returned to Chuck Britz and Western Recorders to lay down the instrumental track. "Life Is for the Living" was an anthem for Brian's own recovery, a funny, high-spirited self-analysis in Sinatra swing style.

A score of other songs were turned out in this period. "My Diane," titled after his sister-in-law, was an all-stops-out tearjerking rock and roller; "That Special Feeling," inspired by rainbows and sunsets over Hanalei Bay, went through some interesting chord changes and spoke of his love for Marilyn. "They're Marching Along" was a prime example of more therapeutic work, off-handed lyrics about kids, school, and the carefree nature of childhood.

At the same time, Dennis Wilson worked on his own album, (working title, *Freckles*). Evolving from plans of the *Sunflower* era, the LP would be the first solo venture for an original Beach Boy and Dennis wanted it to fully reflect his own music and feelings rather than those of the group. The sound was to be coarser, natural, with a rougher, and more environmental and romantic style than the current B.B. material. He worked on every cut extensively; the sound would be in the highly textured production style learned from Brian.

Dennis brought in part of the "Beach Boys family" (guitarists Ed Carter and Earle Mankey, drummers Hal Blaine and Ricky Fataar). He developed a complex instrumental track for "Rainbows," written in '75, and arranged (with Jimmie Haskell) the Double-Rock Baptist Church Choir for "River Song," a haunting, ecological plea, co-written by Carl. Gregg ("Forever") Jakobson shared production duties.

In comparison to the days of *Fifteen Big Ones*, there was a looser attitude in the winter of 1976– 1977. With Brian more confident and comfortable in studio surroundings, he'd often go in and record alone, playing the instruments himself, singing all the parts on new compositions, writing down lyrics quickly, right there at Brother Studios. Among the songs were "Lines," "Hey Little Tomboy," "Shortenin' Bread," "Games People Play," and "H.E.L.P. Is on the Way."

The last two B.B. releases, "It's OK," a classic Love-Wilson summer song put out in September (quite late for the season) and "Susie Cincinnati"/"Everyone's in Love with You" (released rather offhandedly in November) were not hits. Brian seemed unphased.

Dr. Landy was gone and Brian was still active. The eldest Wilson plunged ahead on songs for *two* new albums, the first to be called *The Beach Boys Love You.*

He came in one morning and wrote two or three songs, and for the rest of the

week, he recorded them. . . . "Airplane" was a typical song. Brian went in and laid down a piano track, then a harpsichord track, and maybe an organ track. Then he would come in and put bass on it, and somewhere between the bass and the vocal, he would put the drums on it. The drums were usually only the snare drum or only the bass and snare, simple patterns with space between verse and choruses. Then he'd put a vocal on it. He did that with every song on the album, and then two months later when the guys were in town they'd come in and sing vocals, put on the vocal parts. If the songs had more instruments, that was added on later.

———Earle Mankey, Brother Records engineer

Brian used Arp and Moog synthesizers for a modern, textured instrumental backing. For "Deep Purple" he used charts by Dick Reynolds to get a swirling, romantic style for an orchestrated cover version of the Nino Tempo/April Stevens' classic. A fluttering flute added a gentle highlight and Brian sang lead in a less coarse and more clearly defined voice. His range had improved; "Deep Purple" harkened back to his crooning on "Blue Christmas" in 1964.

By March, there was more than enough completed material for an album. Tracks were selected for the next Warner's release. A group effort from the *Fifteen Big Ones* era, "I Wanna Pick You Up," was included, as was "Ding Dang," a short, syncopated melody casually composed by Brian and Roger McGuinn (formerly of the Byrds) a couple of years earlier. It was a nonsense song, hard-driving and good-natured, with a hysterical "Ding-dang-ding-dang-a-ding-dong" chorus interfaced with some lyrics about trouble with a girl. Brian filled the production with compressed instrumental effects.

It's easier for him to work. . . . There's a lot of speed in what he does. What other people would call adventurous, I think for Brian is just the way you make records. It's not strange for him that he has a song called "Johnny Carson."

———Earle Mankey

Brian's method of producing was very much like it had been in the days before *Pet Sounds*. He'd get an idea for a song and he'd go in and do it. Simple idea, simple method of production—but *incredible* melodies. Even a silly song like "Johnny Carson" — "I was on my way to the studio and I'd been thinking about how I'd seen Johnny on TV the night before and I said to myself, There's gotta be a song about Johnny Carson!"—was brimming with cheerful harmony, inventive use of counterpoint, and an innocent wit.

"Carson" and its musical counterparts—"Love Is a Woman," "The Night Was So Young," and "Let's Put Our Hearts Together"— were charming melodies about everyday occurrences, distinctive in their chord changes and melodic range, interpreted in a textured, contemporary style of production with timeless appeal. The music differed in the degree of Brian and the group's involvement with it. Brian's perfectionist nature had gone into retirement after *Spring* and had yet to return in its old form. Likewise, the Beach Boys' focus had expanded in different directions. Mike was teaching TM, Al and Lynda raised bees and horses, Dennis was busy with his own album and a huge sailboat, Carl was producing a singer (Ricci Martin's first album) solo.

So *The Beach Boys Love You* was more a Brian Wilson album than anything since *Wild Honey*. In many ways, its freshness, simplicity, and upbeat spirit put it very close to *Wild Honey*. As with that album in 1967, *Love You* was both a therapeutic and a creative experience.

Overall I've written twenty-eight new songs. I'm starting to load up. With three new songs and what we have in the can, I think we'll have another album all put together. We're getting into it. I hope we pick the right single. . . . I dunno. I guess I've changed in the way that I've become more adult. I think I've become a more adult thinker over the last year . . . and I've straightened up. The thing is, I'm just pooping along. Some people buzz along. I poop along. I can't help it; that's the way I am. I'm just a pooper.

———Brian Wilson in Crawdaddy, April 1977

A pooper at times, perhaps, but Brian Wilson was still a musician of tremendous talent and drive. The release of *The Beach Boys Love You* in April was greeted with almost unanimous support—from *Rolling Stone* to the *Village Voice*, critics viewed it as an important step from the cover version rock of *Fifteen Big Ones*.

That the Beach Boys are a still-functioning group with a past of such repute is a blessing and a burden. That they have survived fame, disrepute, and insanity with at least some of their innocence intact is amazing.
———*Tom Smucker*, Village Voice

The Beach Boys Love You *pulls off a feat that's eluded, say, Pete Townshend and Mick Jagger—it's almost more juvenile than their original stuff, it's not self-conscious, and it sounds right up-to-date. It's that joyous, roller-rink-in-the-sky sound that always made them the real American Music...and as far as I'm concerned it might be their best album ever.*
———*Lester Bangs*, Circus

If nothing else, *Love You* was rock and roll with a sense of humor, neither self-conscious or hip. The other members of the group delivered Brian's lyrics with a suitably dumb-but-sincere style. Their work preserved the innocence of the songs.

The song "I Wanna Pick You Up" is descriptive of a man who considers this chick a baby and he says, "Well, you still have a baby in you....You just sorta have that thing and I want to pick you up." Even though she's too big to pick up, of course, he wants to; he wants to pretend she's small like a baby, he really wants to pick her up!"
———*Brian*

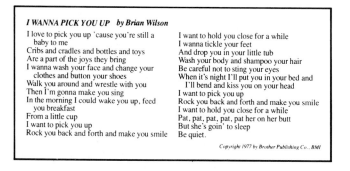

I WANNA PICK YOU UP **by Brian Wilson**

I love to pick you up 'cause you're still a
   baby to me
Cribs and cradles and bottles and toys
Are a part of the joys they bring
I wanna wash your face and change your
   clothes and button your shoes
Walk you around and wrestle with you
Then I'm gonna make you sing
In the morning I could wake you up, feed
   you breakfast
From a little cup
I want to pick you up
Rock you back and forth and make you smile

I want to hold you close for a while
I wanna tickle your feet
And drop you in your little tub
Wash your body and shampoo your hair
Be careful not to sting your eyes
When it's night I'll put you in your bed and
   I'll bend and kiss you on your head
I want to pick you up
Rock you back and forth and make you smile
I want to hold you close for a while
Pat, pat, pat, pat, pat her on her butt
But she's goin' to sleep
Be quiet.

Copyright 1977 by Brother Publishing Co., BMI

Dennis sang "I Wanna Pick You Up" in his raspy, romantic voice, Mike picked up on the inherent humor of "Johnny Carson" and gave it the same silly-smart approach as he had for "Drive-In" over a decade ago.

Two Brian Wilson classics emerged on the album. "The Night Was So Young," a lovely example of "conversational rock" in the tradition of "I Went to Sleep," was enhanced by Carl's vocal. "I'll Bet He's Nice" was coy, very white, very pop, with a stunning chord change and Carl again in rare form on a middle-eight.

Basic rock and roll showed up in three cuts, "Honkin' Down the Highway," "Roller Skating Child," and "Mona," which the band pounded out, Spectorian backbeat and all. Brian left the best ballads in the can and released the mid-tempo "Airplane" and "Let's Put Our Hearts Together," a rather shaky duet with Marilyn. "Good Time" capped the contents, an instrumental throwback to the early seventies, with the original pre-*Spring* B.B. vocal track restored (and lightened background vocals). Brian added a new tag ("Hey!") for the album release.

Plans were made for a follow-up album to tie in with the end of the summer tour in September 1977. These plans and the plans for the tour itself were affected by events before and shortly after the release of *Love You* in April.

With Dennis moving toward the completion of his album for James Guercio's custom CBS Records imprimatur, the Beach Boys announced a deal that would unite them under the same label. For a reported $8 million, the Beach Boys would begin a series of albums for the Columbia/Caribou line. The deal was one of the largest ever made in the history of recorded music and, not surprisingly, it upset Warner's, to whom the Beach Boys still owed one album after *Love You*.

Relations between the group and Warner's had been strained ever since the problem with *Holland*. Even the extensive and obviously successful campaign for *Fifteen Big Ones* had not closed the gap.

Love You fell victim to news of the contract. The record received a one-ad promotion in national and trade magazines, and was then abandoned by Warner's. There was no single to go with the album; "Honkin' Down the Highway" (b/"Solar System") finally showed up in June. While B.B. influenced musicians such as the Eagles, E.L.O., Leif Garrett, and C.S.N. headed up the charts, *Love You* disappeared, another critical success with no sales to back it up. Concert dates were canceled amid the growing entanglements of the label changeover. In July, the group pulled out of an entire European tour, playing one date in London at a convention for CBS Records and then returning to California.

Brian continued to write new songs, including an upbeat Spectorian single with three melodic changes, "It's Like Heaven," for a new version of *Spring*. Joining Diane and Marilyn was Rocky Pamplin, an ex-pinup from *Playgirl* magazine with a voice not unlike Brian's.

Dennis, in the meantime, had delivered the final mix of his album, now titled *Pacific Ocean Blue*, to Caribou. He selected eleven songs, deleting "Taking Off," "Tug of Love," "Schoolgirl," "I Don't Know," and a new version of *Holland*'s "Only With You." CBS released the LP in August and it quickly gathered its share of enthusiastic reviews. Dennis had produced an album of deeply expressive music, much different from the Beach Boys' traditional sound yet vital and romantic in a way that was still very much Californian. The vocals harkened back to "Cuddle Up," but both the pacing and phrasing of the lyrics seemed faster, more fluid, without compromising Dennis's rough but gentle style. *Rolling Stone* called it, "A truly wonderful and touching album...his strong suit is the ballad, and though the tunes are often little more than fragments, they have a way of taking hold of your emotions."

Although the album did not go on to become a major commercial success (the single "Pacific Ocean Blues" did not make the charts), Dennis was exhilarated by the critical reception. Earlier in the year, the Joffrey Ballet had performed their *Deuce Coupe II* in San

Francisco and Dennis's work provided much of its foundation. The piece, by the innovative choreographer Twyla Tharp, based its movements on fragments of Beach Boys' songs and a larger selection of "Cuddle Up."

In the meantime, Brian continued to build up a repertoire of unreleased songs. Many were "throwaways," extemporaneous cuts that would wind up on the shelf. "Sherry She Needs Me" was a melodic combination of Frankie Valli, Bob Crewe, and Phil Spector with both a wall of sound and a chorus of "Sherry Baby." "Lazy Lizzy" was a simple organ piece, a funky slow song ("Lazy Lizzy I saw you walking alone"), mock-Temptations solo ("It's so hard to walk home when you're all a-lonnnnne"), and generally raspy Brian Wilson vocal. "Wild Situation" was more polished, a rolling ballad backed by "Let's Go Trippin'" guitar, drums, Arp synthesizer, strings, and bass.

We've played New York so often that we just decided to give a little back.
————Mike

On Thursday, September 1, 1977, the Beach Boys turned New York City's Central Park into Redondo Beach for the largest concert of their careers. The occasion was WNEW's annual free summer concert, held on the park's Great Lawn. In the sweltering heat between 75,000 and 150,000 people, mostly teenagers enjoying their last days of freedom before school, showed up for a ninety-minute set. Ricci Martin, Carl's protégé, opened the event. The group did their usual mixture of early hits and selected new cuts, most notably a beautiful Al Jardine ballad, "Lady Linda," written in collaboration with Ron Altbach and based on a Bach fugue. The whole show was a family affair—Marilyn and Diane; Carl's wife Annie; her brother, guitarist Billy Hinsche; Audree Wilson; Stan Love; Karen Lamm-Wilson with tambourine onstage; Carnie and Wendy, Brian's daughters; and Brian himself, sporting a baby-blue *American Spring* T-shirt and closely cropped hair. He looked terrific, practically slim, and played both piano and bass for the event.

After the concert, the group flew to Rhode Island for a pair of concerts, then returned to California. There was considerable tension at this time. Plans for the next album were up in the air as the band dealt with their commitments to both Warner and Columbia. Dennis made plans for his second solo album. Brian took a trip to Hawaii. In October, Mike, Al, and Brian regrouped in Iowa for two months of meditation, relaxation, and the production of a new album. The rest of the "family" flew out to join them at the end of the month. Half a million dollars was spent on setting up a small studio in the basement of a dorm at Maharishi International University. Mike supervised most of the arrangements, setting up a regular (if flexible) writing and recording schedule for Brian and a program of natural foods and meditation for the entire Beach Boys' entourage.

What emerged musically was the most impressive vocal performance by the group since *Holland* and the best harmonies since the days of *Sunflower*. The old Beach Boys' "blend" was back—soaring, sweet four-part chorus and even an occasional falsetto by B.W. himself.

Mike sang lead on many of the songs, including two bittersweet ballads, "Matchpoint of Our Love" and the flute-backed "Winds of Change," evocative of "Try To Remember" from *The Fantastiks*. These tracks and the balance of the album would be further "sweetened" and textured by Alan and Ron Altbach in Los Angeles. Alan's influence as a producer on these songs was more substantial and impressive than on any earlier Beach Boys LP. The final results, in late 1978, were a sophisticated blend of horns, strings, synthesizer, and beautiful Beach Boy vocals—a production akin to *Sunflower* in style.

The music as a whole was more vibrant, fuller, and more *finished* than the *Love You* album. Mike's vocals were exceptionally fresh. He was far more involved in this music than he had been in *Love You*.

Perhaps the most startlingly successful cut to emerge from the sessions was "She's Got Rhythm," Brian's answer to the Bee Gees. It was the Beach Boys' first *disco* song since "Dance, Dance, Dance." The track had a dynamic circular pulse, driven right through the roof by Brian's *falsetto*—his first such performance on a new song since the mid-sixties. ("Last night I went out disco dancing, saw a foxy girl out on the floor ... She's got rhythm, she's got something I need.") It was funny, infectious, and a fabulous hit sound.

"How About A Little Bit of Your Sweet Love," "Wontcha Come Out Tonight," and "Our Team" were typical homespun B.B. tunes, cheery, on the order of "Good Time" and once again, a step fuller and more complex than *Love You.* "Kona Coast" was an interpolation of their old "Hawaii" chorus with a new melody built around it. Their sweet background blend was worth the entire album.

At the end of November, the Beach Boys' children joined them in Iowa for a special session—a new Beach Boys Christmas album. Brian and Mike penned two upbeat love songs, "Christmas Day" and "Go Get that Girl," the latter with a driving, contagious melody backed by horns. The unreleased song "H.E.L.P. is on the Way" was divested of its original lyrics and changed to "Santa's Got an Airplane," a bubbling, upbeat song. For the balance of the sessions, the group brought in their kids to sing background chorus, intro, and full vocal parts. They cut two versions of "I Saw Mommy Kissing Santa Claus" and a set of traditional carols. The recordings were cute, high-spirited, and worthy of the genre.

At the end of the year the group played some West Coast dates and made plans for a major tour of Australia and New Zealand. Mike made a guest appearance in *Dead Man's Curve,* a rather melodramatic retelling of Jan Berry's (of Jan and Dean) tragic car crash and subsequent fight for recovery. With Mike and Alan, Brian wrote his first soundtrack material in over a decade, the theme to a Tisch-Davidson movie called *Almost Summer.* Mike and Ron Altbach contributed additional music for the film. With Charles Lloyd, Mike made plans to tour with a TM-oriented band of his own—Waves. Dennis had already neared completion on his second solo album. A beautiful new song called "Baby Blue" made dramatic use of arp and Carl's own vocal range. With Rocky Pamplin, Marilyn and Diane cut Brian's 1972 ballad "California Feeling" and a sensational, country-style cover of Elvis Presley's "Don't Be Cruel."

Alan worked on songs at his combination studio-ranch house. He made plans for his first album, which would probably include "Lady Lynda," and the still-to-be-completed "Loop de Loop."

Brian, Carl, Michael, Alan and Dennis with members of the Joffrey Ballet

Carl continued his long-standing role at Brother Studios, shuttling between Manhattan Beach and Jim Guercio's Caribou Ranch complex in Colorado.

By late winter, Mike Love and Charles Lloyd's group, "Waves," had undergone a name change to "Celebration." Mike incorporated their "Almost Summer" theme into the Beach Boys' act in the spring.

The Beach Boys collectively and individually had fulfilled the promise of their careers. They had the financial and professional security of being the most successful American rock-and-roll band in history. They had outlasted their competitors and had attracted an entire new group of kids to their music. Their last album, their twenty-fifth American LP release, had received good reviews. The future held an $8 million commitment from one of the best record labels in the world. Brian Wilson was returning to old form in the studio. For the first time since 1964, he had become a fully integrated member of their touring band. And, at the same time, Dennis, Mike, Al, Carl, and Brian each had individual careers and talents. As a group and individually as musicians they were respected throughout the rock-and-roll community.

The tapes from the *M.I.U.* sessions were now planned for the group's last Warner Brothers release under the title, *California Feeling*. With the addition of cover versions of Buddy Holly's "Peggy Sue" and "Come Go with Me," the title was changed twice, to *Winds of Change* and finally to *The M.I.U. Album*. A "Peggy Sue" single debuted on the charts in late August with a revised version of "Hey Little Tomboy" on the flip. *The M.I.U. Album* appeared in late September. Brian continued to write new songs for the group.

In the latter part of 1978, the Beach Boys sold Brother Studios and headed down to Miami, Florida to develop their first album for Columbia/Caribou. With Bruce Johnston involved in both the arrangement and production of the record with the Beach Boys, and such tracks as Brian's rousing version of "Shortening Bread" and a 12-minute disco track, the album was scheduled for a late Winter '79 release.

The Beach Boys: To this day the name evokes a picture of blue skies, sunny days, clear water, beautiful blondes, and sleepy summer afternoons. The group never repudiated its roots or its identity. Through seventeen years of music they maintained a continuity of spirit and expression so very uncommon in a business where careers are transitory and success contingent on the length of a trend.

They were—they are—artists.

The Beach Boys: They brought to teenage America a world that existed in the California dream. They preserved that dream in their music. They refined it, expanded it, and reinterpreted it as they grew individually and collectively, but they remained faithful to its expression. The Beach Boys' music was and is the music of innocence and of youth.

The Beach Boys: It has been said that Brian Wilson invented California. At the very least he understood it. Brian was the foremost poet of the California dream. The Beach Boys *were* California. They captured the timeless beauty of its natural wonder in their music.

The Beach Boys: Mike calls them "inseparable from the white middle-class karma." They changed with the rest of America, but they responded to the times without submitting to them. The Beach Boys maintained their identity through hard rock, mellow rock, disco rock, acid rock, folk rock, and even today's punk rock, influencing these movements with their own music or incorporating the new ideas and styles into their own work. They grew musically and personally but retained the sense of optimism, happiness, and fun that they had shared before the group had even recorded.

They stayed young.

The Beach Boys: Musically, the most influential band to emerge in the United States in the sixties and seventies. They changed the complexion of the rock-and-roll medium. When Brian entered the field, rock bands were essentially employees of their labels. Creative roles were secondary; commercial roles came first. Brian defied the

business. He went into the control room, he produced, arranged, composed, and played instrumental tracks for the Beach Boys. He was one the first to take such consistent and extensive control—from composition through actual vocalization—of a record company product. He was an innocent, competitive, and romantic California dreamer.

Brian's work affected not only his rock-and-roll peers but musicians and composers many years his senior. Brian brought to pop music an exciting blend of four-part harmony, dynamic chord changes, forties romanticism, and rhythm and blues. He produced his records as *he* thought they should be produced—not according to the dictums of a record company, but according to the composer himself. Beyond that, he refused to consider his work as "just" rock and roll. He worked as if he were working on a symphony, with respect for the medium and the people who listened to it. He would produce and reproduce a song until he was satisfied. He treated rock and roll as an art form. He experimented. He used nontraditional chord arrangements, eccentric pauses, new recordings of natural sounds. He integrated Moog with four-part harmony and put the theremin into rock and roll. He initiated concept albums, strove for symphonic sound, and he got it. He brought instruments to rock and roll that had rarely, if ever, been used—violins, cellos, harpsichords, banjos, and even plastic waterbottles with drumsticks tapping on the base. He introduced the use of guitar "fuzz" on "Little Honda" and oscillating sound on "Help Me Rhonda." Most of all, he highlighted the simple beauty of the human voice.

The Beach Boys: They were funny when others were pretentious; raw and soulful when others were overproduced. They sang about little birds and carrots when others played electric, and did four-part harmonies when boogie music was the norm. They wore white to the Fillmore and sang "Okie from Muskogee" with the Grateful Dead. They influenced the Beatles, the Who, Elton John, and the entire field of white pop performers to emerge in the seventies. They continued to have impact.

The Beach Boys: Three brothers, a cousin, and a friend. When popularity dipped they played small auditoriums. When teenagers of the seventies popularized their original work they took to the concert circuit with pride. Through it all they stayed together. They represented America's clean-cut suburban youth, and they represented the changes those youths experienced during seventeen of the country's most tumultuous years. Today they represent rock and roll's past and a part of its future. Rock and roll has never grown old before. Its heroes have for the most part disbanded or disappeared, especially the artists whose work was most influential to the development of the music. Brian Wilson and the Beach Boys remain. Their work, their musical future, will be a reflection of rock and roll's past, present, and future—and a reflection of the kids who grew up with it.

The Beach Boys: Foremost exponents of harmony in pop music—vocal, lyrical, and emotional harmony.

The Beach Boys: A shared experience. They made you smile. Seventeen years later, they continue to do the same thing. Changing, revealing their lives in their music, growing yet in some ways staying the same. There's a warmth in the Beach Boys' music—a family feeling that comes from their lives and their values.

Music, like love, must be experienced to be fully understood. The Beach Boys' music, like love, offered *security*—a warm, romantic world where you could go and be free of worries. They offered America a dream and found a place in that dream for themselves and their music.

In so much of the Beach Boys' work, music and love are synonymous. With that in mind, you can see the beauty in the fact that their music makes us want to sing.

Music is always with me. I always have some song I'm humming or whistlin', you know? Music is just like beauty or happiness. It's beauty.
——*Brian*

THE BEACH BOYS /
A CHRONOLOGICAL DISCOGRAPHY

Compiled by Jeff Deutch with additional information from Peter Reum and Ed Engel

KEY: Album (A)
      Single (S)
      Multiple album package (A)S
      Reissue (R)

(B)   Produced and/or written by Brian Wilson
(C)   Produced by Carl Wilson
(D)   Written and/or performed by Dennis Wilson
(BB) Performed by the Beach Boys under another name
(A)   Produced by Ron Altbach

BEACH BOYS /BEACH BOYS LEAD VOCALS /BEACH BOYS PRODUCED AMERICAN LP AND SINGLE RECORDS

Date	Artist	Title	Label	(S) or (A)
12/61	BEACH BOYS	Surfin'/Luau	X 301	(S)
2/62	BEACH BOYS	Surfin'/Luau	Candix 301	(S)
3/62	KENNY & THE CADETS	Barbie/What a Young Girl Is Made Of	Randy 422	(S)
5/62	BEACH BOYS	409/Surfin' Safari	Capitol 4777	(S)
6/62	RACHEL & THE REVOLVERS (B)	The Revolution/Number One	Dot 16392	(S)
11/62	BEACH BOYS	Ten Little Indians/County Fair	Capitol 4880	(S)
12/62	BEACH BOYS	*Surfin' Safari*	*Capitol 1808*	(A)
/63	BOB & SHERRY (B)	The Surfer Moon/Do the Humpty Dumpty	Safari 101	(S)
3/63	BEACH BOYS	Surfin' U.S.A./Shut Down	Capitol 4932	(S)
4/63	BEACH BOYS	*Surfin' U.S.A.*	*Capitol 1890*	(A)
5/63	FOUR SPEEDS (D)	RPM/My Sting Ray	Challenge 9187	(S)
5/63	HONEYS (B)	Surfin' Down the Swanee River/Shoot the Curl	Capitol 4952	(S)
7/63	BEACH BOYS (B)	Surfer Girl/Little Deuce Coupe	Capitol	(S)
7/63	BEACH BOYS (B)	*Surfer Girl*	*Capitol 1981*	(A)
8/63	HONEYS (B)	Pray for Surf/Hide Go Seek	Capitol 5034	(S)
9/63	FOUR SPEEDS (D)	Cheater Slicks/Four on the Floor	Challenge 9202	(S)
10/63	BEACH BOYS (B)	*Little Deuce Coupe*	*Capitol 1998*	(A)
10/63	BEACH BOYS (B)	Be True to Your School/In My Room	Capitol 5069	(S)
11/63	SHARON MARIE (B)	Runaround Lover/Summertime	Capitol 5064	(S)
12/63	HONEYS (B)	The One You Can't Have/From Jimmy with Tears	Capitol 5093	(S)
12/63	BEACH BOYS (B)	Little Saint Nick/Lord's Prayer	Capitol 5096	(S)
1/64	SURVIVORS (BB)	Pamela Jean/After the Game	Capitol 5102	(S)
2/64	BEACH BOYS (B)	Fun, Fun, Fun/Why Do Fools Fall in Love	Capitol 5118	(S)
3/64	PAUL PETERSON (B)	She Rides with Me/Poorest Boy in Town	Colpix 720	(S)
3/64	CASTELLS (BB)	I Do/Teardrops	Warner Bros. 5421	(S)
3/64	BEACH BOYS (B)	*Shut Down Vol. 2*	*Capitol 2027*	(A)
4/64	HONEYS (B)	He's a Doll/Love of a Boy and Girl	Warner Bros. 5430	(S)
5/64	BEACH BOYS (B)	I Get Around/Don't Worry Baby	Capitol 5174	(S)
6/64	GARY USHER (B)	Sacramento/Just the Way I Feel	Capitol 5193	(S)
6/64	SHARON MARIE (B)	Thinkin' 'Bout You Baby/Story of My Life	Capitol 5195	(S)
7/64	BEACH BOYS (B)	*All Summer Long*	*Capitol 2110*	(A)
8/64	BEACH BOYS (B)	When I Grow Up/She Knows Me Too Well	Capitol 5245	(S)
10/64	BEACH BOYS (B)	Wendy/Little Honda/Hushabye/Don't Back Down	Capitol 5267	(ELP)
10/64	BEACH BOYS (B)	*Beach Boys' Concert Live*	*Capitol 2198*	(A)
10/64	BEACH BOYS (B)	*Beach Boys' Christmas Album*	*Capitol 2164*	(A)
11/64	BEACH BOYS (B)	Dance Dance Dance/Warmth of the Sun	Capitol 5306	(S)
12/64	BEACH BOYS (B)	The Man With All the Toys/Blue Christmas	Capitol 5312	(S)
2/65	BEACH BOYS (B)	Do You Wanna Dance/Please Let Me Wonder	Capitol 5372	(S)
3/65	BEACH BOYS (B)	*The Beach Boys Today*	*Capitol 2269*	(A)
5/65	GLEN CAMPBELL (B)	Guess I'm Dumb/That's All Right	Capitol 5441	(S)
5/65	BEACH BOYS (B)	Help Me Rhonda/Kiss Me Baby	Capitol 5395	(S)
7/65	BEACH BOYS (B)	*Summer Days (and Summer Nights)*	*Capitol 2354*	(A)
8/65	BEACH BOYS (B)	California Girls/Let Him Run Wild	Capitol 5464	(S)
10/65	BEACH BOYS (B)	*Beach Boys' Party*	*Capitol 2398*	(A)
11/65	BEACH BOYS (B)	The Little Girl I Once Knew/There's No Other	Capitol 5540	(S)
1/66	BEACH BOYS (B)	Barbara Ann/Girl Don't Tell Me	Capitol 5561	(S)
3/66	BEACH BOYS (B)	Sloop John B./You're So Good to Me	Capitol 5602	(S)
4/66	ANNETTE (B)	The Monkey's Uncle/How Will I Know My Love	Vista 440	(S)

Date	Artist		Title	Label/Number	Format
4/66	BRIAN WILSON	(B)	Caroline, No/Summer Means New Love	Capitol	(S)
5/66	BEACH BOYS	(B)	*Pet Sounds*	*Capitol 2458*	(A)
7/66	BEACH BOYS		*Best of the Beach Boys*	*Capitol 2445*	(A)
7/66	BEACH BOYS	(B)	Wouldn't It Be Nice/God Only Knows	Capitol 5706	(S)
10/66	BEACH BOYS	(B)	Good Vibrations/Let's Go Away for a While	Capitol 5676	(S)
	BEACH BOYS		*Smile*	Capitol 2580	UNR
7/67	BEACH BOYS	(B)	Heroes and Villains/You're Welcome	Brother 1001	(S)
8/67	BEACH BOYS		*Best of the Beach Boys Vol. 2*	*Capitol 2706*	(A)
9/67	BEACH BOYS	(BB)	*Smiley Smile*	Brother 1002	(A)
9/67	BRIAN WILSON & MIKE LOVE	(B)	Gettin' Hungry/Devoted to You	Brother (Capitol)	(S)
10/67	BEACH BOYS		*Deluxe Set*	*Capitol 2818*	(A)S(R)
10/67	BEACH BOYS		*Wild Honey/Wind Chimes*	*Capitol 2028*	(S)
12/67	BEACH BOYS		*Wild Honey*	*Capitol 2068*	(A)
12/67	BEACH BOYS		Darlin'/Here Today	Capitol 2160	(S)
4/68	BEACH BOYS		Friends/Little Bird	Capitol	(S)
5/68	BEACH BOYS		*Friends*	*Capitol*	(A)
6/68	BEACH BOYS	(B)	*Stack-O-Tracks*	*Capitol 2893*	(A)
7/68	BEACH BOYS		Do It Again/Wake the World	Capitol 2239	(S)
8/68	BEACH BOYS		*Best of the Beach Boys Vol. 3*	*Capitol 2945*	(A)
11/68	BEACH BOYS		Bluebirds Over the Mountain/Never Learn Not to Love	Capitol 2432	(S)
1/69	BEACH BOYS		*20/20*	*Capitol 133*	(A)
2/69	HONEYS	(B)	Tonight I'll Be Loving You/Goodnight My Love	Capitol 2454	(S)
2/69	BEACH BOYS		I Can Hear Music/All I Want to Do	Capitol	(S)
5/69	BEACH BOYS		*Close-Up*	*Capitol 253*	(A)
6/69	BEACH BOYS	(B)	Breakaway/Celebrate The News	Capitol 2530	(S)
8/69	DENNIS WILSON & RUMBO	(D)	Sound of Free/Lady	Stateside	UK(S)
2/70	BEACH BOYS		*Good Vibrations*	*Capitol 442*	(A)
3/70	BEACH BOYS		Add Some Music to Your Day/Susie Cincinnati	Brother-Reprise 0894	(S)
4/70	BEACH BOYS		Cottonfields/The Nearest Faraway Place	Capitol 2765	(S)
7/70	BEACH BOYS		This Whole World/Slip on Through	Brother-Reprise 0929	(S)
8/70	BEACH BOYS		*Sunflower*	*Brother-Reprise 6382*	(A)
8/70	BEACH BOYS	(B)	*All Summer Long/California Girls*	*Capitol 500*	(A)S(R)
10/70	BEACH BOYS	(B)	*Dance, Dance, Dance/Fun, Fun, Fun*	*Capitol 701*	(A)S(R)
10/70	FLAME	(C)	See the Light/Get Your Mind Made Up	Brother 3500	(S)
11/70	BEACH BOYS		It's About Time/Tears in the Morning	Brother-Reprise 0957	(S)
1/71	FLAME	(C)	*The Flame*	*Brother 2500*	(A)
1/71	FLAME	(C)	Another Day Like Heaven/I'm So Happy	Brother 3501	(S)
3/71	BEACH BOYS		Cool, Cool Water/Forever	Brother-Reprise 0998	(S)
5/71	BEACH BOYS		Wouldn't It Be Nice (Live)	Ode 70 66016	(S)
5/71	BEACH BOYS		Long Promised Road/Deirdre	Brother-Reprise 1015	(S)
8/71	BEACH BOYS		*Surf's Up*	*Brother-Reprise 6454*	(A)
9/71	BEACH BOYS		Till I Die/Long Promised Road	Brother Reprise 1047	(S)
11/71	BEACH BOYS		Surf's Up/Don't Go Near the Water	Brother-Reprise 1055	(S)
11/71	SPRING	(B)	Now That Everything's Been Said/Awake	United Artists 50848	(S)
3/72	BEACH BOYS		You Need a Mess of Help to Stand Alone/Cuddle Up	Brother-Reprise 1091	(S)
5/72	BEACH BOYS		*Carl and the Passions—Pet Sounds*	*Brother-Reprise 2083*	(A)S
5/72	SPRING	(B)	*Spring*	*United Artists 5571*	(A)
5/72	SPRING	(B)	Good Time/Sweet Mountain	United Artists 50907	(S)
7/72	BEACH BOYS		Marcella/Hold on Dear Brother	Brother-Reprise 1101	(S)
1/73	BEACH BOYS		Sail On Sailor/Only With You	Brother-Reprise 1138	(S)
1/73	BEACH BOYS		*Holland/Mt. Vernon & Fairway*	*Brother-Reprise*	(A)EP
4/73	BEACH BOYS		California Saga/Funky Pretty	Brother-Reprise 1150	(S)
6/73	AMERICAN SPRING	(B)	Shyin' Away/Fallin' in Love	Columbia 45834	(S)
11/73	BEACH BOYS		*Beach Boys in Concert*	*Brother-Reprise 6484*	(A)S
5/74	BEACH BOYS	(B)	*Pet Sounds*	*Brother-Reprise 2197*	(A)(R)
6/74	BEACH BOYS		*Endless Summer*	*Capitol 11307*	(A)
7/74	BEACH BOYS	(B)	Surfin' U.S.A./The Warmth of the Sun	Capitol 3924	(S)(R)
7/74	BEACH BOYS		*Wild Honey/20/20*	*Brother-Reprise 2166*	(A)(R)
8/74	BEACH BOYS		I Can Hear Music	Brother-Reprise 1310	(S)
10/74	BEACH BOYS		*Friends/Smiley Smile*	*Brother-Reprise 2167*	(A)S(R)
12/74	BEACH BOYS		Child of Winter/Susie Cincinnati	Brother-Reprise 1321	(S)
3/75	BEACH BOYS		Sail On Sailor/Only With You	Brother-Reprise	(S)(R)
4/75	BEACH BOYS		*Spirit of America*	*Capitol 11384*	(A)
6/75	BEACH BOYS	(B)	Little Honda/Hawaii	Capitol	(S)(R)
7/75	BEACH BOYS	(B)	Barbara Ann/Little Honda	Capitol	(S)(R)
7/75	BEACH BOYS		*Good Vibrations/Best of the Beach Boys*	*Brother-Reprise 2223*	(A)
8/75	BEACH BOYS	(B)	Wouldn't It Be Nice/Caroline, No	Brother-Reprise	(S)(R)
1/76	RICCI MARTIN	(C)	Stop Look Around/I Had a Dream	Capitol 4164	(S)

Date	Artist	Title	Label/Number	Type
6/76	BEACH BOYS (B)	Rock and Roll Music/TM Song	Brother-Reprise 1354	(S)
7/76	BEACH BOYS (B)	Fifteen Big Ones	Brother-Reprise 2251	(A)
9/76	BEACH BOYS (B)	It's OK/Had to Phone Ya	Brother-Reprise 1368	(S)
11/76	BEACH BOYS (B)	Everyone's in Love/Susie Cincinnati	Brother-Reprise 1375	(S)
11/76	BEACH BOYS	'69/Live in London	Capitol 11584	(A)(R)
4/77	BEACH BOYS (B)	The Beach Boys Love You	Brother-Reprise 2258	(A)
6/77	BEACH BOYS (B)	Honkin' Down The Highway/Solar System	Brother-Reprise	(S)
8/77	DENNIS WILSON (D)	Pacific Ocean Blue	Caribou 34354	(A)
10/77	RICCI MARTIN (C)	Beached	Epic 34834	(A)
10/77	DENNIS WILSON (D)	You and I	Caribou	(S)
4/78	CELEBRATION FEATURING MIKE LOVE (A)	Almost Summer/Lookin' Good	MCA 40891	(S)
5/78	ORIGINAL SOUNDTRACK (A)	Almost Summer	MCA 3037	(A)
8/78	BEACH BOYS (BB)	Peggy Sue	Brother-Reprise	(S)
9/78	BEACH BOYS	M.I.U. Album	Brother-Reprise MSK 2268	(A)

BEACH BOYS ORIGINAL AMERICAN ALBUMS

12/62 SURFIN' SAFARI ... Capitol DT/T 1808 ... *Producer: Nick Venet*
Surfin' Safari; County Fair; Ten Little Indians; Chug-A-Lug; Little Miss America; 409/Surfin';
Heads You Win—Tails I Lose; Summertime Blues; Cuckoo Clock; Moon Dawg; The Shift

4/63 SURFIN' U.S.A. ... Capitol ST/T 1890 ... *Producer: Nick Venet*
Surfin' U.S.A.; Farmer's Daughter; Miserlou; Stoked; Lonely Sea; Shut Down/Noble Surfer; Honky
Tonk; Lana; Surf Jam; Let's Go Trippin'; Finders Keepers

7/63 SURFER GIRL ... Capitol ST/T 1981 ... *Producer: Brian Wilson*
Surfer Girl; Catch a Wave; The Surfer Moon; South Bay Surfer; The Rocking Surfer; Little Deuce
Coupe/In My Room; Hawaii; Surfer's Rule; Our Car Club; Your Summer Dream; Boogie Woogie

10/63 LITTLE DEUCE COUPE ... Capitol ST/T 1998 ... *Producer: Brian Wilson*
Little Deuce Coupe; Ballad of Ole Betsy; Be True to Your School; Car Crazy Cutie; Cherry, Cherry
Coupe; 409/Shut Down; Spirit of America; Our Car Club; No-Go Showboat; A Young Man Is Gone;
Custom Machine

3/64 SHUT DOWN VOL. 2 ... Capitol ST/T 2027 ... *Producer: Brian Wilson*
Fun, Fun, Fun; Don't Worry Baby; In the Parkin' Lot; "Cassius" Love vs. "Sonny" Wilson; The
Warmth of the Sun; This Car of Mine/Why Do Fools Fall in Love; Pom Pom Play Girl; Keep an Eye
on Summer; Shut Down Part II; Louie, Louie; Denny's Drums

7/64 ALL SUMMER LONG ... Capitol ST/T 2110 ... *Producer: Brian Wilson*
I Get Around; All Summer Long; Hushabye; Little Honda; We'll Run Away; Carl's Big Chance/
Wendy; Do You Remember; Girls on the Beach; Drive-In; Our Favorite Recording Sessions; Don't
Back Down

10/64 CHRISTMAS ALBUM ... Capitol ST/T 2164 ... *Producer: Brian Wilson*
Little Saint Nick; The Man with All the Toys; Santa's Beard; Merry Christmas, Baby; Christmas Day;
Frosty the Snowman/We Three Kings of Orient Are; Blue Christmas; Santa Claus is Comin' to Town;
White Christmas; I'll Be Home for Christmas; Auld Lang Syne

10/64 CONCERT ... Capitol STAO TAO 2198 ... *Producer: Brian Wilson*
Fun, Fun, Fun; Little Old Lady From Pasadena; Little Deuce Coupe; Long, Tall Texan; In My
Room; Monster Mash; Let's Go Trippin'/Papa-Ooo-Mow-Mow; The Wanderer; Hawaii; Graduation
Day; I Get Around; Johnny B. Goode

3/65 TODAY ... Capitol DT/T 2269 ... *Producer: Brian Wilson*
Do You Wanna Dance; Good To My Baby; Don't Hurt My Little Sister; When I Grow Up; Help Me
Rhonda; Dance, Dance, Dance/Please Let Me Wonder; I'm So Young; Kiss Me Baby; She Knows
Me Too Well; In the Back of My Mind; Bull Session With "Big Daddy"

7/65 SUMMER DAYS (AND SUMMER NIGHTS) ... Capitol DD/T 2354 ... *Producer: Brian Wilson*
The Girl From New York City; Amusement Parks U.S.A.; Then I Kissed Her; Salt Lake City; Girl
Don't Tell Me; Help Me Rhonda/California Girls; Let Him Run Wild; You're So Good to Me;
Summer Means Now Love; I'm Bugged at My Old Man; And Your Dream Comes True

10/65 PARTY ... Capitol DMAS MAS 2398 ... *Producer: Brian Wilson*
Hully Gully; I Should Have Known Better; Tell Me Why; Papa-Ooo-Mow-Mow; Mountain of Love;
You've Got to Hide Your Love Away; Devoted to You/Alley Ooop; There's No Other (Like My Baby);
Medley: I Get Around, Little Deuce Coupe, The Times They Are A-Changing; Barbara Ann

5/66 PET SOUNDS ... Capitol DT/T 2458 ... *Producer: Brian Wilson*
Wouldn't It Be Nice; You Still Believe in Me; That's Not Me; Don't Talk (Put Your Head On My
Shoulder); I'm Waiting for the Day; Let's Go Away for a While; Sloop John B.; God Only Knows;

I Know There's an Answer; Here Today; I Just Wasn't Made for These Times; Pet Sounds;
Caroline, No

........SMILE .... Capitol 2580 (unreleased) .... *Producer: Brian Wilson*
*Partially or fully produced cuts: Heroes and Villains/Barnyard/The Elemental Suite: My Vega-
Tables (Earth), I Love To Say Da-Da (Water), Mrs. O'Leary's Cow (Fire), untitled piano
instrumental (Air)/Wind Chimes/Wonderful/Old Master Painter/Our Prayer/Cabin-Essence (Home
on the Range)/(Have You Seen) The Grand Coulee Dam/(Who Ran) The Iron Horse/Bicycle Rider/
You Are My Sunshine/Do You Like Worms/Child Is Father to the Man/Good Vibrations/Surf's Up/
Can't Wait Too Long
unscreened rumored cuts: Holidays; I'm In Great Shape; Red Run*

9/67 .... SMILEY SMILE .... Brother ST 9001 (Capitol) .... *Producer: Beach Boys*
*Heroes and Villains; Vega-Tables; Fall Breaks and Back to Winter (W. Woodpecker Symphony); She's
Goin' Bald; Little Pad; Good Vibrations; With Me Tonight; Wind Chimes; Gettin' Hungry;
Wonderful; Whistle In*

12/67 .... WILD HONEY .... Capitol ST 2859 .... *Producer: Beach Boys*
*Wild Honey; Aren't You Glad; I Was Made to Love Her; Country Air; A Thing or Two Darlin'; I'd
Love Just Once to See You; Here Comes the Night; Let the Wind Blow; How She Boogalooed It;
Mama Says*

5/68 .... FRIENDS .... Capitol ST 2895 .... *Producer: Beach Boys*
*Meant For You; Friends; Wake the World; Be Here in the Mornin'; When a Man Needs a Woman;
Passing By; Anna Lee the Healer; Little Bird; Be Still; Busy Doin' Nothin'; Diamond Head;
Transcendental Meditation*

1/69 .... 20/20 .... Capitol SKAO 133 .... *Producer: Beach Boys*
*Do It Again; I Can Hear Music; Bluebirds Over the Mountain; Be With Me; All I Want to Do
(Dennis); The Nearest Faraway Place; Cottonfields; I Went to Sleep; Time to Get Alone; Never
Learn Not to Love; Our Prayer; Cabinessense*

8/70 .... SUNFLOWER .... Brother-Reprise RS 6382 .... *Producer: Beach Boys*
*Slip on Through; This Whole World; Add Some Music to Your Day; Got to Know the Woman;
Deirdre; It's About Time; Tears in the Morning; All I Wanna Do; Forever; Our Sweet Love; At My
Window; Cool, Cool Water*

5/72 .... SURF'S UP .... Brother-Reprise RS 6454 .... *Producer: Beach Boys*
*Don't Go Near the Water; Long Promised Road; Take a Load Off Your Feet; Disney Girls (1957);
Student Demonstration Time; Flows; Lookin' at Tomorrow (A Welfare Song); A Day in the Life of a
Tree; Till I Die; Surf's Up*

5/72 .... CARL AND THE PASSIONS, SO TOUGH.......... Brother-Reprise 2MS 2083.................. *Producer: Beach Boys*
*You Need a Mess of Help to Stand Alone; Here She Comes; He Come Down; Marcella; Hold on
Dear Brother; Make It Good; All This Is That; Cuddle Up*

1/73 .... HOLLAND .... Brother-Reprise MS 2118................... *Producer: Beach Boys*
*Sail On Sailor; Steamboat; California Saga; Big Sur; The Beaks of Eagles; California; The Trader;
Leaving This Town; Only With You; Funky Pretty; Mount Vernon and Fairway (A Fairy Tale); Mt.
Vernon and Fairway—Theme; I'm the Pied Piper; Better Get Back in Bed; Magic Transistor Radio;
I'm the Pied Piper; Radio King Dom*

11/73 .... IN CONCERT .... Brother-Reprise 2RS 6484 .... *Producer: Beach Boys*
*Sail On Sailor; Sloop John B.; The Trader; You Still Believe in Me; California Girls; Darlin';
Marcella; Caroline, No; Leaving This Town; Heroes and Villains; Funky Pretty; Let the Wind Blow;
Help Me Rhonda; Surfer Girl; Wouldn't It Be Nice; We Got Love; Don't Worry Baby; Surfin' U.S.A.;
Good Vibrations; Fun, Fun, Fun*

7/76 .... FIFTEEN BIG ONES............................ Brother-Reprise MS 2251 .... *Producer: Brian Wilson*
*Rock and Roll Music; It's OK; Had to Phone Ya; Chapel of Love; Everyone's in Love With You; Talk to
Me; That Same Song; TM Song; Palisades Park; Susie Cincinnati; A Casual Look; Blueberry Hill;
Back Home; In the Still of the Night; Just Once in My Life*

11/76 .... '69 (LIVE IN LONDON) .... Capitol ST 11584 .... *Producer: Beach Boys*
*Darlin'; Wouldn't It Be Nice; Sloop John B.; California Girls; Do It Again; Wake the World; Aren't
You Glad; Bluebirds Over the Mountain; Their Hearts Were Full of Spring; Good Vibrations; God
Only Knows; Barbara Ann*

.... ADULT CHILD .... (Unreleased) .... *Producer: Brian Wilson*
*Life Is for the Living; Hey Little Tomboy; Deep Purple; H.E.L.P.; It's Over Now; Everyone Wants to
Live; Shortin' Bread; Lines; On Broadway; Two Can Play; It's Trying to Say; Still I Dream of It*

4/77 .... THE BEACH BOYS LOVE YOU .... Brother-Reprise MSK 2258 .... *Producer: Brian Wilson*
*Let Us Go on This Way; Roller Skating Child; Mona; Johnny Carson; Good Time; Honkin' Down the
Highway; Ding Dang Solar System; The Night Was So Young; I'll Bet He's Nice; Let's Put Our Hearts
Together; I Wanna Pick You Up; Airplane; Love Is a Woman*

.... MERRY CHRISTMAS FROM THE BEACH BOYS .. (Unreleased) .... *Producer: Brian Wilson*
*Christmas Day; Go Get That Girl; Santa's Got an Airplane; I Saw Mommy Kissing Santa (Original);
I Saw Mommy Kissing Santa Claus (Standard); Christmas Carole Medley*

9/78 .... **MIU ALBUM** .... Brother-Reprise MSK 2268 (A)................... *Executive Producer: Brian*
Wilson. Producers: Al
Jardine and Ron Altbach

She's Got Rhythm; Come Go With Me; Hey Little Tomboy; Kona Coast; Peggy Sue; Wontcha Come
Out Tonight; Sunday Kind of Love; Bells of Paris; Pitter Patter; Diane; Matchpoint of Our Love;
Winds of Change

ANTHOLOGIES FEATURING BEACH BOYS' MATERIAL

Beach Boys Biggest Beach Hits	ERA	*Chartbusters*	Capitol	*American Graffiti*	MCA
Beach Boys Beach Hits	Orbit	*Shut Down*	Capitol	*Golden Summer*	United Artists
Beach Boys Greatest Hits	Scopton	*Chartbusters Vol. 2*	Capitol	*Surfin' Roots*	Festival
Surfer Girl	Pickwick	*Surfin's Greatest Hits*	Capitol	*The Big Ball*	Warner Brothers Sampler
Wow—Great Concert	Pickwick	*Chartbusters Vol. 3*	Capitol	*Appetizers*	Warner Brothers Sampler
High Water	Pickwick	*Big Hot Rod Hits*	Capitol	*Hot Platters*	Warner Brothers Sampler
Good Vibrations	Pickwick	*Chartbusters Vol. 4*	Capitol	*Hard Goods*	Warner Brothers Sampler
Little Deuce Coupe	Pickwick	*Big Hits*	Capitol	*The Works*	Warner Brothers Sampler
Golden Treasure	Capitol	*Surfin' Oldies Vol. 2*	Capitol	*The People's Record*	Warner Brothers Sampler
		Celebration	Ode '70		

ALBUMS PRODUCED BY OR PROMINENTLY FEATURING THE BEACH BOYS

1/71 .... **THE FLAME** .... Brother LP 2500 .... *Producer: Carl Wilson*

See The Light /Make It Easy /Hey Lord /Lady /Don't Worry Bill /Get Your Mind Made Up /Highs and
Lows /I'm So Happy /Dove /Another Day Like Heaven /See The Light (Reprise)

5/72 .... **SPRING** .... United Artists UAS 5571 .... *Executive Producer: Brian*
Wilson

Tennessee Waltz●/Thinkin' 'Bout You Baby○/Mama Said○/Superstar○/Awake■/Sweet
Mountain○/Everybody●/This Whole World○/Forever○/Good Time●/Now That Everything's
Been Said□/Down Home

Produced by ● Brian Wilson and Stephen Desper ○ Brian
Wilson, Stephen Desper, and David Sandler ■ David Sandler
□ Brian Wilson and David Sandler

8/77 .... **DENNIS WILSON/PACIFIC OCEAN BLUE** .... Caribou PZ 34354 .... *Producer: Dennis Wilson*
and Gregg Jacobson

River Song /What's Wrong /Moonshine /Friday Night /Dreamer /Thoughts of You /Time /You and I /
Pacific Ocean Blue /Farewell My Friend /Rainbows /End of the Show

7/77 .... **RICCI MARTIN/BEACHED** .... Epic PE 34834 .... *Producer: Carl Wilson and*
Billy Hinsche

Stop Look Around /Moonbeams /Belle of the Ball /Everybody Knows My Name /Streets of Love /
Spark of Me /My Old Radio /Precious Love /I Don't Like It /I Had a Dream /Here I Go Again

5/78 .... **ALMOST SUMMER*** .... Original Soundtrack Album .... *Producer: Ron Altbach*

Almost Summer; Sad, Sad, Summer; Cruisin'; Lookin' Good; Summer in the City; It's OK; Football;
Island Girl; Christine and Bobby; We Are the Future; She Was a Lady

*FEATURING CELEBRATION WITH
MIKE LOVE

RECORDING ARTISTS FOR WHOM INDIVIDUAL BEACH BOYS HAVE SUNG BACKGROUND VOCALS

David Cassidy—(RCA)	Angelo—(FANTASY)	Spring—(U.A./COLUMBIA)
Jackie DeShannon—(COLUMBIA)	Warren Zevon—(ASYLUM)	Chicago—(COLUMBIA)
Jan & Dean—(LIBERTY/U.A.)	California Music—(RCA)	Jan Berry—(A&M)
Elton John—(MCA)	Masked Surfers—(UA)	Hale & The Hushabyes—(REPRISE)
Charles Lloyd—(KNAPP/A&M)	Ricci Martin—(CAPITOL)	Blossoms
America—(WARNER BROS.)	Martin & Finley—(MOTOWN)	Asylum Choir—(SMASH)
Henry Gross—(A&M)	Eric Carmen—(ARISTA)	Surfaris—(CHALLENGE)
Johnny Rivers—(EPIC)	Kathy Dalton—(DISCREET)	

MAJOR COVER VERSIONS—OTHER ARTISTS' RECORDING MATERIAL WRITTEN BY THE BEACH BOYS

Artist	Title	Label
Hondells	MY BUDDY SEAT	Mercury
Dino, Desi & Billy	HOLLY	Warner Bros.
	TELL SOMEONE YOU LOVE HER	Warner Bros.
	LADY LOVE	Warner Bros.
Annette	MUSCLE BEACH PARTY	Vista
Jan & Dean	SURF CITY	Liberty
	DRAG CITY	Liberty
	DEAD MAN'S CURVE	Liberty
	SIDEWALK SURFIN'	Liberty
	NEW GIRL IN SCHOOL	Liberty
	RIDE THE WILD SURF	Liberty
	SHE'S MY SUMMER GIRL	Liberty
	SURFIN' WILD	Liberty
	MOVE OUT LITTLE MUSTANG	United Artists
	VEGA-TABLES	United Artists
	GONNA HUSTLE YOU	Sidewalk Surfer New Version
Tokens	DON'T WORRY BABY	Buddah
Sagittarius	IN MY ROOM	Together
Art Garfunkel	DISNEY GIRLS	Columbia
California Music	DON'T WORRY BABY	RCA
Papa Doo Run Run	BE TRUE TO YOUR SCHOOL	RCA
Todd Rundgren	GOOD VIBRATIONS	Bearsville
Spring	THINKIN' 'BOUT YOU BABY	United Artists
	AWAKE	United Artists
	SWEET MOUNTAIN	United Artists
	THIS WHOLE WORLD	United Artists
	FOREVER	United Artists
	GOOD TIME	United Artists
	SHYIN' AWAY	Columbia
	FALLIN' IN LOVE	Columbia
Bruce Johnston (solo)	DISNEY GIRLS Columbia	
	DEIRDRE	Columbia
Johnny Rivers	HELP ME RHONDA	Epic
David Cassidy	DARLIN'	RCA
Captain & Tennille	DISNEY GIRLS	A&M
	CUDDLE UP	A&M
	GOD ONLY KNOWS	A&M
Glen Campbell	GOD ONLY KNOWS	Capitol
Hondells	LITTLE HONDA	Mercury
Keith Moon	DON'T WORRY BABY	MCA
Bryan Ferry	DON'T WORRY BABY	Atlantic
Neil Diamond	GOD ONLY KNOWS	Columbia
Andy Williams	GOD ONLY KNOWS	Columbia
Hugo Montenegro	GOOD VIBRATIONS	RCA
Timers	NO GO SHOWBOAT	Reprise
Ramones	I GET AROUND	Hit
Defenders	LITTLE DEUCE COUPE	Dolfi
Rally Parks	MOVE OUT LITTLE MUSTANG	Imperial
Nick De Caro	CAROLINE, NO	A&M
Henson	GOD ONLY KNOWS	Fame
Exception	GIRL FROM N.Y.C.	Capitol
Mama Cass	DISNEY GIRLS	RCA
Adam Surf	FUN, FUN, FUN	Paladin
Sandy Salosbury	ON AND ON SHE GOES (WITH ME TONIGHT)	Together
Leif Garrett	SURFIN' U.S.A.	Atlantic
	CALIFORNIA GIRLS	Atlantic
KGB	SAIL ON SAILOR	MCA
B. J. Thomas	DON'T WORRY BABY	MCA
Hollyridge Strings	BEACH BOYS SONGBOOK ALBUM	Capitol
Steve Hunter	SAIL ON SAILOR	Atlantic
Troggs	GOOD VIBRATIONS	Pye
Bob McBride	SAIL ON SAILOR	MCA
Wildfire	BREAKAWAY	Casablanca
Marilyn Scott	GOD ONLY KNOWS	Big Tree
Shaun Cassidy	IT'S LIKE HEAVEN	Warner-Curb
The Good Vibrations	I GET AROUND (disco album)	Millenium

BEACH BOYS *Repackaging and Reissues*

7/66	**BEST OF THE BEACH BOYS**	Capitol	T DT	2445	
8/67	**BEST OF THE BEACH BOYS VOL. 2**	Capitol	T DT	2706	
11/67	**DELUXE SET**	Capitol	2813		*Today-Summer Days-Summer Nights-* *Pet Sounds*
6/68	**STACK-O-TRACKS**	Capitol	DKAO	2893	*Beach Boy Songs with original Instrumental* *Tracks Without Vocals*
8/68	**BEST OF THE BEACH BOYS VOL. 3**	Capitol	DKAO	2945	
5/69	**CLOSE-UP**	Capitol	2 LP	253	*Songs From Surfin' U.S.A.* *& All Summer Long*
2/70	**GOOD VIBRATIONS**	Capitol	ST	442	
8/70	**ALL SUMMER LONG/** **CALIFORNIA GIRLS**	Capitol	STBB	500	*Songs from All Summer Long/Summer Days* *Summer Nights*
	DANCE, DANCE, DANCE/ **FUN, FUN, FUN**	Capitol	STBB	701	*Songs from Today & Shut Down Vol. 2*
5/74	**PET SOUNDS**	Brother-Reprise	MS	2197	
6/74	**ENDLESS SUMMER**	Capitol	SUBB	11307	
7/74	**WILD HONEY/20/20**	Brother-Reprise	2MS	2166	
10/74	**FRIENDS/SMILEY SMILE**	Brother-Reprise	2MS	2167	
4/75	**SPIRIT OF AMERICA**	Capitol	SUBB	11384	
	GOOD VIBRATIONS— **BEST OF THE BEACH BOYS**	Brother-Reprise	MS	2223	

BEACH BOYS UNRELEASED

Ba Ba Black Sheep	*Brian Wilson*
The Big Beat	*Brian Wilson*
Land Ahoy ✔	*Brian Wilson*
That Special Feeling	*Brian Wilson*
They're Marching Along	*Brian Wilson*
Bobby Left Me	*Brian Wilson*
When Girls Get Together ✔	*Brian Wilson*
My Solution	*Brian Wilson*
Marilyn Rovell	*Brian Wilson*
It's Like Heaven	*Brian Wilson*
Burlesque	*Brian Wilson*
Boys Will Be Boys	*Brian Wilson*
Sherry She Needs Me	*Brian Wilson*
Lazy Lizzie	*Brian Wilson*
Recreation	*Brian Wilson, Bob Norman, C. Pomoroy*
Rockin' Roadster	*Brian Wilson, Roger Christian*
California Feeling	*Brian Wilson, Steve Kalinich*
Lucy Jones	*Brian Wilson, Steve Kalinich*
You're Riding High on the Music	*Brian Wilson, Steve Kalinich*
Loop De Loop	*Brian Wilson, Alan Jardine*
Snowflakes	*Brian Wilson, David Sandler*
Italia	*Alan Jardine*
Then I'll Be Someone	*Carl Wilson, Tandyn Almer*

Canyon Summer	*Alan Jardine*
Lady Lynda ✓	*Alan Jardine, Ron Altbach*
Country Pie ✔	
Good Timing ✔	*Brian Wilson, Carl Wilson*
Barbara	*Dennis Wilson*
San Miguel ✔	*Dennis Wilson*
Glow Crescent Glow	*Michael Love*
Lisa	*Michael Love*
Phoenix Dream	*Michael Love*
Our Life, Our Love, Our Land	*Michael Love*
I've Got a Friend	*Dennis Wilson*
10,000 Years	*Dennis Wilson*
School Girl	*Dennis Wilson*
Tug of Love	*Dennis Wilson*
Time	*Dennis Wilson*
Holy Man	*Dennis Wilson*
I Will Be in Heaven When My Angel Comes ✔	*Carl Wilson*
Wild Situation	*Carl Wilson*
Baby Blue ✔	
Michael, Row the Boat Ashore (adaptation) ✔	*Alan Jardine*
Mrs. O'Leary's Cow (*Elemental Suite*) ✔	*Brian Wilson*
Cabinessense (Home on the Range) ✔	*Brian Wilson, Van Dyke Parks*
Who Ran the Iron Horse ✔	*Brian Wilson, Van Dyke Parks*
The Grand Coulee Dam ✔	*Brian Wilson, Van Dyke Parks*
Air (Untitled-*Elemental Suite*) ✔	*Brian Wilson*
Old Master Painter ✔	*Brian Wilson, Van Dyke Parks*

Bicycle Rider ✔	*Brian Wilson, Van Dyke Parks*
Barnyard ✔	*Brian Wilson*
Do You Like Worms ✔	*Brian Wilson*
Can't Wait Too Long	*Brian Wilson*
You Are My Sunshine	*Brian Wilson (adaptation)*
Life Is for the Living ✔	*Brian Wilson*
H.E.L.P. Is On the Way ✔	*Brian Wilson*
It's Over Now ✔	*Brian Wilson*
Everyone Wants to Live ✔	*Brian Wilson*
Lines ✔	*Brian Wilson*
Two Can Play ✔	*Brian Wilson*
It's Tryin' to Say ✔	*Brian Wilson*
Christmas Day ✔	*Brian Wilson, Mike Love*
Go Get That Girl ✔	
Santa's Got an Airplane (Same melody as "H.E.L.P.")	*Brian Wilson* ✔
I Saw Mommy Kissing Santa Claus (Original) ✔	
I Saw Mommy Kissing Santa Claus (Standard) ✔	
Our Team	
How's About a Little Bit of Your Sweet Lovin' ✔	

UNRELEASED COVER VERSIONS

Come to the Sunshine	He's So Fine	Honeycomb
Sea Cruise ✔	Shake, Rattle & Roll	On Broadway ✔
Ruby Baby	Money Money	Deep Purple ✔
Working in a Coal Mine	You've Lost That Lovin' Feelin'	